ATLANTIC

IRELA...

London

NETH.

GERMANY

POLAND

BELGIUM

CZECHOSLO

FRANCE

SWITZ

AUSTRIA

Vichy

ITALY

YUGOS

Corsica

PORTUGAL

SPAIN

Sardinia

Sicily

Algiers

Mers-el-Kébir

Oran

Mehdia-Port Lyautey

Rabat

Casablanca

TUNISIA

Safi

Marrakech

MOROCCO

ALGERIA

LIBYA

TROPIC OF CANCER

FRENCH WEST AFRICA

Dakar

SENEGAL

Bathurst

GAMBIA

NIGERIA

Freetown

SIERRA
LEONE

GOLD
COAST

Monrovia

LIBERIA

EQUATOR

☐ French North Africa

☐ French West Africa

☐ British West Africa

SOUTH ATLANTIC

CAPTAIN MCCREA'S WAR

The World War II Memoir of Franklin D.
Roosevelt's Naval Aide and USS *Iowa*'s
First Commanding Officer

CAPTAIN McCREA'S WAR

The World War II Memoir of Franklin D. Roosevelt's Naval Aide and USS *Iowa*'s First Commanding Officer

VICE ADMIRAL JOHN L. MCCREA

EDITED WITH AN INTRODUCTION AND AFTERWORD BY JULIA C. TOBEY

Skyhorse Publishing

Skyhorse Publishing books may be purchased in bulk at special discounts for sales promotion, corporate gifts, fund-raising, or educational purposes. Special editions can also be created to specifications. For details, contact the Special Sales Department, Skyhorse Publishing, 307 West 36th Street, 11th Floor, New York, NY 10018 or info@skyhorsepublishing.com.

Skyhorse® and Skyhorse Publishing® are registered trademarks of Skyhorse Publishing, Inc.®, a Delaware corporation.

Visit our website at www.skyhorsepublishing.com.

10 9 8 7 6 5 4 3 2 1

Library of Congress Cataloging-in-Publication Data is available on file.

Cover design by Rain Saukas
Cover photos: Editor's collection; AP Images

Print ISBN: 978-1-5107-1323-9
Ebook ISBN: 978-1-5107-1324-6

Printed in the United States of America

Contents

∞∞

Foreword   vii

Preface   xi

Introduction   xiv

Chapter 1: The United States Goes to War   1

Chapter 2: Reporting to the President   11

Chapter 3: Zeroing In   19

Chapter 4: The Map Room   24

Chapter 5: Press Relations   33

Chapter 6: Yarn: A Lesson on the White House Steps   43

Chapter 7: Foreign Relations   47

Chapter 8: Informal Diplomacy   61

Chapter 9: White House Visitors   67

Chapter 10: Yarn: A Tour of Hyde Park   78

Chapter 11: Special Jobs   83

Chapter 12: FDR   99

Chapter 13: Sea Duty and War Production   110

Chapter 14: The Invasion of North Africa and Preparations
for the Casablanca Conference   123

Chapter 15: The Casablanca Conference   133

Chapter 16: Return to the White House and Detachment   148

Chapter 17: *Iowa* Goes into Commission   156

Chapter 18: Shakedown   164

Chapter 19: Aground   171

Chapter 20: Plans for a Secret Mission   175

Chapter 21: Voyage to Algeria   184

Chapter 22: Three Transatlantic Crossings   193

Chapter 23: War Preparations   203

Chapter 24: *Iowa* Joins the Fight   211

Chapter 25: The War in the North Pacific   223

Afterword   232

Endnotes   238

Bibliography   253

Acknowledgments   257

Index   260

Foreword

By Craig L. Symonds

To many, President Franklin D. Roosevelt was, and is, an enigma: to all appearances a relentlessly cheerful man full of good will and bonhomie despite the physical and political burdens he bore as president. Both contemporaries and historians have occasionally wondered if this demeanor was a kind of disguise or a coping mechanism, and some have sought evidence of a darker, more troubled man underneath the veneer. Only a very few ever got close enough to offer testimony about him: his wife Eleanor, his old political pal Louis Howe, Edwin "Pa" Watson, Harry Hopkins, and a few others.

One of them was U.S. Navy Captain John McCrea, who in the days immediately following Pearl Harbor was astonished to be plucked from a pending appointment to command a cruiser and assigned instead as the president's naval aide. He served in that capacity throughout the critical year of 1942—that is, from Pearl Harbor through Casablanca—during which time he spent part of every day with the president. He did not keep a diary, for that was forbidden by Navy regulations, but many years later, upon the urging of his family, he did write a memoir, which is published here for the first time.

McCrea saw the president every day when he was in Washington, generally once in the morning and again in the afternoon, though he often spent hours or even days in continuous proximity to him. If there was a darker persona lurking under Roosevelt's veneer, McCrea never saw it. "Invariably," McCrea writes, "he was in good spirits and eager to talk." On many of these days, the president was still in bed when McCrea arrived, and occasionally the Navy captain, wearing his service dress blue uniform, sat on the toilet in the bathroom to read briefing papers aloud to the president while he shaved. As the president was pushed to his office in his wheelchair each morning, he greeted everyone he passed with a large smile and a cheerful hello. Cooks, gardeners, maintenance men: he knew their names and their children's names, and often inquired about their health or their interests. As McCrea noted, "his zest for living was enormous."

McCrea became FDR's go-to man for all sorts of errands, from tracking down errant visitors to providing war stories for the president's Fireside Chats. He set up FDR's Map Room in the basement of the White House, and he supervised the modifications to the mountain cabin that became Roosevelt's retreat, initially called Shangri-La and subsequently renamed Camp David. He even attended church services with the president and at least once had to come up with a couple of dollars for the collection plate when FDR forgot to bring his wallet.

Nor was theirs a relationship confined to the White House. He accompanied the president to Hyde Park and got a hair-raising high-speed tour in FDR's old Ford with its special hand-operated controls. McCrea also supervised the secret trip from Washington to Casablanca for the conference with Churchill. As McCrea writes, "I had the honor and pleasure of coming to know him on a personal basis."

The topics of their conversations ranged widely. There was a lot about the Navy, of course, a subject always near to the president's heart, but there were many other topics as well. Once at Hyde Park, the president asked McCrea if he knew much about the history of the Hudson Valley. When McCrea professed ignorance,

FDR proceeded to fill him in. As McCrea puts it in the memoir, "He would start off, 'Well, I've been thinking about so-and-so,' and he would talk."

In addition to Roosevelt, McCrea's memoir also offers intimate glimpses into the lives and personalities of many of the principal players in those heady and perilous days. He had a close relationship with FDR's gatekeeper, Edwin "Pa" Watson, a major general in the Army reserve who acted as FDR's appointments secretary. He dealt with Navy Secretary Frank Knox, Secretary of State Cordell Hull, former Vice President John Nance Garner, and of course with the chief of naval operations, the stern and forbidding Admiral Ernest J. King.

McCrea's portrait of King does little to diminish the Admiral's reputation as cold, judgmental, and quick-tempered. King once counseled McCrea that, while he had the makings of a good officer, he had "one outstanding weakness." When McCrea asked him what it was, King told him: "you are not a son of a bitch." "A good naval officer," King insisted, "has to be a son of a bitch." Nevertheless, McCrea got on well with King, whom he admired for his professional efficiency, and on more than one occasion he was even able to elicit a "gentle chuckle" from the famously humorless Navy Chief.

But it is always FDR who shines brightest in this memoir. There was the president's great love of the Navy (which he liked to call "my navy"), his suspicion of the State Department (which he considered "leaky"), and his bantering relationship with the press. The president could be blunt if necessary, even to Churchill, but he always managed to lighten the mood afterward with a kind word or a story, often throwing his head back and laughing aloud. Indeed, laughter seems to have been one of FDR's principal weapons, deployed frequently and deliberately to fend off enquiries as well as to lighten the mood.

During the conference at Casablanca, Roosevelt tasked McCrea to deliver an invitation for dinner to the Sultan of Morocco, and

McCrea paints a vivid word portrait of his reception by the Sultan. "No Hollywood director could have put on a more dazzling spectacle," he writes. At the dinner, where the sultan presented a gold dagger for the president and a gold tiara for Mrs. Roosevelt, Churchill was visibly upset that in deference to the sultan, no alcohol was served.

McCrea left his job as the president's naval aide in January of 1943 to take command of the new-construction battleship USS *Iowa*. His relationship with the president was not at an end, however. Very likely at Roosevelt's suggestion, King selected the *Iowa* to carry the president and his staff to Algeria, the first stop on the trip to the Cairo and Tehran conferences. The voyage across the Atlantic included a then-secret but subsequently notorious accident in which a U.S. Navy destroyer inadvertently fired a live torpedo at the *Iowa* while the president was on board.

In his description of this and other events, McCrea shows why he was successful in his job. His prose is direct, clear, and uncluttered with just the right amount of illuminating detail. Judy Tobey has done a tremendous service to students of the Second World War and of the Roosevelt administration by carefully editing and bringing to publication this elegant yet unpretentious account of the war service of Vice Admiral John McCrea.

Preface

⁓⁓⁓

The story of how this book came to be is a saga of over forty years. When Vice Admiral John McCrea became my stepfather in 1965, he was seventy-three, retired from the navy, and engaged in a second career at John Hancock Mutual Life Insurance Company in Boston, Massachusetts. I quickly learned that he was a marvelous raconteur, with an eye for detail and an ear for dialogue. Endowed with the memory of an elephant, he was a student of history and human nature, and he delighted in sharing stories—"yarns," he called them—about his life and naval career.

The richness of his personal experience was extraordinary. He had witnessed countless events of historic interest and encountered an astounding array of world-famous figures. To cite just a few examples, he had heard William Jennings Bryan speak, watched the surrender of the German High Seas Fleet at the end of World War I, worked closely with President Franklin D. Roosevelt, and known Winston Churchill. His yarns about his past were fascinating.

Many urged him to write a book, but he claimed that others had already capably chronicled what he would write about. However, at the urging of family, he began to make a record of his life shortly before his retirement from John Hancock in 1966. Over a period of more than ten years, working entirely alone, he dictated his recollections into a cassette tape recorder, sometimes writing out scripts beforehand as an aid to dictation. Ultimately, he created a continuous narrative on tape covering his family history and childhood through the death of Franklin D. Roosevelt in April 1945, with a few fragments of later material. For significant details, he relied on a huge collection of personal papers, naval documents, speeches, and other materials that he had accumulated during his careers. Most of these papers are now in the Manuscript Room at the Library of Congress in Washington, D.C.

In 1982, Paul Stillwell, a naval historian and then-director of oral history at the U.S. Naval Institute, interviewed John twice and was taken by his personality, his narrative gifts, and the historic value of his recollections. When Paul learned of the cassette tapes in the mid-eighties, he was pleased to learn that John had already created an extensive memoir and helped to arrange for the transcription of the cassettes. John died in 1990 at the age of ninety-eight before the transcriptions were completed.

Starting in the mid-nineties, I began to read the tape transcripts, viewing them as an opportunity to catch up on the yarns I had missed because I didn't live in the Boston area. I quickly discovered that, despite the memoir's great length, organizational flaws, and holes where John's dictation was unintelligible, much of it was delightful and full of intriguing details, some of interest to family and some to historians. I decided to edit the memoir to make it more accessible. My approach was not to cut, but to organize, eliminate duplication, and make the text as accurate and readable as possible while preserving John's language and voice. I corrected transcription errors, verified names and facts to the extent possible, and supplemented the text with some first-person material from John's interviews, speeches, and letters. I added a table of contents, chapter titles, and explanatory footnotes for a general reader with no particular knowledge of the navy or World War II.

During the editing process, which continued intermittently over some fifteen years, I was in regular contact with Paul Stillwell.

Paul served as an advisor on all things naval and as a guide to others with specialized naval expertise. He also read every chapter and offered substantive comments. The product of this effort was an unpublished electronic document (PDF format) entitled *A Naval Life: The Memoirs of Vice Admiral John L. McCrea, U.S. Navy (Retired),* edited by Julia C. Tobey.

After completing *A Naval Life,* I wanted to publish at least a portion of the memoir because I felt it deserved a wider audience. The obvious choice was the section on World War II, the period that John regarded as the high point of his career. To create *Captain McCrea's War,* I extracted this section from the long memoir, cut and further edited it, and again added a few excerpts from John's writings.

Captain McCrea's War includes a lot of dialogue in quotation marks. John spun his yarns with dialogue, which could change slightly with each telling, so the dialogue is only an approximation of what was said. Materials indented in block quote form are exact quotations.

J.C.T.
January 2016

Introduction

What did you do during the war? That simple question has elicited a flood of intriguing stories about World War II. Among the most historically significant are these recollections by John McCrea, possibly the last memoir to emerge from the White House of President Franklin D. Roosevelt. Front and center at the heart of the navy's war effort, McCrea spent the first fourteen months of the war working with President Roosevelt and top Allied leaders, and later held two important commands at sea.

McCrea's memoir begins with the attack on Pearl Harbor and ends in April 1945, shortly after President Roosevelt's death. During that time, McCrea held four successive jobs: aide to the chief of naval operations (CNO); naval aide to President Roosevelt; first commanding officer of the battleship USS *Iowa*; and commander of a North Pacific task force based in Alaska. Although he subsequently rose to higher rank and held other important posts, he regarded these assignments as the highlight of his career. He participated in top-level war planning at the Navy Department and at the first U.S.-British military conference held after the United States joined the war. At the White House, he assisted the president in an astonishing variety of wartime assignments as disparate as setting up the White House Map Room and escorting British Prime Minister Winston Churchill. The president and McCrea spent many hours together, and they developed a warm personal friendship. On leaving the White House, McCrea put the country's newest and largest battleship into commission, transported the president and the country's top military brass across the Atlantic, and fulfilled his dream to command in battle. In *Iowa*, he was responsible for turning the new crew of a new ship into a fighting team with well-honed battle skills and high morale. Afterward, as the commander of a small task force based in the Aleutian Islands of Alaska, he implemented U.S. strategy to make Japan fear invasion from the north by leading bombardment raids on Japan's Kuril Islands, north of the Japanese homeland. McCrea's war was nothing if not eventful.

John Livingstone McCrea was born on May 29, 1891 in Marlette, Michigan, a small farming town about fifty miles from Detroit. His father was a country doctor, a Presbyterian Church elder, and a dyed-in-the-wool Republican. His mother was a housewife who cared for the couple's six children and a stepdaughter, and occasionally served as a surgical assistant for her husband.

McCrea's school years did not augur well for professional success. He was bright, but a lazy and indifferent student. In high school, he was consumed by a passion for athletics—principally baseball and football—and let his studies slide. With the stern disapproval of his scholarly father, he barely managed to graduate, standing dead last in the class of 1909. He immediately went to work at the Marlette telephone exchange because his father, suffering from diabetes, could no longer afford to send him to college.

The following winter, the father of one of McCrea's school friends, then a midshipman at the Naval Academy, asked McCrea if he had any interest in the navy. He indicated that he could arrange for McCrea to get an appointment to the Naval Academy and have the opportunity to take the entrance examination. McCrea had never given any thought to a naval career and doubted he could pass the entrance exam, but he thought he'd like to give it a try. As he traveled to Annapolis, Maryland, to see the academy, he was filled with misgivings. But after one look at the beautiful campus, he decided then and there to do whatever it took to become a part of that impressive institution. In the fall of 1910, he attended a preparatory school in Annapolis for those intending to take the academy entrance examination. Casting distractions aside, he hit the books hard, knowing how much schoolwork he had to make up. He took the exam in the spring of 1911, passed, and entered the academy that summer.

McCrea graduated from the Naval Academy in 1915 with a class standing firmly in the bottom half of his class. Fleet Admiral Ernest J. King, who led the navy during most of World War II, and Fleet Admiral Chester A. Nimitz, who commanded naval operations in the Pacific and succeeded King as chief of naval operations, were respectively fourteen and ten classes senior to McCrea. Both had graduated near the top of their classes. However, despite McCrea's lackluster academic performance, he possessed qualities that made him stand out as an officer. He rose through the navy's ranks to work closely under King and Nimitz, and they regarded him highly. The story of his development as a naval officer will help to explain why he was entrusted with great responsibility during the war and illuminate the source of some of his core beliefs and practices. His upward naval trajectory was propelled by a combination of personality, job performance, and a bit of good luck.

McCrea had a natural air of authority and looked like a military officer. He was tall, erect, and always impeccably dressed. He also had what was once described as "an attractive personality." He was quick-witted, charming, and tactful, with a fine sense of humor. In company, he was an engaging raconteur. He liked people and understood them, and they liked him. In 1942, a Washington society columnist once described him in print as "popular Capt. John McCrea." He was proposed as President Roosevelt's naval aide in part because his personality would be a good fit with the president's.

Other traits contributed more directly to McCrea's naval success. He possessed sound judgment and an exceptional memory, and he was devoted to the navy. Principled and modest, he was secure enough in his authority to entertain a subordinate's suggestion if he felt it had merit, and he was not intimidated by high rank or powerful personalities. He was willing to speak his mind to his superiors if he felt the matter important, and he was comfortable and effective in the higher echelons of the navy.

Although McCrea's personality made him an attractive shipmate, it was his performance of duty that primarily fueled his rise. At the Naval Academy, he showed a gift for leadership. During his final year, he was awarded two rotations as company commander in the student military organization, and he discovered that he liked command. In his first two assignments after graduation, he again showed ability, and he developed standards and practices that would become his signature in later years.

McCrea's first assignment was on the USS *New York*, a battleship known for the excellence of its officers. McCrea served there for four years, including two years during World War I, when *New York* was the flagship of a division of U.S. battleships that served with the British Grand Fleet in the North Sea. McCrea absorbed *New York*'s high standards and applied them on other vessels for the rest of his career. One executive officer (second-in-command of the ship) had a particularly profound influence on him. The officer took a personal interest in the well-being of his subordinates, both officer and enlisted. He showed them respect and occasionally shielded them from the displeasure of higher authority about matters of little significance. In return, the men respected and liked him and gave him superb performance. As will be evident in McCrea's command style on *Iowa*, he adopted this approach to leadership.

Just a lieutenant in 1919, McCrea's second assignment was as the most junior member of the staff of Admiral Hugh Rodman, the first commander in chief of the Pacific Fleet. Rodman had served on *New York* as commanding officer and later as the admiral in command of the battleship division loaned to the British during the war. Rodman was greatly impressed by McCrea, and when he got the Pacific Fleet command after the war, he asked McCrea to serve as his aide.

Rodman liked to test young officers by giving them assignments beyond their experience to see how they handled themselves. With full knowledge that the Pacific Fleet would soon be downsized and face an acute personnel shortage, Rodman assigned McCrea as fleet personnel officer in charge of fleet staffing. McCrea had grave doubts about his competence for this duty, but he took it on, and, with judgment beyond his years, he performed well, despite heavy criticism from senior fleet officers that their staffing needs were receiving short shrift. As personnel officer, McCrea demonstrated a quality that he prized in others, the ability "to roll with the punches," to take on any assignment without question and perform well under pressure. This quality would be much in evidence in McCrea's work at the White House.

At the end of his tour of staff duty, McCrea returned to more rank-appropriate assignments. As was typical in navy practice, he alternated between periods of sea duty and shore duty. When ashore, he took advantage of educational opportunities. He spent a year at the Naval War College, and later he participated in the navy's challenging postgraduate program in law, working full-time in the Office of the Judge Advocate General (JAG) while earning a bachelor's degree in law. In two subsequent tours in the JAG Office, he earned a master's degree in law (although the navy did not require one) and served briefly as acting assistant attorney general.

Although McCrea enjoyed the War College and the law, his passion was sea duty. With his love of command and the challenges and camaraderie of shipboard life, he wanted to be a "line officer," one who commands in battle. Higher authority took note of some of his impressive early accomplishments at sea. In 1925, in command of his first ship, his quick response to a distress signal on a foggy night in Chefoo, China, enabled him to rescue the passengers on a grounded steamship. As chief of staff to the commander of the Special Service Squadron based in the Panama Canal Zone, he developed a disaster plan for civilian earthquake relief by the U.S. military, and his plan was immediately put into effect when a major earthquake struck Nicaragua. Shortly afterward, he took command of a destroyer judged "a non-effective unit of the fleet" and turned it into a successful performer in less than a year.

By 1936, the chief of the Bureau of Navigation (the navy's personnel office) had sufficient confidence in McCrea to make an example of him for his fellow officers. Since the turn of the nineteenth century, the navy had operated a naval base and the local government on the island of Guam, an American possession in the mid-Pacific. However, Guam duty was extremely unpopular because naval officers, particularly line officers, viewed assignment there as a sign that their careers were on the rocks. To remove the stigma attached to this duty, and over McCrea's vigorous objections, the bureau ordered McCrea to the island as executive of the naval base and aide for civil administration to the governor. McCrea was most unhappy about having to expose his family to the primitive conditions and isolation of his new post. He had married Estelle Murphy in 1925, and by this time the couple had two young daughters, Meredith, nine, and Annie, not yet one.

About the time McCrea received his orders, the chief of the Bureau of Navigation wrote him, promising that if McCrea performed as well as expected on Guam, he would subsequently get "a good job in the fleet." McCrea saved the letter as insurance.

McCrea threw himself into the problems of Guam's government, employing his law school training in civil subjects for the first and only time. When he started, Pan American Airways was in the process of establishing trans-Pacific passenger service between San Francisco and Hong Kong, with intermediate stops at Honolulu, Midway Island, Wake Island, Guam, and the Philippines. McCrea worked with Pan Am as it set up and staffed its operations, negotiating employment contacts for Guamanian workers and establishing Pan Am's obligations to the island government.

Discovering that Guam's sole fresh water source was rain, McCrea hired two geologists and initiated a drilling program that produced sixteen fresh water wells during the next year and a half. He stabilized the finances of the Bank of Guam, served as a court magistrate, drafted a disaster plan for earthquakes and typhoons, and improved island education. By the fall of 1937, when McCrea left the island, he had compiled a remarkable record of achievement.

Returning to Washington for his final tour in the JAG Office, Commander McCrea immediately established friendly relations with his detail officer in anticipation of negotiating the "good job in the fleet" he had been promised. In November 1938, he landed a prize assignment: executive officer of the battleship USS *Pennsylvania*, the flagship of the U.S. Fleet and one of the navy's most prestigious vessels. As executive, he was responsible for the administration of the ship's day-to-day operations. He focused hard on preparing for war. Most in the navy, including senior officers, thought it highly unlikely the U.S. would ever go to war.

In August 1940, Captain A. Trood Bidwell, McCrea's new detail officer and an old friend, contacted McCrea about his next assignment. Bidwell indicated that McCrea would likely be selected for the rank of captain that November, and if so, he could have command of a light cruiser. McCrea was delighted. However, a month later, in a complete change of plan, McCrea was ordered to Washington, D.C., to report to Admiral Harold R. "Betty" Stark, the chief of naval operations (CNO), to prepare a paper entitled "Are We Ready?," a study of the navy's preparedness for war.

McCrea had always been lucky in his naval career. Much of this luck involved being an eyewitness to history or a participant in noteworthy events. Later, he would describe these incidents to fascinated listeners in reminiscences that he called "yarns." One of his yarns from the summer of 1911 was about his role in launching the navy's third airplane, the very first plane he had ever seen. Built by the Wright brothers and shipped to the Naval Academy in boxes, the biplane was assembled overnight in the armory. It had enough power to fly, but not enough to take off. McCrea had the luck to be one of twenty or so midshipmen selected to run down the parade ground pulling the plane with lines until it achieved enough momentum to take flight. Luck struck again on the *New York*. In 1915, McCrea was detailed to explain the operation of a 14-inch gun and its firing chamber to an extremely deaf Thomas A. Edison, then studying the effect of heat on metal alloys. Still later, in 1918, McCrea happened to be stationed on the bridge of *New York* when the German High Seas Fleet surrendered to the British at the end of World War I, and he had the honor of recording the surrender in the ship's log. He always seemed to be present when something interesting was taking place.

Assignment to the Office of the Chief of Naval Operations was another stroke of luck, far more significant than an occasion to acquire yarn material. The "Are We Ready?" project would give McCrea a chance to acquire broad knowledge of naval operations and war preparedness as war loomed on the horizon. More importantly, he would have the opportunity to work with, and earn the confidence of, the men in charge of the navy.

At the Navy Department, McCrea was assigned an office along the front corridor. He "hoisted aboard" the details of the "Are We Ready?" study as quickly as possible, got Admiral Stark's approval to say he was acting in Stark's name, and made significant progress during the fall of 1940. The results met with Stark's approval, and McCrea felt they hit it off pretty well.

Shortly after McCrea reported to the Navy Department, Captain Richmond Kelly Turner arrived as head of the War Plans Division. He moved into the office next to McCrea's with a connecting door in between. Turner was a whirlwind who quickly made his presence felt. He took an immediate interest in McCrea's study. A few days later, he breezed into McCrea's office and announced that the navy's Orange war plans for armed conflict with Japan were completely inadequate, and he was going to write new ones. He needed peace and quiet, so he was going to lock his front office door, and told McCrea to intercept any uninvited visitors. As the fall progressed, McCrea saw more of Turner, who showed a continuing interest in McCrea and his work.

Early in Thanksgiving week, Turner announced, to McCrea's surprise, that he wanted McCrea to deliver and explain the new Orange war plans to the commanders in chief of the U.S. and Asiatic Fleets. In minutes, Stark summoned McCrea to his office and indicated he and Captain Turner wanted McCrea for an important, top secret officer messenger assignment to Admiral James O. Richardson, commander in chief of the U.S. Fleet in Pearl Harbor, and Admiral Thomas C. Hart, commander in chief of the U.S. Asiatic Fleet in the Philippines. He was to depart in early December on a trip of at least a month, and no one but the three of them was to know about it.

Turner gave McCrea a crash course in the war plans. Besides studying, McCrea had many arrangements to make. He was to fly to Asia on civilian aircraft, traveling incognito as a civilian.

As Christmas approached, he felt increasingly uncomfortable keeping the trip from his wife. Finally, a week before his departure, he obtained Stark's permission to tell Estelle he would be traveling over Christmas without giving her any details. She was taken aback and disappointed, but she promised to keep the trip a secret.

On December 13, McCrea flew out of Washington, D.C., with a briefcase of war plans. He would not reach his destination in the Philippines for twenty-four days, largely due to the inability of the aircraft of the day to cope with bad weather. McCrea's experience flying across the Pacific provides a striking glimpse of the best in commercial aviation in the early 1940s.

McCrea booked flights to Honolulu and the Philippines on Pan American's trans-Pacific Clipper service, the same service he had helped to organize in Guam and the only one offering flights across the Pacific. In the late afternoon at San Pedro harbor in Los Angeles, he boarded his Clipper—a large, luxury seaplane. On

On Admiral Stark's instructions, McCrea met with General MacArthur, who was then temporarily retired from the U.S. Army and serving as military advisor to the Commonwealth Government of the Philippines. The general talked about the war in Europe and North Africa. He spoke while striding up and down in his office with cigar in hand, occasionally shaking it in McCrea's direction by way of emphasis. He remarked that the Germans had missed their chance to win the war when they failed to overwhelm the British at Dunkirk and invade the British Isles. He attributed this failure to the Germans' inability to resist the temptations of Paris. McCrea wondered cautiously about U.S. involvement in the war. MacArthur's thundering reply: "It is inevitable that we, the United States, will actively participate in this war. Do you think we would build up a $20 billion machine and not use it?"

Admiral Hart had described MacArthur as being "positive in his views," and knowing "many things that are not so." When McCrea reported the general's remark about the Germans' inability to resist the temptations of Paris, Hart dismissed it out of hand. He thought the Germans lacked the amphibious capability to invade England. It was clear to McCrea that Hart did not think highly of MacArthur.

McCrea left Manila on January 20. With the exception of two hours flying at an altitude of two hundred feet to avoid turbulence, McCrea's Clipper flights east were without incident. Since McCrea's departure from Washington, Admiral Richardson had been ordered to be detached as commander in chief, U.S. Fleet, and Rear Admiral Husband E. Kimmel had been named as his relief. Kimmel, a long-time friend of McCrea, was already at Pearl Harbor, and McCrea met with both admirals on his return trip. Both expressed the view that Pearl's air defenses were inadequate, and the situation needed immediate attention.

On returning to Washington, McCrea gradually finished the "Are We Ready?" project. Not long afterward, Admiral Stark asked him to move into his office to serve as his third aide. McCrea spent takeoff, the Clipper immediately encountered stiff headwinds and bucked about. At about eleven o'clock in the evening, the plane captain appeared in the passenger lounge for a cup of coffee and told an astonished McCrea that they were headed back to California. Pan Am required its planes to return to the coast if they got halfway to the Hawaiian Islands with less than a required amount of gas. The next morning, at the captain's invitation, McCrea joined him on the bridge as he attempted to land the plane. Heavy fog blanketed southern California, so they headed north. When they finally set down in San Francisco Bay, they had flown 22 hours and traveled, as the crow flies, a distance of only 400 miles.

McCrea stayed at a hotel waiting for the next westbound Clipper, but bad weather persisted. After four days, Pan Am told him that a plane was leaving that afternoon, but it would take no passengers. Pan Am's contract with the U.S. Post Office required that mail be given preference at all times, and much mail had accumulated. McCrea immediately called Admiral Stark, who called the postmaster general and asked him to offload enough mail so McCrea and another officer could reach Pearl Harbor. On boarding the plane, they discovered that all the seats had been removed to accommodate the cargo, and that night, after a stiff drink, they slept fully clothed on sacks of mail.

McCrea arrived at Pearl Harbor on December 21. He spent several days briefing Admiral Richardson and his staff about the revised war plans. Afterward, he was delayed again by weather in Honolulu and by engine trouble at Midway. He finally reached Manila on January 6, 1941. Just two years later, President Roosevelt would fly another Clipper with similar limitations across the Atlantic during wartime.

In the Philippines, Admiral Hart invited McCrea to stay in his cabin on board his flagship. The opportunity to get to know Admiral Hart was a highlight of McCrea's trip. McCrea was impressed by Hart's thoughtful analysis of the international situation, and the two discussed the war plans and naval and local government affairs at length.

much of his time on the admiral's heavy correspondence with the commanders afloat. Communications from the fleets were usually filled with questions, and McCrea drafted replies with information he dug out of the bureaus and offices. He found this work most interesting, and delighted in seeing how fast he could get answers to the people in the field. He also prepared Admiral Stark for meetings with President Roosevelt, and from time to time the admiral told him what the president had on his mind. During the summer, McCrea was promoted to the rank of captain.

As 1941 progressed, the international situation deteriorated. Stark received a visit from Admiral Kichisaburo Nomura, the Japanese ambassador to the United States. Nomura had sought the meeting because the field of diplomacy was new to him, and he felt more at ease talking to another sailor than to a diplomat. He was disturbed at the trend of diplomatic negotiations between Japan and the United States. He stated that the military in control of his government were highly provincial, with little knowledge of world affairs. He felt the United States would win any war with Japan because it had virtually unlimited resources, but his government didn't seem to understand Japan's limitations. Nomura assured Stark he would make every effort to avert a war.

By fall, most in the Navy Department thought war was imminent, although those on the front corridor were aware of efforts to negotiate with Japan. On November 27, Kelly Turner, by then a rear admiral, handed Admiral Stark a dispatch he had drafted. It was from the chief of naval operations to the commanders in chief of the Asiatic and Pacific Fleets. Turner recommended that the dispatch be sent at once. Its opening sentence read, "This dispatch is to be considered a war warning." It indicated that a Japanese aggressive move was expected shortly in the Philippines or Southeast Asia.

Admiral Stark immediately called a conference. Those present were Rear Admiral Turner; the president of the navy's General Board, an advisory body comprised of senior officers; the assistant chief of naval operations; and two of Stark's aides, including McCrea. Admiral Stark read the proposed dispatch aloud. He questioned the bluntness of the opening sentence. Pointed discussion followed. In the end, the war warning remained, and the dispatch was sent.

During the fourteen months preceding the transmission of the war warning dispatch, McCrea had acquired a unique combination of knowledge, experience, and trust. He had earned the confidence of the chief of naval operations. He was familiar with the CNO's interactions with the fleet commanders in the Pacific, he had written the report on the navy's war preparedness, and he knew as much as anyone about the navy's revised plans for war with Japan. He was poised to become an invaluable figure in the navy's war effort.

Chapter 1

The United States Goes to War

Everyone old enough to remember the attack on Pearl Harbor has his tale to tell about what he was doing that day. This is mine. On the morning of 7 December 1941, a Sunday, I noted in the paper that newsreels of the Army-Navy football game would be shown at the Trans-Lux Theater that afternoon. My daughter Meredith and I thought it would be fun to go.

After lunch, we took off for downtown Washington. I stopped at the Army-Navy Club to cash a check. While I was at the desk, a brother officer who lived at the club came rushing down the stairs and asked if I was headed for the Navy Department. I countered that I was taking my daughter to the movies.

"Evidently you haven't heard, John," said he. "Pearl Harbor is under enemy attack."

Of course, that called for an immediate change in plans. Meredith assured me she could make her way home by public transportation. My friend and I drove to the Navy Department in my Ford.

Arriving at the department, I found that my boss, Chief of Naval Operations Admiral Stark, was already there. As was his habit, he had come to the office on Sunday morning to work.

When I entered his office, he was trying to establish long-distance scrambler contact with Admiral Claude C. Bloch, commandant of the Fourteenth Naval District at Pearl Harbor. At Admiral Stark's direction, I manned the telephone on my desk, which had a switch to Admiral Stark's line. After some little delay, contact was made with Admiral Bloch. The conversation went something like this.

"Claude," said Admiral Stark, "tell me all you can about the attack. Is the damage severe?"

"Betty, how secure is this scrambler telephone?"

"I really don't know, but go ahead, Claude, and give me all the information you can."

"The damage is severe, Betty, but at this moment I can't tell you how severe. I can only talk in generalities."

And then Admiral Bloch proceeded to give us one bit of bad news after another. Finally, Admiral Bloch said, "If anyone other than Admiral Stark and I have overheard this conversation, I beg of them, as loyal citizens, to keep the nature of this conversation to themselves." I scratched out a longhand memorandum of the conversation and gave it to Admiral Stark. He disappeared down the corridor to the office of Frank Knox, secretary of the navy.

At a free moment, I called my wife, Estelle, to find out if Meredith had made it home. I told Estelle to get out my service uniforms, because an order was going out that afternoon that all naval personnel from here on would be in uniform. "No, I don't know when I'll be home. I'll let you know when I leave the office. Keep tuned to your radio. You're bound to hear items of interest."

The telephone jangled all afternoon as more information became available. There were a number of telephone calls between Admiral Stark and Admiral Bloch. I monitored all these calls and prepared memoranda about the details. Admiral Stark called Captain John Beardall, naval aide to President Roosevelt, so that Beardall could keep the president informed. The admiral also made many visits to the office of Secretary Knox.

The extent of the damage was staggering. The only positive news was that the Japanese had not attacked the navy yard installation or the tank farm, where thousands and thousands of barrels of fuel oil were stored.

Between 6:30 and 7:00 p.m., Admiral Bloch called again with more information. I wrote up another memorandum and took it in to Admiral Stark.

"John," said he, "run this down to the secretary. He has seen enough of me this afternoon. Besides, I am a bit weary." I proceeded to the secretary's office and announced that I had a memorandum for him. "Go right in," said the officer in the secretary's outer office.

I entered the secretary's inner office, but I did not see him. I stood there a moment or two, unsure of what to do. I thought I heard a noise coming from his washroom. I coughed to make my presence known, and Secretary Knox stuck his head out of the washroom.

"Oh, it's you, Captain," said he. "Come right in. Come right in. This has been a strenuous afternoon, and I was preparing a small drink of bourbon for myself in the hopes that it would raise my spirits a bit. Won't you join me?"

"Well, Mr. Secretary," said I, "I have never had a drink in the Navy Department, but I agree that this has been a strenuous afternoon. Of course, I can hardly decline an invitation from my chief."

The secretary had the bottle in his hand, and he poured a drink for himself and one for me. He raised his glass and said, "Now that the war is here, despite its tragic start," said he, "I am counting on the navy to acquit itself well."

"I can drink to that, Mr. Secretary," said I. And between sips, we discussed the happenings of the day and the memo that I had in my hand.

In due course, I thanked the secretary for his hospitality and withdrew. I went immediately to acquaint Admiral Stark with the details of my visit. "I was wondering what was keeping you," he said, with a smile on his face and in his voice. "It's been a rugged afternoon, hasn't it?" I had to agree.

One of the visitors to the office early that evening was Admiral Richmond Kelly Turner. He went in to see Admiral Stark and stayed a considerable time. On his way out, he stopped to speak to me.

"You will recall that shortly after I reported as chief of war plans, I detailed you to watchdog duty to keep people out of my office. Now that war has arrived, Admiral Stark will be busier than ever. He will have much to do, and he will have to do a lot of thinking. Because of Admiral Stark's nature, it's going to be very hard for him to say 'no' to visitors. You must keep people out of his hair." Admiral Turner was most emphatic.

"That's a big job," I responded. "I can do my best to persuade people not to go in, but lacking an order to do so, my position wouldn't be very sound."

"I'll think about it," said Admiral Turner.

I got home between 2:30 and 3:00 a.m. and snatched a couple of hours' sleep. Then I got into uniform and went back to the office. On my desk, I found a memorandum to the effect that, because of hostilities, the availability of the chief of naval operations would be sharply limited, and anyone who wished to see Admiral Stark should call Captain McCrea regarding an appointment.

I had hardly finished reading when Admiral Turner appeared in my office. He told me that the evening before he had counseled Admiral Stark that he must conserve time and energy and he needed to work without distractions. Pointing to the memorandum, Turner said, "I whipped this up last night, and right now some 900 copies are being distributed in the Navy Department. Let me know as soon as Admiral Stark comes in. I wish to tell him what I have done. I think he will approve."

A few days later, after I had learned more details about the Japanese attack, I recalled the evening in January 1941 when

Admiral Hart and I had discussed Japan's high-ranking naval officers. Admiral Hart's intelligence officer, Commander Redfield
"Rosie" Mason, was also present. I had suggested it might be of
interest to have thumbnail sketches of the flag officers most likely
to be met in combat, should war occur. They came up with sketches
of six officers.

I checked my trip notes to see whether Admiral Yamamoto had
been one of the officers discussed that night.[1] He was number two
on the list. My notes read:

> Energetic. Highly able. Bold in contrast to most, who are
> inclined to be cautious. Decisive. He has an American view-
> point. Formerly naval attaché in Washington. London Arms
> Conference delegate. Well versed in international affairs. A
> wounded veteran, having lost two fingers at Tsushima.
> Highly thought of by rank and file of the Orange Navy. Per-
> sonally likes Americans. Plays excellent bridge and poker.
> Alert in every way. Very air-minded.

I was impressed with the accuracy of the sketch.

Of course, my friend Admiral Kimmel was in command of the
naval forces at Pearl Harbor at the time of the Japanese attack. He
was relieved of command immediately afterward and subsequently
blamed for many of the navy's failures in connection with the attack.
My heart went out to him. I know of no one who worked harder at
being a good naval officer. In my opinion, if we had had Horatio
Nelson and Napoleon Bonaparte out there, Pearl Harbor would
still have happened as it did. The country simply wasn't ready for it.

Events moved rapidly during the month of December. During
Christmas week, Prime Minister Winston Churchill and the British joint chiefs arrived in the United States in a large and heavily

---

1   Admiral Isoroku Yamamato, commander in chief of the Combined Fleet of
    the Imperial Japanese Navy, conceived of the plan to attack Pearl Harbor.

armed Royal Navy ship. The ship anchored in Annapolis Roads, a short distance from the Naval Academy. President Roosevelt drove to Annapolis to welcome the prime minister. On their arrival in Washington, the prime minister took up residence in the White House. He set up his traveling war room, and he was in business.

On Sunday, 23 December, Admiral Stark called to say that the president had called a conference at the White House for 6:00 p.m. that evening, and the admiral wished me to accompany him. The meeting was held in the president's second-floor study. Admiral Stark introduced me to the president. We were all introduced to the prime minister, who in turn introduced his chiefs of staff.

The president presided at the meeting. After a few general remarks, he announced that the prime minister would acquaint us with his views on the current crisis. This the PM did, with his well-publicized eloquence. He deplored the despicable philosophy of Nazism and the violence that it had produced on the continent. "Our immediate objective is to destroy the economy of the enemy, which enables it to support its military operations. With this accomplished, our next objective should be to meet the enemy on the continent and bring about its total military destruction."

The meeting lasted an hour or so. A drink was had, and a cracker or two. When the group broke up, Admiral Stark and I walked back to the Navy Department. On the way he said, "Well, John, what did you think of it?" After stumbling a bit, I remarked that I had had the privilege of attending a historic conference, for which I thanked him. He agreed that the conference might well be considered historic.[2]

---

2 The meeting McCrea attended was part of the first Washington conference of President Roosevelt and Prime Minister Churchill after the United States became a belligerent. The conference was code-named Arcadia (December 22, 1942–January 14, 1943). At the conference, the president, the prime minister, and top U.S. and British military leaders met to review the status of the war and plan for the future.

A senior British-U.S. military group—that is, the British joint chiefs and U.S. representatives of the army and navy—commenced a series of meetings the very next afternoon. The U.S. leaders were the chief of staff of the army, General George Marshall, and the chief of naval operations, Admiral Stark. The British joint chiefs were First Sea Lord Admiral Sir Dudley Pound, chief of the Royal Navy; Air Chief Marshal Charles Portal, chief of the Royal Air Force; and the head of the British Army, Field Marshal Sir Alan F. Brooke, whose title was chief of the Imperial General Staff.

General Marshall designated Colonel William Sexton to be the army's secretary at these meetings. Admiral Stark designated me as secretary for the navy. This was the first time I had ever done anything along that line, and I was far from pleased with my performance.

While these meetings were going on, matters of personal importance took place. On the afternoon of 2 January 1942, I was at my desk struggling with my notes of the meetings when Rear Admiral Randall Jacobs, chief of the Bureau of Navigation, stuck his head in my office door. "John, how fast can you move?"

"Awfully fast," said I, quickly on my feet, "especially if it's the cruiser command that I understand Captain Carpender has been saving for me."[3]

"Well," said Admiral Jacobs, "forget the cruiser, John. But it's an important job just the same."

The door closed and he was off, leaving me in a state of wonderment. My little secretary, the charming Miss Margaret Dudley, said, "What does he mean?"

"I wish I knew," was my reply.

---

3   Before the Pearl Harbor raid, Captain Arthur S. Carpender, assistant chief of personnel at the Bureau of Navigation, offered McCrea a command in a cruiser division Carpender was to command. McCrea eagerly accepted.

In about ten minutes, Admiral Jacobs returned. He handed me a copy of a memorandum signed by the secretary of the navy, which stated:

Memorandum for the President
It is my desire to appoint Captain John R. Beardall, U.S. Navy, at present serving as your naval aide, to the recently vacated position of superintendent of the United States Naval Academy, Annapolis, Maryland, provided such appointment is satisfactory to you. I nominate as his relief in his present position as your naval aide, Captain John L. McCrea, U.S. Navy. Captain McCrea has served in naval operations for a period of about fifteen months and for the past seven months has been aide to the chief of naval operations. He is thoroughly conversant with the present state of naval affairs. His professional record and his personality are such as to indicate that he would be an excellent naval aide for you.

Frank Knox

Before I had finished reading, Admiral Jacobs had gone.

As far as I knew, Admiral Stark knew nothing of this memorandum. I immediately entered his office. Admiral Ernest J. King was with him, engaged in friendly conversation.[4] Getting straight to the point, I told Admiral Stark about the memorandum and said I did not know how it had come about. I told him about the promised cruiser command. Then I listed rather heatedly all my reasons for not wishing to go to the White House, including my view that the assignment would be an expensive one that I could not afford.

---

4   Stark thought highly of King's abilities. He appointed King commander in chief of the U.S. Fleet, a position restructured after the Pearl Harbor attack to confer authority over all U.S. naval forces wherever located.

Both admirals King and Stark sat there quietly until I had finished. Admiral Stark remarked, "I have been aware of this proposal for some days. Admiral King and I agree that you should be made available to the president. We talked it over with the secretary, and that is how this memorandum came to be. We both wish you luck."

At this point, Admiral King broke in crisply, saying, "This country is at war, and you can afford anything your assignment might require. Besides, you will get a modest additional aide's allowance in that job."

As to Admiral King's first remark, I thought it well not to remind him that it had been common knowledge around the Navy Department that he had not so long ago left a Washington assignment early because he couldn't afford Washington duty. As to an allowance, I quickly responded that there was no allowance for the job of naval aide to the president. That was a surprise to Admiral King.

At this point, Admiral Stark joined the conversation. "I'm sure that the president will accept you as his naval aide, and, in that event, I think it wise for me to give you a bit of advice that I think you need. When you are naval aide to the president, and you find yourself in disagreement with him, I recommend that you not raise your voice to him as you do to me when you disagree with me."

Of course, I was taken aback. Admiral Stark laughed lightly. Admiral King smiled somewhat. I remarked, "Admiral Stark, if I raised my voice to you, it was not in any way in disrespect. If I raised my voice, it was because of my earnestness in whatever proposition that I was supporting. And I am grateful to you for the caution that you have just given me." All three of us laughed, and the incident was over. I withdrew.

On 3 January 1942, the secretary's memorandum to the president was returned to the secretary. On it, in large capital letters in the president's handwriting, was the notation:

FK
OK
FDR

My orders for this change of duty were carried out on 16 January 1942. And that is how I came to go to the White House as naval aide to FDR.[5]

---

5 McCrea reported to the White House after the Arcadia Conference, where several significant actions were taken. The conferees decided that the defeat of Germany would take priority over the war against Japan. They executed a Declaration by the United Nations, affirming that none of the countries at war with the Axis Powers would make a separate peace with the enemy. Finally, they gave the task of developing U.S.-British war strategy to a new body called the Combined Chiefs of Staff based in Washington, D.C. By mid-summer 1942, the United States was represented on the CCS by a Joint Chiefs of Staff, whose membership would remain constant for the rest of the war: Admiral William D. Leahy, chairman, chief of staff to the commander in chief of the U.S. Army and Navy; General George C. Marshall, chief of staff of the U.S. Army; Admiral Ernest J. King, chief of naval operations and commander in chief of the U.S. Fleet; and General Henry H. "Hap" Arnold, chief of the army air forces.

Chapter 2

Reporting to the President

The first person I met at the White House when I reported as naval aide was Major General Edwin M. Watson, the president's military aide.[6] No one around the White House ever addressed him by his military title. He was known to everybody simply as "Pa"—Pa Watson. He had known the president as a young officer, and a high degree of rapport existed between them.

Pa came from Virginia. He talked with a Southern drawl, radiating goodwill and cheer with every word. Pa's father was a tobacconist who made some of his own products. His specialty was chewing tobacco. Pa delighted in telling that one of his father's most successful creations was a chewing plug named "Little Edwin" after him. "People started chewing me when I was just a little shaver, and they've been doing it ever since," he would say, followed with an uproarious laugh.

---

6   An aide, short for aide-de-camp, is an officer who acts as a personal assistant or secretary to a senior officer, in this case the commander in chief. In Roosevelt's day, "military aide" referred to an officer of the army, and "naval aide" to a naval officer. Subsequent presidents have had aides from the army, navy, and other services.

When President Roosevelt was elected in 1932, he requested that the army assign Pa as his military aide. Pa joined the president in that capacity in March 1933 and continued there until his death at sea, returning from the Yalta Conference in the early spring of 1945.

In addition to serving as the military aide, whose duties in peacetime were none too arduous, Pa was the president's appointments secretary. He liked the job immensely, and he was good at it. Almost everyone in Washington wanted to see the president at one time or other. Probably not one in a hundred ever made it.

It was a real circus to hear Pa on the telephone saying "no" to a would-be presidential visitor. "Now, Ernie"—I pick this name at random—"I can't tell you how good it is to hear your voice. What have you been doing lately with yourself?" and on and on.

"So you want to see the president, do you? Well, I must be frank with you, Ernie, and tell you that he is up to his neck in work. He is so darn busy that I, myself, who must see him many times a day, often stand outside his door and say to myself, 'Isn't there some way, Pa, that you can spare him this interruption?' I always feel better about it when I can say, 'Yes, Pa, there is. Just don't go in.' I can't tell you, Ernie, how good it makes me feel to keep from going in.

"So, Ernie, you can see how it is. I know the boss well enough to know that there isn't anyone in Washington whom he would more rather see than you. But he just can't make it today or any day soon, so far as I am able to forecast. I'll tell you, why don't you ring me up in a week or ten days from now, and maybe we can work something out.

"It's been so good, Ernie, to hear from you, and it's fine to know that you are so understanding. I'll tell the president of your call at the risk of catching hell for not letting you in. It's been so good to talk to you, Ernie. But you can see how it is."

And with that, Pa would hang up the phone. "Jesus, John," he would say, "if I let that guy in to see the president, I'd find myself fired from here and on duty with troops in about forty-eight hours." Another big uproarious laugh.

Pa was a perfect foil for the president's lighthearted ribbing. The president would tweak Pa about odds and ends. Pa used an aftershave lotion that was fragrant in the extreme. Once the president, Pa, and I went to the Lincoln Memorial for a wreath-laying ceremony. Pa's aftershave lotion was most notable. "What do you think of Pa this morning, John?" said the president. "Doesn't he smell pretty? Do you suppose all army officers smell pretty like this so early in the morning?" Pa laughed uproariously. All this, of course, was in high good humor and greatly enjoyed by Pa.

On the day I was to report to the White House, I had a call from Pa, whom I had not yet met. He said he wanted to put me on the president's appointment list at 4:00 p.m. and asked that I come to his office at that time. "Beardall will be here, too," Pa added, referring to Captain John Beardall, whom I was to relieve. Of course, I arrived in plenty of time. Promptly at 4:00 p.m. I was ushered into the president's office by Pa, who introduced me to the president and withdrew. Captain Beardall left shortly afterward.

The president was most cordial. He proceeded to startle me with what he knew about me and my career. "You know, Captain," said he, "when I was a boy in Hyde Park, one of my playmates was a John McCrea Livingston. I note that you are John Livingstone McCrea. Your Livingstone has an 'e' in it. His didn't. Is there any connection between your families?"

"None, Mr. President," said I. "My father and mother were both first-generation Canadians, and I suspect that your friend was one of the social Livingstons from up the river in New York." He concurred.

The president noted that I had served in the North Sea with the British Grand Fleet in the battleship division commanded by Admiral Hugh Rodman, and later with Rodman in the Pacific Fleet. He said that when he was assistant secretary of the navy, he had known the admiral, who was then a member of the navy's General Board.

I told the president that no doubt he had forgotten, but in 1920, when I was aide to Admiral Rodman, he had taken the admiral and me to his home for lunch with his family. When issuing the invitation, he had told Rodman that he didn't think his kids had ever seen an admiral in uniform.

"Of course, I remember the incident," the president said. "But I didn't associate you with it."

After telling an amusing story about Admiral Rodman, the president got down to business. He outlined my duties. "You know I have always liked the navy. It was one of my earliest ambitions to go to Annapolis, but my mother vetoed that idea. I enjoyed greatly my association with the navy when I was the assistant secretary of the navy during the Wilson years.

"I would like you to be my eyes and ears in the Navy Department. I'm sure you won't burden me with nonessentials, but I confess that little things about the navy will be of more interest to me than the same sort of things about the other services.

"I shall be seeing you twice daily, in the morning and the late afternoon. I'll see you seven days a week, if I'm in town. I'm sure you will arrange to be available at other times.

"One other thing. I hold two press conferences a week, one on Tuesday afternoon for the benefit of the morning papers, and one on Friday morning for the benefit of the afternoon papers. Rightly or wrongly, I got the impression when I was assistant secretary of the navy that you naval officers live a largely cloistered existence. I want you to attend my press conferences, because I know of no better way for you to understand what is on the minds of the people about our navy and government than by attendance at these conferences."

I assured the president that I would attend. With this, our talk seemed at an end, so I excused myself and was gone.

On my way out, I again encountered Pa Watson. "Who runs the plan of the day around here?" I asked him, by way of trying to pick up a little information.

"There is no plan aside from the president's appointment list," said he. "I generally see him when he is at breakfast. We make up his appointments for the day from the list of those who want to see him and those he wishes to see. The list, at times, becomes formidable. Besides appointments, regular meetings with the leaders of Congress, and press conferences, little else happens but the routine signing of mail. Mr. Rudolph Forster, who has been here since the Cleveland days, is the executive secretary, and he looks out for all routine matters."

Pa continued. "Another item. Within a few days, if the past is any indication of the future, you are going to be on a first-name basis around the White House. Have you a nickname?"

"No," said I. I suppose I could have told him that aboard the *Pennsylvania,* I was known in the junior officers' mess as "Tough John." This information hardly seemed appropriate for Pa's purposes.

"Well, what would you prefer to be called? Mac, Jack, John, or anything else?"

"If a choice has to be made, I would prefer to be called John," said I. And thus it was that within the week I was addressed as John by the top echelon, and as Captain by those on the lower levels.

"And one more thing," continued Pa. "I've been around here a long time, and I've picked up a few things. I want to give you the benefit of my experience. When I was a young officer, my colonel once told me that I was being paid about six times my worth, and I was getting that because of the amount of punishment that I could absorb. A healthy young second lieutenant can absorb plenty of punishment, you know.

"Well, every so often around here, I feel that I have to absorb more than my share of punishment. Accordingly—and I think this important—I try to keep out of sight. I would much rather have them say, 'Where's Pa?' than have the thought flash across their mind, 'There he is again.' Be available, but be out of sight. Get it?"

I got it. And it was good advice, too.

"By the way," said Pa. "It's five o'clock. Let's go into my private office." In his office, Pa pulled out a drawer, and from it, a couple of glasses and a bottle of bourbon whiskey.

"Now," said Pa, "my doctor is Walter Bloedorn. You must know him, John. He's a retired navy doctor, and he's also the dean of the medical school at George Washington University. Walter says that a little bit of bourbon is good for me in the evening. This is about the time for my two fingers of bourbon. Walter also says, 'Pa, don't drink too much,' and I always remember that. I take two fingers of bourbon. If in an hour I don't feel like a man, I take another two fingers."

This was my introduction to duty as naval aide to President Roosevelt. It was both interesting and pleasant.

Upon my return to the Navy Department, I left word with Admiral King's aide that I had reported to the president. Since my detachment orders had been delivered by Admiral Stark, I thought it appropriate to inform Admiral King of their execution. In no time flat, Admiral King sent for me.

After I was announced, Admiral King proceeded sternly about as follows. "I need hardly tell you, Captain McCrea," said he, biting off his words, "that you have achieved a minor degree of notoriety by being assigned to duty as naval aide to the president of the United States. Experience has led me to the conviction that if anyone succeeds by hard work, rare good fortune, or both, to raise his head this far above the herd, there are untold numbers of sons of bitches standing by, ready and willing to knock him down a peg." The admiral indicated the distance by holding his thumb and forefinger about an inch apart.

"Another thing that will, no doubt, amaze you is the number of people senior to you, people who have heretofore never given you a tumble, who will now address you as 'John, old boy.' Don't be flattered by it. It's just part of the pattern that I have described.

"Now, as to our relations. I expect, from time to time, to make use of you to transmit matters to the president. You are to attend the morning conferences held by the secretary of the navy. You are to have access to all top secret, secret, and confidential dispatches, and the communications people have been so informed.

"I wish you luck in your new assignment. I think you will ably represent the navy at the White House. Otherwise, Admiral Stark and I would never have recommended you to the secretary for this assignment. Don't hesitate to consult me at any time you think it advisable to do so."

The next person to send for me was Secretary Knox. During my time with Admiral Stark, I had occasion to see a lot of the secretary. He was a pleasant, outgoing personality, greatly interested in the navy. He was a lifelong Republican and had been Alf Landon's running mate in the presidential elections of 1936.[7] During President Roosevelt's second administration, he asked Knox to be secretary of the navy, and Henry L. Stimson, another Republican, to be secretary of war. The appointments were made when the president concluded that the Hitler menace in Europe posed a potential threat to this country.

When I met with Secretary Knox, he remarked, "I asked that you come by, Captain, to tell you that I am pleased at your new assignment. I trust it will be a pleasant one. You are welcome to attend my morning conferences. In fact, I expect you to attend. At the conferences, we will try to bring all the happenings of the previous twenty-four hours into focus. These summaries, no doubt, will be helpful to you in keeping the president advised."

"Thank you, Mr. Secretary," said I. "The president has told me that he wants me to be his eyes and ears insofar as the navy and the Navy Department are concerned. I tell you this so that if there is anything that you don't want the president to know, I trust you will not speak about it to me."

---

7   In the election of 1936, Alf Landon, governor of Kansas, and Frank Knox, publisher, were the Republican candidates for president and vice president. They were defeated in a landslide by the incumbents, Franklin D. Roosevelt and John Nance Garner.

I continued, "Captain Carpender had me lined up for a cruiser command, so this assignment is not particularly welcome. Now I find myself in a job that, I suppose, has some political overtones. I have never voted. However, I was raised a Republican, and as far as I know, I am no New Dealer."

Secretary Knox responded with a belly-shaking laugh. "Well, Captain, what do you think I am? A New Dealer? Not a bit of it. I'm a thoroughgoing Republican serving a Democratic president. When I was asked to take this job, I considered the political implications that seemed to go with it. Taking the job wasn't easy on my political conscience, but I'm delighted that I did. I have greatly enjoyed knowing and working with President Roosevelt. The cabinet associations have been splendid, and I've found that the New Dealers in the cabinet have the same love of their country that I do. My bet is that you will enjoy this assignment. I may utilize you from time to time to take messages to the president. We'll work this out to the advantage of all of us."

With that, I withdrew and went to my office to contemplate the good advice and offers of assistance that I had received from Admiral King and Secretary Knox.

Chapter 3

Zeroing In

———⟨∞⟩———

My first days at the White House were focused on "zeroing in," if I may use that expression, on my new responsibilities. I established my regular routine and gave thought to what the role of naval aide should be now that the country was at war. I knew the job would be vastly different than it had been in peacetime, when the duties were largely ceremonial.

Every morning about 7:30 I went to the Navy Department and read through the night's incoming dispatches in the office of Admiral Ernest J. King, then commander in chief of the U.S. Fleet.[8] I pulled out the dispatches I thought would interest the president. At 8:30, I attended the daily conference of the secretary of the navy. The chief of naval operations, the bureau chiefs and department heads in the Office of the Chief of Naval Operations, and the commandant of the U.S. Marine Corps attended the secretary's conferences. I was the only officer below flag rank.

---

8   Admiral King assumed the duties of commander in chief of the U.S. Fleet (CominCh) on December 30, 1941. On March 26, 1942, he relieved Admiral Stark as chief of naval operations, and remained in both positions throughout the war.

After the secretary's conference, I went to the president's bedroom at the White House to update the president on overnight events. To save his time, I read the dispatches to him. Often I perched on the toilet cover and read to him while he shaved. I met with the president again in the late afternoon to brief him on the day's events. These meetings took place in his office or sometimes in the White House office of his physician, Rear Admiral Ross T. McIntire, Medical Corps, U.S. Navy.

I conveyed to the president, as soon as need be, documents and information relating to the war and other urgent matters. Less important papers that I thought would be of interest to him I accumulated in the dispatch box on my desk. These generally involved the administration of the Navy Department. On Sunday mornings, I took the papers from the dispatch box to the White House along with the important dispatches that had come in overnight. The president didn't go to his office on Sunday mornings, so he was free to talk and look at non-urgent papers.

A friend who had once served as President Roosevelt's naval aide paid me a "well-wishing call" when my appointment was announced. He told me that the president was genuinely interested in all that the navy did, and that he had the memory of an elephant. My friend advised that I inform myself thoroughly about the things that seemed to interest the president because he was likely to refer to them again. This advice proved to be good indeed in preparing for briefing sessions.

Rapid communication with the White House was a must for my job. Immediately after I reported to the White House, telephone men appeared at my home to install two telephones, one in my bedroom and the other on the first floor. Both phones connected directly to the White House switchboard. They were off-limits to my family and were to be answered only by me, or, in my absence, by my wife. I had an office in the Navy Department, and it, too, had a direct line to the White House switchboard. The direct lines allowed me virtually instant communication with the

White House. I kept the White House switchboard informed of my whereabouts at all times so I could be located any time, day or night.

As part of "zeroing in" on my job, I thought it important to acquaint myself with the inner workings of the White House. Pa Watson introduced me to the heads of all the offices. He knew everyone on a first-name basis, including most of the secretaries. I should note here that, throughout my time as naval aide, I made it my business to maintain friendly relations with the employees who made the White House and its offices tick. This practice was pleasant and interesting, and it often paid dividends as well.

The dean of the office employees was Mr. Rudolph Forster, the executive secretary. Mr. Forster had been at the White House since the days of President Cleveland, and he had the workings of the offices well in hand. I had first met him nine years before when I served as aide to the judge advocate general. When I needed to get the president's signature on an urgent paper, I would to bring the paper to Mr. Forster, explain the matter, and wait while he got the signature.

One day early in FDR's first administration, I remarked to Mr. Forster that he had seen a lot of presidents come and go. "That's right," said he, "and that one was the greatest of them all," pointing to a framed photograph of President Theodore Roosevelt on his desk. After a short pause, he said, "Every so often, I see flashes of greatness in the Roosevelt in there now." By the time I arrived in the White House as naval aide, Mr. Forster was convinced that FDR was doing well in the competition with TR for greatness. "But in different directions, of course," he said.

The White House Secret Service detail, an arm of the Treasury Department, was responsible for safeguarding the president. Colonel Edmund Starling was the nominal head of White House security. However, he had been at the White House for years and had long since lost his effectiveness for security purposes. Whenever the press saw him outside Washington, they recognized him and knew that a presidential visit was imminent. The de facto head of the Secret Service detail was the able Michael F. Reilly.

Shortly after I reported to the White House, Mike Reilly paid me a visit to instruct me about security when I accompanied the president in his automobile. Said he, "Charles Fredericks, the president's Secret Service bodyguard, will be in the front seat alongside the chauffeur. If the president is endangered in any way, you are to throw yourself across his body and try to drag him down to the bottom of the car. Remember, stay on top of him." Whenever I rode with the president, I always had Mike Reilly's instructions in mind.

Miss Louise Hackmeister, a lovely person in every way, presided over the switchboard, which was tended by some six or eight attractive gals. The switchboard personnel were tops, all intelligent and resourceful to a high degree. As time progressed, I would occasionally visit this important cubicle, bringing a cheery greeting and, invariably, a box of candy. A bribe? Maybe so. But I can assure you that I got superb service from the Hackmeister crew. If I ever told the switchboard that it was important that I get through to the president, I went to the top of the list, even ahead of cabinet officers on a couple of occasions.

I made contact with the staff of the pressroom. The president's press secretary, Stephen T. Early, was in charge. Steve's high-powered assistant was William D. Hassett, who also served as the president's correspondence secretary. I was introduced to the president's two secretaries, Miss Grace Tully and Mrs. Dorothy Jones Brady. They were my check-in points any time I wished to see the president, other than on my regular morning and late afternoon appointments.

I also acquainted myself with the workings of the White House proper. Mr. Howell Crim, chief usher and master of the White House, administered White House operations, ably assisted by two assistant ushers and doormen. Of course, the First Lady supplied guidance for these activities. Receptions and state dinners were under the supervision of the protocol division of the State Department. The orchestra section of the Marine Band furnished the music for these affairs.

Mrs. Henrietta Nesbitt presided over the basement kitchens that prepared all the food served in the White House. The president was a gourmet, and he didn't care much for Mrs. Nesbitt's food or her menus. However, because of his immobility, his physician watched his diet carefully. Accordingly, Mrs. Nesbitt shouldn't be faulted exclusively for the fact that her food often did not measure up to presidential expectations.

My introductions completed, I got down to work. It was wartime, and there was much to be done.

Chapter 4

The Map Room

The attack on Pearl Harbor brought about many changes at the Navy Department and the White House. Dispatches about naval operations poured into Washington. Some found their way to the White House. At the same time, the geography of the world's oceans suddenly assumed huge importance. Detailed maps were essential for planning and for evaluating reports of naval action.

As I saw it, my first priority as naval aide was to collect as much naval information as possible at the White House and to make it easily available to the president. Naval dispatches had to be organized and filed, and the president needed maps suitable for wartime use. The White House had no appropriate geographic aids. There were a couple of globes and a set of National Geographic maps behind the president's desk that he used in connection with his stamp collection. As an aside, I note that the president's knowledge of world geography was amazing. I once remarked about this, and he replied, "If a stamp collector really studies his stamps, he can pick up a great deal of information."

After Pearl Harbor, a few large charts were brought into the White House. They were kept in the old cabinet room, which had a table large enough to handle them. However, the cabinet room was used as a waiting room for people with appointments to see the president. When visitors were present, the charts had to be turned facedown. This arrangement was clearly unsuitable for my purposes.

At some point, it was suggested that a room be set aside where records of naval matters could be kept for the president. I do not recall the details. Perhaps the idea came from the president himself. In December 1941, he had seen what Prime Minister Churchill called his "traveling map room," a condensed visual version of the records maintained in the Admiralty Map Room. At any rate, the need for some such arrangement was immediately apparent to me, and I thought that something had to be done at once.

Head scratching was in order. I did not know where to begin. I contacted the chief usher, Howell Crim. I acquainted him with my need for a space that could serve as an office for the naval aide and a storage facility for information essential to the president. He informed me that there was a room that might suit me on the basement level of the White House, between the doctor's office and the diplomatic reception room.

Mr. Crim and I looked the place over. The room was of modest dimensions, perhaps the size of a couple of small living rooms thrown into one. It had plenty of wall space, enough to mount charts. It also had its own bathroom facilities. The feature that particularly caught my eye was the room's location. Ease of access for the president was essential for our operation. The room was across the corridor from the elevator the president used when going to and from his living room on the second floor of the White House. And it was next door to the office of the president's physician, Ross McIntire, where the president received treatment almost nightly for his sinus condition and massage therapy for his crippled lower legs and feet.

The room seemed ideal for my purposes, and I told Mr. Crim so. Within hours, the room was cleaned out, and its odds and ends of furniture sent elsewhere. A couple of desks, a locked file cabinet of generous proportions, and several chairs were moved in. Towels and coat racks were installed in the facilities, and we were in business. The facilities room was a refinement that turned out to be most important once the Map Room got into operation. It served as a coat closet and a dressing room.

At one of my first meetings with the president, he took a small stack of papers from his desk drawer and told me they were dispatches between Prime Minister Churchill and himself. Turning them over to me, he said he was sure I would safeguard them and "that their contents would not find their way into any of the news columns originating in Washington or elsewhere." The stout, locked cabinet in my basement office provided a secure repository for that stack of papers, and the subsequent dispatches that flew back and forth between the prime minister and the president.

Soon after contacting Mr. Crim, I learned by chance that a U.S. Naval Reserve officer had spent some weeks as an observer in the map room of the British Admiralty. This officer was on duty in Washington in the Office of Naval Intelligence. His name was Lieutenant (junior grade) Henry Montgomery, otherwise known as Robert Montgomery, the movie actor, to a large and appreciative public. I immediately got in touch with him. I wanted to know what he knew about the Admiralty Map Room.

I was impressed with Montgomery's personality, his intelligence, his modesty, and his eagerness to do something helpful. I was also impressed that, as a civilian early in the war, he had driven a Red Cross ambulance in France. From the very start, I liked Bob Montgomery. As time went on, I became genuinely fond of him. He had initiative and enterprise, and was not hesitant in speaking out. But once a decision was made, he could "roll with the punches" with the best of them. Rear Admiral Alan G. Kirk, chief of the Office of Naval Intelligence, agreed to release Montgomery to me.

I told Montgomery of my goal to create a Map Room at the White House. He thought the size of our space was suitable. I instructed him, "Based on your experience in the Admiralty Map

Room, I want you to draw up a plan for an installation of the same sort here. Recall, if you can, just what information the Admiralty chaps thought important. In that way, we can reduce trial and error to a minimum."

For visual aids, we obtained large-scale charts of the Pacific and Atlantic from the Coast and Geodetic Survey. Once mounted, they covered at least two walls of the room. We also mounted smaller charts covering other combat zones, namely Southeast Asia and Indonesia, the Mediterranean, North Africa, and the east coast of Africa, including the Red Sea, the Suez area, and the Persian Gulf. Much progress was made in a hurry.

The Map Room started out as strictly a naval affair. A few days after it was under way, I invited General Watson in to see what we were doing. He was impressed. "But," said he, "where is the army part of this?" I told him I had thought that since he was the military aide to the president, he would arrange to keep the president informed in those matters. "But how can I?" said he. "I'm also the appointment secretary to the president, and believe me, that is a full-time job."

My reply went something like this. "I'll tell you what I'll do. I started out to make this room a center of naval information for the president, and that was as far as my authority would seem to carry me. If you want pertinent army information here as well, I'll be glad to do it, so long as the whole operation is under my direction and control, and so long as the army helps out by supplying personnel who, while here, are subject to my direction."

"That's no problem," said General Watson. "I'll have my assistant report to you at once. Of course, I would still like to have his services from time to time."

"That is satisfactory to me," said I. "But I note that your man is a captain. At the rate promotions are going forward in the army, it won't be long before he will be advanced in rank. I have my eye on a naval reserve lieutenant and Naval Academy graduate, whom I expect to bring over here as my assistant and the executive of this operation. Since promotion is much slower in the navy than in the army, your man may eventually outrank my man. I would like your man to know that this is a strictly naval operation and will be run that way. In my absence, my lieutenant will be acting on my behalf."

"Agreed," said the general. "It's a deal."

The naval lieutenant I had in mind was Lieutenant William C. Mott, Naval Academy class of 1933, and a graduate of George Washington University Law School. Mott was passed over for a navy commission because he had defective vision. He instead obtained a commission in the naval reserves and went on active duty in the Office of Naval Information. While I was working for Admiral Stark, I saw a lot of Mott. I liked the cut of his jib. He was intelligent, quick-witted, and a doer. Since much of my time would be spent in my Navy Department office, I needed a deputy in the Map Room who was a "take-charge" guy. Another consideration in his favor was the likelihood that his visual handicap would disqualify him for sea duty.

The Map Room started to grow, really grow. Some early experiments were discarded, but in the end, progress was made. Soon the operation became a twenty-four-hour-a-day undertaking, receiving urgent messages from the service departments around the clock. The Map Room knew where I was at all times and could get in contact with me day or night, as necessary.

What information did we keep in the Map Room? By far the most important was the file of ultra-secret dispatches about the conduct of the war that passed between the president, Prime Minister Churchill, Chiang Kai-shek of China, and Joseph Stalin of Russia. This file was a progressive outgrowth of the small collection of dispatches the president had handed me shortly after I reported to him. For security reasons, all the president's outgoing dispatches went by the navy communication system, and all his incoming dispatches were received by the army communication system. The Map Room had the only complete file of outgoing and incoming dispatches. Aside from Map Room personnel, access to the dispatch file was limited to the president, Harry Hopkins,[9] and later, Admiral William D. Leahy, the president's chief of staff.

The Map Room also housed what we called "The Magic Book."[10] It contained top secret enemy dispatches that had been intercepted and decoded. What a help these dispatches were in planning! They allowed us to know what our enemies and their friends were up to. The Magic Book was handled with great care, I assure you.

The Map Room's visual aids showed the location and numbers of United States forces—army, army air forces, navy, and marine corps—throughout the war zone. In addition, we posted the day-to-day locations of military and merchant convoys, naval task forces, capital ships, and the like.

As our operation developed, the president came to the Map Room with increasing frequency. He visited on the way to his office in the morning, and on the way up to his quarters in the late afternoon. Of course, we were always pleased to see him. However, early on, I became concerned about conserving his time and energy. I felt that matters of interest could be communicated to him without his having to come to the Map Room.

---

9   Formerly an architect and administrator of the New Deal, Harry Hopkins was President Roosevelt's good friend and became probably his most influential advisor on the war. Widowed and serving as secretary of commerce while suffering from a disabling disease, in May 1940 Hopkins spent a night at the White House and, at Roosevelt's urging, took up residence there for the next three and a half years. Illness forced his resignation from the cabinet that August, but due to Hopkins's proximity and devotion to the president, his keen intellect, and his analytic ability, he quickly became an invaluable advisor and sounding board for the president. Starting in January 1941, despite bouts of illness, he began to assist Roosevelt in a host of other ways, including acting as his personal representative in meetings abroad with Churchill and Stalin; administering Lend-Lease, the program under which the United States provided war materiel to the U.K., the U.S.S.R., and other allies; and participating in the president's major wartime conferences with Churchill and others.

10 The U.S. cryptographic operation engaged in decoding secret Japanese messages was known as "Magic."

I talked to Ross McIntire, and he agreed to allow me to brief the president during his afternoon therapy sessions so he could go directly to his quarters after the sessions. I read the president the dispatches he would have seen in the Map Room. Of course, he was particularly interested in the decoded enemy dispatches in the Magic Book. The president read these dispatches himself so no one would overhear me reading them aloud.

Despite the "no admittance" sign on the door, the Map Room had visitors from time to time. Admiral Stark paid us a visit one afternoon in early April. He was impressed, and that very day he wrote a highly complimentary letter to the chief of personnel on my behalf. Admiral King and General Marshall also visited us on occasion. Of course, the president used the Map Room regularly. Often he was accompanied by Mr. Hopkins, who visited our operation daily.

In the summer of 1942, Admiral William D. Leahy, our ambassador to Vichy France, was recalled, and the president appointed him as his chief of staff. After the president announced the appointment, I asked him if Admiral Leahy's new assignment made any change in our relationship. "Not in the slightest," said the president, "and I've taken care to tell Bill Leahy so."

Later, I overtook Admiral Leahy in the corridor. I wished him well in his new job, and invited him to see the Map Room. A few weeks later, he remarked, "McCrea, I think there's more information about the war concentrated in your Map Room than in any other single place in Washington."

Once our operation got up to speed, the Map Room personnel consisted of my deputy, Bill Mott, and maybe twelve to fourteen officers in total. As I recall, aside from two regular army officers, the staff was all reserve personnel, about equally divided between the army and the navy. Both the army and the navy were generous in sending us some good people. The watch officers were intelligent, alert, anxious to be helpful, and knew how to keep their mouths shut. Of these fine qualities, a shut mouth was the most important.

I must say a final word about Bob Montgomery, who was so helpful in guiding our early efforts in the Map Room. Through no fault of his own, Bob was a target for attention. He was well-known in uniform, and he was spotted going to and from the White House. As his association with our operation continued, he attracted some unwelcome attention. From time to time, the press carried critical items about him and his association with the White House. One day, a well-placed friend in the White House asked if I knew I had a rabid Republican working in the Map Room. He was referring to Montgomery. I responded that a Republican in the Map Room didn't worry me one bit, and it was nitpicking to complain about the politics of a junior lieutenant in wartime. "But this is the White House," said my friend.

One fine Saturday morning at about the same time, Bob rang me up in the Navy Department. He said there were a couple of reporters in the White House press office who wanted him to pose with Diana Hopkins, Harry's daughter, for a photograph showing her feeding pigeons on the White House lawn. Bob said he didn't feel at liberty to do so without my permission. "Bob," I replied, "tell those chaps that as far as I'm concerned, they can take all the pictures they want of Diana Hopkins feeding pigeons on the lawn, but you are working for a stinker who will not permit you to appear in such a picture."

From time to time Bob had told me that he hoped to have sea duty one day. Given the attention he was attracting, I thought this might be a good time for him realize that ambition. I talked to Bob at length. I told him that his services in the Map Room had been helpful in every respect. I pointed out, too, that he was a target because of his fame. He was a national figure. "And I think you will agree, Bob," said I, "that only one national figure can be associated with 1600 Pennsylvania Avenue."

Bob understood and was enthusiastic about the prospect of sea duty. Despite the fact that he was thirty-nine years old, he expressed a preference for service in the PT boats. He went to the PT boats, and he did well there. My appraisal of Bob Montgomery is that he was a thoroughly good officer.

During my time at the White House, the Map Room started from scratch and grew into something of real importance to the president. We are all familiar with the axiom, "Big oaks from little acorns grow." Years later, I had the pleasure of visiting the White House during the early days of the Kennedy Administration, and I was shown the Situation Room. It was a grown-up version of the Map Room with many, many refinements, and the capacity to keep the president fully informed about all the things he needed to know. The Map Room of 1942, a little acorn, had grown into a big oak, the Situation Room, and become an important adjunct of the White House. Since then, I suppose it has only grown in importance.

Chapter 5

Press Relations

One of the regular duties the president assigned me when I reported as naval aide was attendance at his press conferences. He regarded these conferences as vital because they allowed him to reach a vast and important audience, the people of the United States. He thought my attendance would be "good for me," because I would get a feel for the views of the press and the country.

The press conferences were organized by Steve Early, the president's press secretary. There were two regular conferences per week: one on Tuesday afternoon at 4:00 p.m. for the benefit of the morning papers, and one on Friday morning at 9:30 a.m. for the afternoon papers. The conferences were held in the president's office. Generally, about 150 newsmen attended. Most questions were impromptu, but sometimes questions were submitted in advance to Steve Early. The latter were the sort that required special briefing for the president.

The president's staff had assigned seats. All the newsmen stood, except Earl Godwin, the dean of the Washington press corps. He sat at the corner of the president's desk. On signal from Steve Early, it was he who would terminate the conferences with, "Thank you, Mr. President."

The Washington press corps is the elite of the domestic news industry. Washington's foreign correspondents are tops, as well. Thus, it is not surprising that Washington newsmen think highly of themselves and their abilities. They are a confident and nervy group, and among them are experts at framing embarrassing and needling questions.

I was always impressed with the way the president handled questions at the conferences. He spoke well and was generally most gracious. Much lighthearted banter prevailed. Personally, I thought his performance with the press contributed much to Americans' understanding of their government.

For the most part, the reporters treated the president with respect and were grateful for his remarks, which assured them a good story. While I often thought I detected some annoyance in his voice, he responded to questions without evident resentment. However, there were occasions when reporters were downright rude, and thus disrespectful of the presidency. Steve Early told me about an incident prior to my time at the White House when a reporter managed to get under the president's skin.

According to Steve, after a particularly annoying performance by Drew Pearson[11] at a press conference, the president remarked, "Steve, Drew Pearson is a son of a bitch. I've put up with his insolence and scurrilous columns long enough. I want you to pick up his press pass."

Steve said to the president, "Boss"—Steve always called the president "Boss"—"I completely agree with you about Drew Pearson. But the press conferences are held for the benefit of 180 million people. In that number, I am sure there are many, many sons of bitches, and they have a right to representation at these confer-

11 Drew Pearson was a muckraking journalist. In the early 1940s, he wrote a syndicated column called the *Washington Merry-Go-Round* and had a radio news commentary show on NBC. He used journalism to attack policies and people he did not like. In the service of his goals, he was known to play fast and loose with the truth.

ences." Steve told me he meant his comment to be funny, but the president didn't see the humor. He remarked coldly, "Pick up Drew Pearson's press pass."

Steve withdrew and thought over the president's order. The next morning he went in to see the president. Steve reiterated his agreement with the president's view of Pearson, and said that he, too, resented Pearson's abusive and often inaccurate columns. Nevertheless, Steve stated he thought it unwise to withdraw Pearson's pass. The president looked Steve dead in the eye and said, "Pick up Drew Pearson's press pass and bring it to me."

Steve drew a deep breath and said, "Of course, Boss, I'll do exactly as you say, but when I deliver the pass to you, it will be accompanied by my resignation as your press secretary."

The president looked a bit startled and responded, "Well, Steve, if you feel that strongly about this, maybe we had better put off making a final decision for a few days. I feel strongly about it, too, you know. I'll think it over for at least three days, and let you know my final decision."

Steve said the president never brought up the subject again. Steve added that he thought he had kept the president from making a bad mistake.

Newsmen are in the business of "telling," and even the best of them will tell when they shouldn't, no matter what the consequences. In the first part of 1942, I participated in two incidents where the country's war effort and the news business's interest in telling collided. Both incidents involved Mr. Elmer Davis.[12]

In the late thirties and early forties, Elmer Davis was a well-known newsman and news broadcaster with a considerable following. Mr. Davis was one of the regular attendees of the president's news conferences, and his pointed questions and remarks reflected

---

12 Elmer Davis was one of the most respected journalists of the mid-twentieth century. A former Rhodes scholar and writer for the *New York Times* editorial page, in 1942 he had a highly successful radio news program on CBS.

criticism of the quantity and quality of the war news released by the administration. He was particularly persistent in asking about U.S. war losses. The president, as always, was exceedingly tactful in handling Mr. Davis.

I vividly recall the distress in the president's voice one day after a press conference when he said: "John, catch Elmer Davis before he gets away. Take him aside and see if you can get across to him the idea that he can't publish everything he wants to about our losses. Steve Early tells me he can make no headway with him, and I haven't the time to take him on."

I caught Mr. Davis and tried to explain that the release of information about war losses, particularly those unknown to the enemy, created serious problems for the administration and the armed services. Mr. Davis was, I thought, remarkably naïve. He responded, "The American public has a right to know what's going on. If the administration released a daily summary of U.S. losses, the information would only be covered in the U.S. press, and the enemy would know nothing about it. I suspect you fellows in the military have something to cover up if you don't want your losses known in this country."

"Mr. Davis," said I, "I don't know you well, but you have a fine reputation among the news fraternity, and there is hardly anyone in your profession who has a greater following. I have in mind something to tell you, but I shan't do so unless you are willing to promise that you will never repeat or make reference to it in your writing, broadcasting, or your private conversation or correspondence. If you give me this assurance, I will tell you. If not, we might as well forget any future conversations." After a moment's hesitation, Mr. Davis agreed to my terms.

I continued, "You have told me that a daily press report of U.S. losses could not benefit the enemy. You are absolutely wrong in this. Nightly, an embassy here in Washington sends a coded dispatch to its government's foreign office containing a digest of all military news in our press. The country engaged in this activity is supposedly neutral, but we have proof positive that the military information transmitted by its embassy is reaching the Axis powers. I am not going to name the neutral country or tell you how we know the information is reaching the enemy. You will have to take my word for it. However, I am sure that you, as a patriotic American, would not want to give aid and comfort to our enemies. Do you need further proof of the wisdom of censoring our losses?"

"Well, no. But we can't let censorship take over." Mr. Davis still felt the people had a right to know, although he allowed that the issue of "when" they were entitled to know might be relevant. I do not recall that Mr. Davis ever again asked about our country's losses at a presidential news conference.

In early June 1942, the Office of War Information (OWI)[13] was established to consolidate U.S. government information services. President Roosevelt appointed Elmer Davis as director of OWI. One of OWI's functions was to control the release of war news that might damage the war effort. Because of OWI's role in censorship, I doubt Mr. Davis accepted his appointment with any degree of enthusiasm, but he did accept it. No doubt President Roosevelt felt this job would bring home to Mr. Davis the necessity for considered judgment in releasing information on military losses.

In early 1942, the United States was hampered by a lack of aircraft carriers, so crucial in the Pacific War. The Japanese knew about this deficiency and directed much of their combat effort against our carriers. At the time, USS *Lexington* was one of our two largest carriers. On 8 May 1942, at the Battle of the Coral Sea, *Lexington* was subjected to air attack. She suffered much damage.

---

13 In the United States, OWI was in charge of coordinating the release of war news and developing radio programs, movies, posters, and other media designed to encourage American patriotism and create support for the war effort. Abroad, it conducted a massive propaganda campaign designed to undermine enemy morale.

Every effort was made to save her, but to no avail. She was abandoned, and she sank during the night.[14]

Because of the circumstances of *Lexington's* sinking, the enemy was unaware that the ship had been lost. Our high command felt it imperative that this significant loss not be publicized because the information would be of great value to the enemy. Accordingly, no information was released. Very few people in the Navy Department knew about the loss. Even the Map Room carried the *Lexington* as "active" on the wall charts of the South Pacific. Among the Map Room staff, I alone knew the truth, or at least so I thought.

One Saturday afternoon, some weeks after the sinking, I was in my office in the Navy Department, reviewing a few dispatches that I intended to discuss with the president, who was then in Hyde Park. The telephone rang. It was Admiral King.

"Captain McCrea, I know you are aware of the loss of *Lexington*. I have just learned that Elmer Davis, the director of OWI,

---

14 By the end of April 1942, Japan had swept through southeast Asia and the nearby Pacific islands, seizing Malaya, Singapore, Thailand, the Philippines, Guam, the Dutch East Indies, and parts of New Guinea. By decoding Japanese messages, the United States learned in early May that Japan intended to dispatch naval forces to seize one of the Solomon Islands and Port Moresby on Australian New Guinea. From there, it planned to bomb Australia and attack vital U.S.–Australian supply lines. To counter this move, the United States sent two carrier forces to the Coral Sea, one with the carrier *Lexington*; the other, with *Yorktown*. On May 8, two Japanese fleet carriers and the two American carriers, out of sight of one another, exchanged air attacks. *Yorktown* was damaged and *Lexington* was mortally wounded. However, during the battle, the United States sunk a small Japanese carrier, heavily damaged a large one, and decimated the aircraft complement of a third. As a result, Japan had to call off the invasion of Port Moresby.

The Battle of the Coral Sea was significant because it was the first naval action by ships out of visual range exclusively using aircraft as offensive weapons. It confirmed the lesson of the Pearl Harbor attack that the aircraft carrier, with its airborne firepower, had superseded the battleship as the most potent warship in the naval arsenal. It was also the first time in the war that the Allies prevented a Japanese invasion force from achieving its objective.

intends to release information about the *Lexington* to the press this afternoon. This should not be done. I have talked to Mr. Davis, and I have been unable to dissuade him. He is insistent that the public has a right to know. I have persuaded him not to make the release until he has talked to the president. Please take it from here and do the necessary."

I immediately took up my White House phone. Through the White House switchboard, I was connected to Miss Louise Hackmeister, then manning the Hyde Park switchboard.

"Hackie," said I, "please answer me this. Has Mr. Elmer Davis talked to the president today, and if not, has he got a call in for him?"

"Mr. Davis has not talked to the president, but he does have a call in," she answered.

"Now, Hackie, I know you girls handle calls in order of receipt, but it is most important that I talk to the president before he talks to Mr. Davis. I trust you can arrange that."

"The president has a guest with him now. As soon as he is free I will put him on, Captain." As I hung up, I reflected that my courtesy calls on the switchboard, with the occasional box of candy, were not without effect.

In about a half hour, my telephone rang. It was Miss Hackmeister. "I'll put the president right on," said she.

The conversation ran about like this. "Good afternoon, Mr. President. I have some dispatches which will be of interest," and I proceeded to tell him about them.

"And there is another item, Mr. President. Admiral King called a short time ago to tell me that Mr. Elmer Davis is planning to release news of the loss of *Lexington* to the press this afternoon. Admiral King hopes this won't be done. He has talked with Mr. Davis and has been unable to dissuade him. However, Mr. Davis has agreed not to make the release until he has talked to you. I think that is about all, Mr. President."

The president responded, "You should be up here today, John. The weather is perfect. This Hudson River Valley can turn out wonderful weather from time to time. How is it in Washington?" He went on in this vein for a few minutes, and signed off.

After thanking Miss Hackmeister for letting me through, I called Admiral King.

"What did the president say?" asked Admiral King.

"He talked about the beautiful weather in the Hudson Valley and wondered about the weather in Washington. But he got your message, Admiral," said I.

The next morning, I picked up the *Washington Post* and the *Sunday Star* from my front porch and nervously scanned the front pages of both papers. I was sure that an important item like the loss of the *Lexington* would be front-page news, but there was no word about it. What had happened?

About 10:00 a.m. I called Hyde Park. "Hackie, good morning, and how is everything up there?" said I. "Oh, fine," was the reply. "Hackie, tell me. Did the president talk to Mr. Elmer Davis yesterday?"

"You know, Captain, right after you called, the president told me he was going to take a nap and didn't wish to be disturbed. I told him about Mr. Davis's call, and he said he would get to that later. When he awakened, he went for a drive to take advantage of the fine weather. Then there were some guests in for tea, and they stayed awhile. There were a few guests for cocktails and dinner. The president retired about ten o'clock. He never did get around to talking to Mr. Davis."

"Thank you, Hackie, thanks a lot," I said.

Later in the morning, I reported what Hackie had said to Admiral King. He had a gentle chuckle. The president obviously understood that sometimes much can be done by doing nothing. A few weeks later, the loss of the *Lexington* was disclosed at a time deemed appropriate by the president and Admiral King.[15]

---

15 The loss of *Lexington* was publicly acknowledged on June 15, 1942, after the decisive U.S. victory over Japanese naval forces at the Battle of Midway (June 4–7). At Midway, the Japanese planned to seize the American base and destroy the U.S. Pacific Fleet. However, through exceptional

[continues on following page]

There is a footnote to the sinking of *Lexington* involving a member of the Map Room staff. Some weeks after the loss, I had occasion to take on an additional watch officer. I selected a young naval reserve officer then on duty in the Office of Naval Communications, Ensign Charles Nelson Berry of Oklahoma City, Oklahoma.

When the loss of *Lexington* was finally announced, Ensign Berry confided in me, "You know, Captain, I knew all along that *Lexington* had been lost." I asked how he knew.

"I decoded the top secret dispatch received in the Office of Naval Communications reporting the loss."

"Why didn't you say something to me?" I asked.

"When I came to work in the Map Room and saw *Lexington* being carried as active, it was on the tip of my tongue to tell you about the loss. But thinking it over, I concluded that you probably knew, and for reasons I didn't understand, you were carrying the ship as active. Then, too, if you didn't know, I couldn't properly tell you because the dispatch I decoded was top secret. So I said nothing."

My response was, "Young man, what a pleasure it is to have you working here. You possess a fine trait of military character, the ability to keep your mouth shut." From that day forward, whenever a communication officer was required on a presidential trip, Ensign Charles Berry was my selection for the job.

A final note about the press. It has been my pleasure to meet and know many newsmen. However, with rare exceptions, I am not sure I ever understood them. I could not understand their desire to tell all at the risk of damaging the country's war effort. Nor could I understand their casual attitude towards their craft.

---

intelligence work, the United States learned in advance of this plan and surprised the Japanese. U.S. forces, including three aircraft carriers (*Enterprise*, *Hornet*, and *Yorktown*), destroyed four Japanese fleet carriers and many aircraft at the cost of one carrier (*Yorktown*). After the Battle of Midway, the balance of naval power in the Pacific shifted away from Japan to parity between Japan and the United States.

Many blithely dismissed criticism of inaccuracies and misinformation in their reporting.

I am equally sure that newsmen never understood me. I was friendly with the reporter in charge of the Washington office of the *New York Herald Tribune.* He usually stood behind my chair at news conferences. On a number of occasions he remarked on the contents of "my diary." I took this as idle talk, until one day he told me in all seriousness that he wished I would let him look at my diary sometime. I told him that since the outbreak of hostilities, the Navy Department had ordered that no personal diaries be kept.

"Oh yes, I know that," said he, "but I would still like to see your diary."

"What would you say if I told you I do not keep one?"

"I would say that you are either a liar or a damn fool."

"Well, call me a damn fool then, because I'm not lying." My friend could not understand that I valued following orders and preventing leaks of confidential information more than the personal and potential financial rewards of keeping a diary.

Chapter 6

Yarn: A Lesson on the White House Steps

―∞―

Duty at the White House during wartime was often strenuous. There were many long days and plenty of pressures of one sort or another. But the duty also had its lighter side. Here I record a yarn about one of the light moments, my encounter with the well-known American wit, commentator, and writer, Alexander Woollcott.[16] This episode might be entitled, "A lesson in the English language on the White House steps."

One Saturday afternoon in early 1942, at about 5:30 p.m., I went to the White House intent on going to the Map Room to get ammunition for my 6:00 p.m. meeting with the president. As was my custom, I stopped at the chief usher's office to have a word with the officer on duty. The ushers were knowledgeable about all the White House goings-on. They knew the whereabouts and activities

---

16 The multifaceted Alexander Woollcott (1887–1943) was a drama and book critic, commentator, editor, book author, playwright, CBS radio personality, actor, and member of the Algonquin Round Table.

of the principals and could be counted on to have the latest information about past, present, and future White House activities.

On this particular afternoon, the usher on duty remarked as follows, "Captain, if you saw a gentleman in the main lobby as you came in, you might have recognized him as Mr. Alexander Woollcott. He had tea with Mrs. Roosevelt this afternoon and has been in the lobby about fifteen minutes. He asked me to get a cab for him, but even the magic of a call from the White House often fails to produce a cab in these days of gasoline rationing. I asked Mr. Woollcott if he would like to sit here in the office, but he declined and has been busy pacing up and down the lobby. I think he is too important to be left to amuse himself in the lobby without attention from anybody on the staff. Do you suppose that you could entertain him for a few minutes? A cab should be here shortly, I would think."

I agreed with the usher about the degree of hospitality due Mr. Woollcott, so out I went to take him on. He was not in the lobby. I inquired of Jackson, the uniformed doorman, as to Mr. Woollcott's whereabouts.

"The gentleman who was here has gone outside, and he is sitting on the front steps. I don't think he should be sitting out there, but I hesitate to tell him so, since he is Mrs. Roosevelt's guest."

Outside I went. I introduced myself to Mr. Woollcott, and inquired if I might be of assistance. He said he wanted a cab, but he understood the difficulty in getting one and was resigned to the delay. I stood. Mr. Woollcott sat. I asked if he wouldn't like to come inside where we could await the arrival of the cab in comfort.

"It's such a pleasant day, I think I prefer to stay outside."

By way of trying to get him on his feet, I inquired if he would like to see some of the unusual shrubbery on the White House grounds. He was completely uninterested. Finally, convinced that I couldn't move him, I sat down beside him. Mind you, this was the front steps of the main entrance to the White House, 1600 Pennsylvania Avenue, in full view of passersby on the street. I didn't like doing this, but hesitated to tell him that I thought it inappropriate that the two of us be seen sitting there.

We talked briefly about the Roosevelts. He was lavish in his admiration of both Mrs. Roosevelt and the president. I told him how much I enjoyed the humor of his radio broadcast and that my wife and I greatly enjoyed reading his book *While Rome Burns*. Just for good measure, I told him that I envied those who could pleasingly and effectively put words together. It was an art that brought much pleasure to many.

"Writing isn't so difficult," he said. "I admit one must have some aptitude in that direction, but after all, it shouldn't be too hard to write. Recording one's feelings is relatively easy. It can be done simply."

"Ah," said I, "like most naval officers, I have difficulty writing simple declarative sentences."

"That is not too hard to learn," he said. "If you are engaged in an interesting operation or experience, try making a record of it. You should describe the event and your feelings about it. If you keep at it, something good will often result. There is no one correct approach. Every professional writer has his own way of expressing things, and that is what ultimately becomes his trademark."

Mr. Woollcott continued, "Of course, who undertakes to write must observe certain basics. First off, he needs to be a competent judge of words. Now, there are strong words, and there are weak words. As a general rule, I would say that one should avoid the use of weak words.

"Let me ask you, Captain, what is the weakest word in the English language? You don't know? You use it daily, and so do I, in conversation. But when I write, I avoid it like the plague. The weakest word in the English language is the word 'very,' V-E-R-Y. If ever you feel when writing that you would like to use the word 'very,' just don't do it. Maybe that's a little too strong. Evaluate its use. Put it to the test. Try substituting the word 'damn' for 'very.' Ordinarily 'damn' will improve the sentence immeasurably.

"Let me illustrate. This is a fine day. Some would be inclined to say this is a very fine day. In speaking, I would say this is a damn fine day. But in writing, I would say this is a fine day, and let it go at that. And it is a fine day, isn't it, Captain?"

A cab arrived at the northwest gate, halted a moment by the gate guard, and then proceeded slowly up the gravel drive to the main entrance. "It is *very*"—with much emphasis—"nice to have met you, Captain." And Mr. Woollcott was off.

On reflection that evening, I decided that the day had been most eventful. I had met the great wit and distinguished man of letters, Mr. Alexander Woollcott. I had had a lesson in the importance of the use of words, with emphasis on the use of "very." And I had sat on the front steps of the White House. The last item, I might add, was a never-to-be-repeated experience. As to weak and strong words, my meeting with Alexander Woollcott occurred some thirty years ago, and to this day, I try to avoid the use of that weak word "very." Rarely, however, do I substitute for it the word "damn."

Chapter 7

Foreign Relations

President Roosevelt maintained a certain distance from his Department of State. He was fond of Cordell Hull, the secretary of state, and showed him many little courtesies. However, Mr. Hull was not well. He was absent from his offices for days at a time, and occasionally he was hospitalized. The president always inquired about his health, and was pleased when the news was favorable, but he did not cut Hull in on too much information that a secretary of state might be expected to know.

The president did not fully trust the State Department. He thought the department was, in his words, "leaky." He could never be sure that highly classified information would remain secret once State got its hands on it. He had seen items of a confidential nature in the newspapers that could only have come from the State Department, and this annoyed him.

When the president conducted business with State, he did so mostly through Sumner Welles, the under secretary. Welles was a professional and knew his business. The president thought him capable, especially in his specialty of Latin American matters. But since Mr. Hull was so often unavailable, the president was pretty much his own secretary of state, assisted on occasion by Sumner Welles.

The State Department knew very little about the Map Room. James Dunn, the assistant secretary, was aware of its existence; I'm not sure what others knew. I am certain that State leakiness was the reason the president kept the Churchill/Stalin/Chiang Kai-shek dispatch file in the White House. No doubt this was also the reason the president assigned me certain duties involving representatives of foreign governments and secret matters relating to the war.

Shortly after my arrival at the White House, President Roosevelt decided to form a group that he called the Pacific War Council. He discussed the idea with Mr. Churchill, who thought well of it, even urged it, I am told. The council was to be made up of the senior representatives of the Allied nations that had an interest in the war in the Pacific, namely the United Kingdom, the Netherlands, Canada, New Zealand, China, and Australia. The president was to preside at the meetings.[17]

The council's beginnings were informal. About a week in advance of the first meeting, the president asked me to get in touch with the senior diplomatic representatives of the six countries involved: Lord Halifax,[18] U.K. ambassador to the United States; Alexander Loudon, Dutch ambassador to the United States; Leighton McCarthy, Canadian minister to the United States; Walter Nash, the ambassador from New Zealand; T.V. Soong, the Chinese minister for foreign affairs; and Herbert V. Evatt, the Australian minister to the United States. The president asked me to explain to each of them his proposal for a council, and to invite them to meet in the cabinet room for an

---

17 The Pacific War Council held its first formal meeting on April 1, 1942. The council was an advisory body formed to discuss the war and the availability of war materiel. Any council recommendations about the conduct of the war were referred to a committee of the Combined Chiefs of Staff chaired by President Roosevelt, which had operational control of the war.

18 Edward Frederick Lindley Wood, first earl of Halifax.

informal discussion of the war to date. As I recall it, the first meeting was scheduled for a Tuesday in late March 1942. All the invitees accepted with alacrity.

The day of the meeting came. When all had arrived, I so reported to the president. He got into his wheelchair, I at the handles, and promptly at 9:30 a.m. we entered the cabinet room. On our way out of his office, the president said over his shoulder in an offhand manner, "Of course, John, I want you to stay at this meeting and the others that I expect will grow out of this one."

After greeting the gathering, the president proceeded about as follows: "For some time now, I have thought it would be well for those of us who are concerned with the war in the Pacific to meet occasionally, say once a week—no oftener, ordinarily—and to discuss problems in the area of our mutual concern. In this way, we can keep in close touch with each other. This will be helpful, I think, for all of us. We shall be able to speak frankly here, in agreement or otherwise.

"One subject that I am sure will be of interest is our war production figures. Harry Hopkins has assured me that he will have weekly figures available for us, and the discussion of these will be helpful. There will be other items we will wish to discuss. I hope you will have no hesitancy in suggesting discussion topics. I think it would be best to keep these meetings completely informal. There will be no agenda, and each person can speak his mind.

"Any group like this needs a messenger boy. My naval aide, Captain McCrea, whom you have met, has consented to be our messenger boy. He will advise you of the place and time of our meetings. Unless there is good reason to do otherwise, I think Tuesday at 9:30 a.m. is a good hour to meet. I would hope for good attendance. Setting a date and hour now should achieve this. If any of you have any questions about the meetings, just get in touch with John. He can be reached through the White House switchboard anytime."

My description of the president's remarks is rough, but it is generally correct. I always liked to hear FDR talk off the cuff. I thought he was superb at it.

Well, there it was. The first meeting of the Pacific War Council was in session, and not until I heard the president say so that morning did I know that I was to attend these meetings and to be the liaison/messenger boy for the council. But as so often happened at the White House, I said to myself, "The man has spoken," and it was done.

After the meeting, I accompanied the president back to his office. He asked me to prepare a memorandum for the file about each meeting, indicating who attended and what was discussed. "Keep no notes. I am sure you can recall enough to come up with a report. I would like to see the reports before they go to the file."

My first report was of little consequence. The second was longer and more involved. The president read it carefully. Handing it back to me, he said, "If this is the way you're going to handle these reports, don't bother to show them to me anymore. This one is done just the way I want it."

In early May 1942, Manuel L. Quezon, president of the Commonwealth of the Philippines, joined the council. Mr. Quezon's attendance at meetings was sporadic because of his deteriorating health. When he was absent, the vice president of the Philippines, Sergio Osmena, represented the islands.[19]

Of course, it was a privilege to sit weekly with this distinguished group, with their varied personalities and points of view. Lord Halifax, a former viceroy of India, was a real gentleman. He was courteous, thoughtful, and exceedingly quiet. T.V. Soong of China, a brother-in-law of Chiang Kai-shek, was also quiet and

---

19 In January 1942, as the Japanese were consolidating their control of the Philippines, President Quezon and Vice President Osmena moved from Manila to Corregidor, from which they were evacuated by U.S. submarine in February. By May, the Philippine government was operating in exile in Washington, D.C.

somewhat withdrawn. Loudon, a Hollander of distinguished name, was highly nervous and a great admirer of FDR. The light-hearted Mr. Nash of New Zealand often discussed the economic impact of the war, and deplored the loss of the Japanese market for his country's agricultural and dairy products. President Quezon was spirited and nervous, and he spoke a lot. Whenever he attended, the conversation was interesting and lively. Of course, he was greatly distressed with what his country was experiencing at the hands of the Japanese, and he spoke of this often.

Dr. Evatt of Australia was an odd character. He spoke with a strong cockney accent and was completely lacking in humor. I found it uncomfortable to listen to him. When he addressed the president, I felt he was almost disrespectful. During some early meetings, he addressed questions to me, short-circuiting the president entirely. I reluctantly spoke to him about this, and he admitted he was in error. Later, Evatt was succeeded by Sir Owen Dixon, a grand person and a thorough gentleman, who spoke "educated" English.

All the meetings of the Pacific War Council were interesting. Opinions were frankly expressed about a variety of subjects. Most discussions were about the conduct of the Pacific War, but some ranged to totally unrelated topics. For the most part, the discussions were in good spirit and good taste, even when widely divergent views were expressed. As I recall, I missed but one meeting of the council, when the president sent me on another assignment. Harry Hopkins substituted for me on that occasion.

As the president predicted, the U.S. war production figures were always of interest. Each member seemed to think that his country was not as well served as it should be, and that Russia was getting too much of our war materiel output. Each time this argument was made, President Roosevelt would point out—quite effectively, I thought—that Russia was heavily engaged with the enemy on the Eastern front, and that every German casualty inflicted by Russia now would eliminate a German soldier who could oppose an Allied assault in Western Europe in the future.

When Winston Churchill visited the United States in the summer of 1942, he attended a meeting of the Pacific War Council at the president's invitation.[20] He participated in the give-and-take around the table in high good humor, adding zest to the meeting. Just before the gathering broke up, the president asked the prime minister if he would care to say a "few words" to the council.

Mr. Churchill was sitting directly across the cabinet table from me. There were only ten of us in the room: the seven members of the council, the president, Mr. Churchill, and myself. Mr. Churchill opened his remarks on a light tone. "I am glad to see old friends and to participate in the deliberations of this body," said he. He had a pencil in his hand. He looked directly at the table, never once raising his eyes, and as he talked, he tapped the table in a slow rhythm with the pencil's eraser. Literature rolled off his tongue. The gist of his remarks was: "We are engaged in a mighty, mighty struggle. Our every effort at this time should be directed at bringing about the complete disruption of the German economy, which at the moment supports that country's war effort. In the end, we shall prevail. Of that I am certain."

One memorable incident relating to the council occurred after one of its meetings. While a meeting of the Pacific War Council was of no great significance, it brought several representatives of the Allied countries together. When the members filed out of the cabinet room, the White House press made the most of the opportunity to question them. "Any statement today, sir? What was discussed at the meeting?" Usually the members would remark that broad aspects of the Pacific War were discussed, or, "No, I have no statement to make," or, "If any statement is to be made, it should be made by the president." That put an end to the questions, and

20 The Prime Minister attended a Pacific War Council meeting on June 25, 1942, while he was in Washington, D.C., for the Second Washington Conference (June 17–25, 1942) with President Roosevelt and top military leaders from the United States and the United Kingdom.

the press would retire to the pressroom to await the next White House visitor.

Dr. Evatt liked to talk to the press. One day after a meeting, I saw him at the center of a group of twelve or fifteen reporters. All the council members escaped without making pronouncements worthy of print, save Dr. Evatt, whose remarks were reported in the paper the following morning.

At about 8:30 a.m., I received a call at my office from Dr. Evatt. After an exchange of greetings, he said, "I'm calling to ask you, Captain, if you think I made a mistake yesterday."

"Why, Dr. Evatt, you have the advantage of me. I don't know to what you refer."

"But, Captain, it's in the morning paper, which you must have seen."

Lying barefacedly, I said, "I'm sorry, Dr. Evatt, I haven't gotten around to the morning paper. I have been up to my eyes in dispatches."

"Well, you know how the boys of the press question us after the council meetings. They're all nice fellows, and I like to help them out. Yesterday, I told them what we discussed in the meeting. The news article states that I said the president said so-and-so with reference to certain military aspects of the Pacific War. I'm not denying I told them that, but I wonder if I made a mistake. If I did, I'm sorry."

Of course, I had already seen the article. When I read it, I knew that if Evatt had made the remark attributed to him, the president would be greatly annoyed. Now here was the good doctor admitting that he had made the remark.

"I'm sure you understand, Dr. Evatt, that no one around here speaks for the president. Sometimes his press secretary issues a statement for him, but those statements are always authorized by the president."

"Well, if I've done wrong, I trust I'll be forgiven."

"Thank you for your call, Doctor." I signed off saying that I would get to the paper in a few minutes.

In ten minutes, Dr. Evatt called again.

"Captain, I think this incident should be cleared with the president. Would you be good enough to set up an appointment for me to see him as early as possible?"

"I'm afraid you are asking for something outside my area of operation. The chief of protocol in the State Department, Mr. George Summerlin, has jurisdiction over all calls made on the president by representatives of foreign governments. Call Mr. Summerlin and ask him to set up the appointment. Sometimes there is a little delay in such things. Meanwhile, I suggest that you not worry about this incident."

I knew my suggestion would carry little weight. He would worry, and I thought it would be good penance for him to do a little worrying. He had a good idea he had committed a *faux pas*, or he would not have called me.

In a few minutes, I was off to the White House with the morning dispatches and a copy of the morning paper under my arm. I showed the item in question to the president. He didn't like it. I told him of my conversation with Dr. Evatt, of lying to him, and of referring him to the chief of protocol to get an appointment with the president. The president looked up with a twinkle in his eye. "Good, John. You did just right. One more thing. Call Summey and tell him that I am going to be very busy for the next three or four days. That will give the doctor time to decide that he will never again quote POTUS to the press." (I should add that POTUS is an acronym for president of the United States. The president was fond of referring to himself by that name from time to time.)

Another task I was assigned in "foreign relations" was certainly something that the State Department would be expected to handle. In early 1942, control of the island of Madagascar, a French colony, became a matter of grave concern for the Allies. After France fell to the Germans in June 1940, Allied influence in the

French colonies diminished rapidly.[21] Frenchmen abroad were split in their loyalties. Some were loyal to Marshal Henri Philippe Pétain, head of the Vichy government in unoccupied France that collaborated with the Germans. Others were inclined to follow General Charles de Gaulle, who fled to London after the fall of France, and there organized the Free French Movement. The colonial government of Madagascar remained loyal to Vichy.

Situated off the eastern coast of Africa on an important shipping route, Madagascar was of great strategic importance to the Allies. When Germany abandoned its nonaggression pact with the Soviets and declared war on the Soviet Union, the Soviets suddenly found themselves taking the full blow of the German war machine. They desperately needed war materiel from abroad, and keeping them supplied became a high priority and a problem of the first magnitude for the Allies.

Allied convoys used two principal sea routes to supply the Soviet Union: the northern route across the Atlantic Ocean to Murmansk and Archangel, and the southern route around the Cape of Good Hope through the Indian Ocean to the Persian Gulf. The British also needed war materiel for its North Africa campaign. Most of these supplies were convoyed along the Cape of Good Hope route to the Red Sea. The German submarine menace to Allied shipping was substantial, whatever route was used.

For some time before the United States entered the war, U.S. cryptographers had been working on cracking Japanese codes and ciphers. By the time Japan struck Pearl Harbor in December 1941,

---

21 Following the surrender of France, a French government headed by Marshal Philippe Pétain in Vichy entered into an armistice with Germany. Under the armistice agreement, the French were allowed to retain control of French colonies and territories. Most of the colonies were loyal to Vichy. To maintain contact with their former ally, the United States and Britain granted full recognition to the Vichy government, but Vichy soon broke off relations with Britain after the British destroyed a French fleet at Mers-el-Kébir, French Algeria, fearing that Germany would take control of the ships.

we were fairly adept at reading the Japanese diplomatic code. As a result, we learned that the Axis powers were planning to seize Madagascar and establish submarine bases there, from which they would prey on Allied convoys bound for the Red Sea and the Persian Gulf. It was essential that this plan be thwarted. In early spring 1942, Mr. Churchill and President Roosevelt exchanged dispatches about the situation. They decided that a British naval task force should make an assault on Madagascar and seize it before the Japanese did.

The political implications of the seizure were complex. France was an ally at heart, albeit an impotent one. Here were her allies, planning to take one of her territories by force. The president and the prime minister thought it appropriate to explain to France the nature of the operation, the reasons for it, and that the Allies had no desire to keep the island permanently. To whom should this explanation go—to Pétain in Vichy, or de Gaulle in London? Ultimately, they agreed that the president would inform Marshal Pétain. For security reasons, notification could not be given in advance. The ideal moment would be just as the assault was getting under way.

Madagascar was seized on a Tuesday early in May 1942.[22] About a week before the assault, the prime minister sent the president an eyes-only dispatch explaining the details of the operation, and stating that the attack would go forward without de Gaulle's knowledge.

The prime minister's dispatch also explained how the president would be notified that the invasion was commencing. When the task force commander was committed to the assault, the prime minister would send a dispatch containing a code word. The code word was to be conveyed in the prime minister's next dispatch to the president. Some hours later, a dispatch arrived from the prime minister bearing a single word, "Adonis."

22 The British invasion of Madagascar began on Tuesday, May 5, 1942.

On the Saturday morning preceding the assault, the president said he wanted to talk to me in his office. He proceeded about as follows: "John, you are aware of the Madagascar operation next week. Winston wants me to let Marshal Pétain in on it as soon as the operation is under way. I would like you to draft a dispatch for me to send to the marshal."

After a few pleasantries, I left the president and went to my office in the Navy Department. In my time at the Naval Academy, we often drew lots for class recitation topics. Slips were placed facedown on the instructor's desk, each bearing a question to be discussed orally or in writing on a blackboard. We each took a slip. Often a midshipman drew a question for which he was poorly prepared. In such a case, hesitation and indecision were in order. The midshipmen lightly referred to this period of rumination as "chewing chalk."

Thus, on a beautiful Saturday morning in May, I found myself chewing chalk over how to proceed. Questions passed through my mind. Why was I caught in this predicament? Wasn't this a matter for the State Department, rather than the president's naval aide? How does one prepare a dispatch from one head of state to another? But "the man had spoken," and that was that.

I drafted one dispatch after another. They were all inadequate. They did not reflect the president's personality. They did not have the gentleness and kindliness that I knew he would want to convey to Marshal Pétain in these circumstances. After many attempts, I concluded that despite the gravity of the situation, I could best accomplish what I wanted in a relatively informal letter. And so here, in substance, is what I wrote:

My dear Marshal Pétain,
I recall with much pleasure meeting you in France in 1918 when the Allies were engaged in the First World War with the German war machine. You were actively engaged with your military duties, but you thoughtfully took time out to

greet me when, as assistant secretary of the United States Navy, I visited the Western Front. Your kindness to me on that occasion has remained a pleasant memory.

Regretfully, we again find ourselves engaged in a mighty struggle, this time with the great Axis powers of which the German war machine is such a potent part. Our intelligence people have made available to the Allies conclusive evidence that the enemy proposes to seize Madagascar for the purpose of establishing submarine bases there to operate against Indian Ocean shipping. This, of course, we cannot allow. By the time that you receive this dispatch, a task force of the British Royal Navy will be in the process of seizing Madagascar to prevent the enemy from carrying out its plans. The Allies will hold it in trust and protect France's interest in this important island, and when peace is again achieved, and it is appropriate to act, Madagascar will be returned to France. May that day come soon.

With great respect, I am most sincerely yours,
Franklin Delano Roosevelt
President of the United States

Of course, the foregoing is a rough sketch of the draft I presented to the president that evening. He read it over and remarked, "We'll think it over until Monday." I had no reason to think the president approved of what I had done.

Monday morning came, and again I accompanied the president to his office. When settled at his desk, he reached into the side pocket of his jacket and brought out my draft. "I think this is all right. I like your treatment of it on a personal basis and making a letter of it. I have made a few changes. I trust you can read them all. You will want to work with the State Department on this. I think that Jimmy Dunn is the chap you should talk to."

I took the draft back to my office and had it retyped with the president's changes. I put the letter in an envelope addressed to the

State Department duty officer, together with instructions which read substantially: "On direction of the naval aide to the president, the attached is to be sent 'in the clear'"—that is uncoded—"by the fastest possible channel to the U.S. *chargé d'affaires* in Vichy for immediate delivery to Marshal Pétain." To ensure that no one could get advance notice of the attack, the envelope was sealed, and the outside bore the notation, "This envelope is not to be opened except on the direction of the naval aide to the president."

I talked with Mr. Dunn, the assistant secretary of state. I told him that the president had an important message for Marshal Pétain that he wanted delivered immediately upon receipt by the *chargé* in Vichy. I also told Dunn to alert the *chargé* in France to be ready after 6:00 p.m., Washington time, to handle an important message. I did not apprise Dunn of the message's contents.

Early on the day of the attack, I advised the British mission that if they received a message for President Roosevelt, they should contact me at my Navy Department office. Shortly after 8:00 p.m., my office telephone rang, and a clipped, female voice with an English accent asked for Captain McCrea. When I identified myself, she told me she had a one-word message for the president: "Adonis."

I called the State Department duty officer and told him to open the envelope I had sent and carry out the instructions inside. About fifteen minutes later, he called to say that the *chargé* in Vichy had acknowledged receipt of the message. I called the president and told him that the British were committed to the Madagascar assault, our *chargé* at Vichy had received the message to Marshal Pétain, and if the president had nothing further, I was going home.

He expressed appreciation that things had gone so smoothly. I left word with the Map Room that I was headed home via the residence of Rear Admiral Brent C. Young, Supply Corps, in Chevy Chase, Maryland. Mrs. McCrea had dined with the Youngs that evening while I had been excused because of duties elsewhere.

The Madagascar assault was a Royal Navy operation. Since the Admiralty was usually quick to make operations announcements to the press, I assumed there might be something about the assault on the WMAL ten o'clock news broadcast. There was nothing, however, so I was deprived of telling the Youngs and my wife what I knew. But more was to come.

About 10:15, the telephone rang and Brent Young answered it. "John, the call is for you." I identified myself. A high-pitched old man's voice, which I recognized immediately as that of Secretary of State Cordell Hull, asked, "Is this Captain McCrea?"

"It is," I replied.

"Well, this is the secretary of state, and I'd like to know what in hell is going on."

The secretary listened patiently as I explained, punctuating his listening with an occasional unintelligible grump, which I could only interpret as annoyance at his not being apprised earlier as to what was "going on."

In the Madagascar operation, the president chose to involve the State Department as little as possible. It was a *fait accompli* before any responsible person at State knew about it. No doubt some will fault the president's handling of this matter, but I cannot. The operation required the greatest secrecy, and secrecy was preserved. I am sure the president employed me to draft the letter to Marshal Pétain because of his concern that State was leaky. I note that the Royal Navy assault on Madagascar was successful, and by November 1942 Madagascar was in Allied control for the remainder of the war.

Chapter 8

Informal Diplomacy

—∞∞∞—

President Roosevelt was fond of engaging in what he sometimes called informal diplomacy. He enjoyed meeting with foreign leaders and representatives in informal settings, sometimes at Hyde Park, and he liked dealing with them outside the usual State Department channels. As his aide, I found myself participating in a peripheral way in these activities.

In mid-summer 1942, Queen Wilhelmina of the Netherlands; her daughter, Princess Juliana; and the princess's two daughters spent a long weekend as the guests of President and Mrs. Roosevelt at Hyde Park.[23] The royal family was then living in exile near Stockbridge, Massachusetts. The big house at Hyde Park was well suited for such a visit, and the setting was ideal for long, informal talks between the president and the queen.

---

23 Queen Wilhelmina (1880–1962) was queen of the Netherlands from 1890 to 1948. Three days after the German invasion of the Netherlands on May 10, 1940, Wilhelmina and her family were evacuated to Britain, and there she took charge of the Dutch government-in-exile. She became a symbol of Dutch resistance to the Nazis through her radio broadcasts to her people from London. Princess Juliana was the queen's only daughter. Juliana's daughters at Hyde Park that weekend were Princesses Beatrix and Irene.

On the morning of our guests' arrival, the president called me in and remarked about as follows: "John, the queen tells me that Crown Princess Juliana is carrying her third child. The queen says that the princess's doctor wants her to walk a couple of miles daily, morning and afternoon. Of course, she can't go out and walk alone. Will you and a Secret Service chap be good enough to make yourselves available to escort the princess on her walks?" Thus, while the president spent time with the queen, I was detailed to entertain the princess.

From conversations with Aleck Loudon, the Dutch ambassador, I gathered that Queen Wilhelmina was a determined and stubborn woman. I saw none of this in the princess. Juliana, then thirty-four, was friendly, gracious, and exceedingly courteous.

During the weekend, the princess and I were scheduled to be together daily at luncheon, dinner, tea, and for an hour or so in the morning and the afternoon. With all that time together, what to talk about was a concern. Meals were not a problem, because the president and the queen pretty much controlled the conversation. Queen Wilhelmina sat on the president's right. Princess Juliana sat on his left, and I, on the princess's left. The president was enthusiastic about his Dutch ancestors. His knowledge of the Dutch in America was extensive, and, in my judgment, he made a delightful host. There was no table-talk strain on me.

The walks were different. Fortunately, the princess was easy to talk to. She asked lots of questions, and tactfully suggested topics of conversation. "Where did you come from? Why, that is in the Midwest, is it not? And how did it happen that you went into the navy?"

She was particularly interested that I had visited the Dutch East Indies, spending time in Tanjung Priok, the seaport of Batavia,[24] and Palembang in Sumatra. She had never been to the Indies. I described how, in October 1925, as commanding officer

24 Now Jakarta, Indonesia.

of the USS *Bittern*, I had taken a party of U.S. astronomers from Manila to Sumatra, where they planned to view a total eclipse of the sun. It was my pleasure to tell her stories of that trip and how kindly I had been received by her countrymen.

I related my yarn about the dinner given for me by the burgomaster in Palembang, when an obscure hymn was played in my honor instead of "The Star-Spangled Banner." We guests had all stood at attention for this particular bit of music, and I had assumed it was the Dutch national anthem. The error was discovered when I could not name the piece for the burgomaster's daughter. "How remarkable, not knowing the name of one's own national anthem," she had commented. The princess was greatly amused.

I also told the princess about my conversations in Batavia with a captain of the Dutch Navy. The captain feared for the Dutch East Indies because he thought Japan would like to grab them. The princess and I discussed how things had changed in the Pacific since those relatively peaceful days in 1925. Singapore had fallen. The Dutch East Indies had been occupied. In June 1942, things looked dark indeed, and the United States and its Pacific allies had not recovered from the initial shock of war.

While Queen Wilhelmina was at Hyde Park, the president talked many, many hours with her. Although I do not know much about their discussions, I learned a few details one evening about 11:00 p.m., when the president invited me to join him in a nightcap. He said the queen had told him that evening that she personally favored much more colonist participation in government, but the idea was difficult politically. She had said that once the war was over, she would use what influence she had to bring about a liberalization of Dutch colonial rule. Of course, President Roosevelt had decided ideas about colonies and believed strongly that colonists should participate in their own government.

The royal visit was a pleasant one. I thoroughly enjoyed my part in the proceedings. To be present at Hyde Park on this occasion was a remarkable experience, one of a long parade of fortunate experiences that made up my service in the navy.

The naming of ships provided another opportunity for President Roosevelt's informal diplomacy. In this particular series of events, I played the role of emissary. At the Battle of Savo Island, the Australian cruiser HMAS *Canberra* was sunk on 9 August 1942, with heavy loss of life. It was a great blow to the Australians, particularly as members of many of Australia's first families were among the casualties.[25]

Some weeks later, I took a list of proposed names for new heavy cruisers to the president for his approval. In the course of our conversation, he remarked about as follows: "John, I've been turning over in my mind something that I think I'll try out on you. What do you think of the idea of naming one of our new heavy cruisers *Canberra* as a tribute to the Australian *Canberra* lost at Savo Island?"

"Well, sir," said I, "off the top of my head, I like the idea. I suppose it would be agreeable to the Australians, but further inquiry would be in order."

"You're dead right," said he. "The formal way to take up this matter would be through the State Department. But," said he, with a twinkle in his eye, "what do you say that you and I indulge in a little bit of informal diplomacy? Get in touch with Sir Owen Dixon, and see what he thinks about the idea. If he doesn't like it, we'll forget it. If he likes it, I'm sure you will pursue it further." Sir Owen Dixon was the Australian ambassador and a member of the Pacific War Council.

---

25 The Battle of Savo Island, fought in the Solomon Islands during the night of August 8–9, 1942, took place shortly after the Allies commenced landings on Guadalcanal to capture a nearly completed Japanese airfield, from which the Japanese could threaten vital U.S.–Australian supply lines. During the battle, Japanese ships surprised a U.S.–Australian naval force screening transports bound for Guadalcanal. The results for the Allies were disastrous. The Allies lost four cruisers, two destroyers suffered heavy damage, and many lives were lost.

I called Sir Owen and made an appointment to see him. At our meeting, I explained the president's proposal to name a new U.S. heavy cruiser after the *Canberra* that was lost. I said that the name would not be used unless the Australian government approved.

Sir Owen was deeply moved. I thought I detected a tear in his eye. "How thoughtful of the president to make such a proposal. I shall refer it to my government with the recommendation that it be approved." He asked me to tell the president how much he appreciated his thoughtfulness.

Shortly afterward, the ambassador informed me that his government was pleased to accept the president's offer, and I so informed the president. He was delighted and remarked, "You know, John, this cruiser is going to need a sponsor. Would you be good enough to ask Sir Owen if Lady Dixon would be willing to christen the ship? If so, I shall be pleased to extend an invitation to her."

The following morning, I went to the Australian Embassy and met with Sir Owen again. When I delivered the message about Lady Dixon christening the ship, there was no doubt about a tear in Sir Owen's eye. In a choked voice, he said, "Of course, I cannot speak for my wife, but I suspect she will be most pleased to be the sponsor of the new *Canberra*. And on behalf of my government and myself, please let me again say how deeply we appreciate the president's proposal." The president invited Lady Dixon to christen USS *Canberra*, and she accepted.

There is a sequel to my *Canberra* story. Years later, after my retirement from the navy, I was living in Boston, and Sir Owen Dixon was the chief justice of the Australian Supreme Court. Quite by accident, I discovered that he was in town at Harvard Law School. I left a message for him, and shortly afterward, my wife and I received an invitation to tea with the Dixons.

At tea, we talked about Washington, and what had happened to us in the intervening years. Lady Dixon remarked, "You know, I am often asked about my family, and I have a stock answer to that question. I always say I have a large family: two sons, two daughters, and a heavy cruiser." What a nice ending, thought I, to FDR's informal diplomacy.

Alexander Loudon, the Dutch ambassador, offered an interesting view of President Roosevelt's style as a diplomat. We talked in the spring of 1946, when the Roosevelt home at Hyde Park was turned over to the country. Loudon remarked, "I tell you, McCrea, it was this way with FDR. Mine is a small country, but he made us feel it was large and important."

Chapter 9

White House Visitors

In 1942, the first year of the war, foreign dignitaries and missions flocked to Washington, most of them intent on availing themselves of the U.S. production of war materiel. During that year many, many royal visitors, heads of state, and high government officials made their way to the White House. As I recall it, these included at least two kings, a queen, two princes, and many presidents and prime ministers. The list was impressive.

When the president entertained distinguished visitors, I was called upon to perform a variety of duties. I accompanied the president to speeches and functions. I laid wreaths. I met and accompanied dignitaries on the president's behalf and assisted with organizational details. I also coped with the unexpected.

Since the president's time and mobility were limited, I was assigned escort duty on a number of occasions. I missed a meeting of the Pacific War Council when the president sent me to Baltimore to welcome the king of Greece on his behalf. When Vyacheslav Molotov, the Soviet Union's minister of foreign affairs, paid a visit to the White House, the president asked me to accompany Mr. Molotov and his party to the airport for their flight home. There I waited with Secretary of State Cordell Hull and others until Mr. Molotov's heavily loaded plane struggled into the air, barely clearing the trees at the end of the runway.[26]

In February 1942, I had a more extended escort assignment. The president asked me to arrange a visit to the Naval Academy for Crown Prince Olav of Norway and his wife, and requested that I accompany the royal couple on the trip. The prince had come from London, where he spent the war years, to visit his wife, Princess Märtha, then living in Washington with her children. Märtha was a great favorite of the president's and a frequent White House visitor. I made arrangements with the superintendent of the Naval Academy for a weekend of activities for the royal couple, and they thoroughly enjoyed their visit. I had the opportunity to discuss the Nazi occupation of Norway with his Royal Highness, and to hear his views on Vidkun Quisling, the Nazi stooge, then in control of the Norwegian government. It was a most interesting weekend.

The most memorable of my escort missions was in June 1942, when Prime Minister Winston Churchill visited the United States to meet with the president.[27] On the day of Mr. Churchill's arrival, the president was in Hyde Park. He wanted Mr. Churchill to join him there, a change in the prime minister's itinerary not previously agreed upon. The president directed that I welcome the prime minister on his behalf so I could convey his wish that the PM join him at Hyde Park, and explain the transportation options available at the PM's convenience.

The day of arrival came. The prime minister's Boeing seaplane landed on the Potomac River and taxied to the landing float at the Naval Air Station. A large crowd was on hand, including Secretary of State Cordell Hull; Lord Halifax, the British ambassador; and many other important personages. As a navy captain, I ranked well

---

26 On May 29, 1942, Molotov held a secret meeting with President Roosevelt to urge him to launch a "second front" against Germany in 1942.

27 Prime Minister Churchill came to Washington to meet with the president and military leaders, arriving by flying boat on June 18.

below the other members of the welcoming committee. I managed to get close to the gangway leading to the landing float, but the gangway was crowded with dignitaries.

As the prime minister emerged from the plane, Mr. Hull turned around and said in his high-pitched, old man's voice, "Captain McCrea, I have been informed that the president has directed that you welcome the prime minister to these shores on his behalf. You better get out there."

I mumbled something about not wishing to push dignitaries into the water, and made my way to the float. I introduced myself to Mr. Churchill, and gave him the president's messages. As to transportation to Hyde Park, I informed the PM that I had a special train standing by. Or, if he preferred, I could have air transportation available the following morning.

The PM was given to making unexpected remarks, and so it was in this case. He listened attentively to his options and then remarked gravely, "I shan't make this important decision until after I have had my bath."

With that I withdrew, and Mr. Hull, Lord Halifax, and the others proceeded to extend greetings. Of course, my role in these proceedings was rather insignificant, but I did have the honor of welcoming the leader of our most important ally ahead of our secretary of state.

On the final evening of Mr. Churchill's visit, President Roosevelt again called me into service, this time to escort the prime minister to Baltimore to meet his seaplane for the flight home. Thus, I found myself in a car making conversation with the great prime minister. I cannot say that my efforts were an unqualified success.

It was quickly evident that the PM did not need me to keep him entertained. Out the window, he caught sight of a sign advertising Valley Forge Beer. "How clever, how deucedly clever," he remarked. "History and relaxation at once!"

As we rode along, it occurred to me that the prime minister might know what had become of Admiral of the Fleet Sir Ernle

Chatfield, a British naval officer in whose career I had taken an interest. I decided to broach the topic.

A little background is necessary for the yarn that follows. During World War I, I served on the USS *New York*, the flagship of a division of U.S. battleships that operated for a time as part of the British Grand Fleet. On our arrival in Scotland in late 1917, one of the first British officers to pay a call on our admiral was Captain Ernle Chatfield, commander of the flagship of the commander in chief of the British Grand Fleet.

Captain Chatfield had an engaging and powerful personality. We young naval officers were most impressed with him, and thought he would go far. I knew that he had become first sea lord, the head of the Royal Navy, but by June 1942, he no longer held that position.

I was aware that Chatfield did not get on well with Mr. Churchill. These were two brilliant people with totally different personalities. A British admiral once described their relationship: "The PM was the kind of chap who would send for the first sea lord, and greet him thus: 'I say, Chatfield, what about sending a cruiser division somewhere to take something?' Chatfield never rose to that sort of bait. His answer would be, 'But Mr. Prime Minister, can't you be more specific?' Whereupon, the prime minister would roar that he expected more cooperation from the Royal Navy."

With considerable caution, I approached the subject of Chatfield. I described how I had met him and followed his career, indicating that I had lost track of him. Continuing, I timorously remarked that I supposed Admiral Chatfield was currently retired or "unemployed," a Royal Navy term meaning one who has been detached from one assignment and has not yet gone to another.

"Unemployed? Unemployed?" roared the prime minister. "Not a bit of it. He races up and down England making speeches against my government to all who will listen to him. He couldn't be more employed!" With that, the prime minister changed the subject.

Distinguished visitors to the White House were entertained formally at lunch or dinner. While the chief of protocol at the State Department, George "Summey" Summerlin, staged the state functions at the White House, there were always details and formalities that demanded my attention. When I attended these affairs, as I did often, my place at the table was in accordance with my rank, always well "below the salt" at the far end from the president.

State dinners and luncheons were always followed by an exchange of toasts. I was impressed with the character of the talks made by the president on these occasions. In my judgment, they were little gems of friendliness, graciousness, and wisdom. He spoke without notes, and no record was kept of his remarks. It occurred to me that a record should be made, if only for his protection.

The state luncheon for the prime minister of Poland stands out for the attention given to the president's toast. Thirteen had been invited to the luncheon, but after I remarked to the president that some might regard a party of thirteen as a bad omen, and suggested that I be removed from the guest list, he invited Under Secretary of State Sumner Welles to expand the group to fourteen.

At the luncheon, the Honorable James F. Byrnes, an associate justice of the U.S. Supreme Court, was seated on my left. Our conversation settled on the president's "table talks," and I remarked on how splendid I thought them and how worthy of preservation they were. Mr. Byrnes was inclined to agree.

At one time, Mr. Byrnes had been a court reporter. When the president started his post-luncheon toast, Mr. Byrnes drew an envelope from his pocket and began to write. A couple of hours after the luncheon, a messenger appeared in my office with a copy of the president's remarks and a note from Mr. Byrnes indicating that he agreed that a record should be kept of such talks. I talked to Steve Early and the president about the idea. Steve was enthusiastic; the president less so, but he went along. Steve arranged to have future talks recorded by John Romagna, his brilliant shorthand stenographer. I have no idea what ultimately became of this operation, but it was a worthy endeavor.

Every White House visit had its little problems, but the Washington stay of Queen Wilhelmina of the Netherlands was marked by incidents of a more serious nature. One was quickly resolved, but the other had the potential to cause a serious international misunderstanding.

The queen arrived in early August, some weeks after the weekend at Hyde Park I described earlier. Her visit was an important event for the Roosevelts and the Dutch Embassy. The White House had arranged a full day of activities for her. She was to address a joint session of Congress, accept a patrol vessel from the United States, lunch on board the presidential yacht, and visit Mount Vernon and Arlington National Cemetery. In the evening, she was to be the guest of honor at a state dinner at the White House. On subsequent days, the queen was scheduled to attend a Dutch Embassy reception and an investiture ceremony at the embassy, where she was to award decorations to American military personnel.

During the daytime activities, the president and I accompanied the queen. At our first port of call, the Capitol, the president remained in the car while I escorted the queen to the door and turned her over to Vice President Henry Wallace and Sam Rayburn, the speaker of the House of Representatives.

Our next stop was going to be the Washington Navy Yard, where the president was to speak at the ceremonies marking the transfer of a patrol vessel to the Dutch. Whenever the president went any place where he was to speak, Charlie Fredericks, his Secret Service bodyguard, carried a black book containing an outline of the remarks the president expected to make. I never had anything to do with the book. I just knew that it was invariably in Charlie's lap in the front seat of the president's limousine.

When I returned to the car after bringing the queen into the Capitol, I remarked to Charlie that I supposed he had the president's black book. "No, I don't," he said. "The president didn't give it to me this morning."

I quickly spoke to the president. "That's right," he said. "I didn't give it to Charlie. It was on my desk in the oval room in the White House."

I dashed over to the officer in charge of our motorcycle escort and told him to immediately dispatch one of his men to the White House to pick up the book and bring it to me at the Capitol, or at the Washington Navy Yard, if we had moved on. Away went a motorcycle officer with a roar, White House–bound. I dashed into the basement entrance of the Capitol, found a pay phone, and called Howell Crim at the White House. I told him to get the black book and deliver it to the motorcycle policeman.

In due course, the queen reappeared and took her place in the president's car. There was no motorcycle policeman in sight. I told the president's chauffeur to head for the Washington Navy Yard, whispering that he should drive slowly. To my relief, just as we entered the navy yard, the motorcycle officer appeared, in great haste.

On that bright and sunny morning, I made up my mind that henceforth, whenever we went where the president was to speak, a copy of his prepared remarks would be in my hip pocket, just in case there was no motorcycle officer on hand to make a dash to the White House. What is an aide for, anyway?

A few days later, at an investiture ceremony, Queen Wilhelmina was to award decorations to some Americans who had served with the Dutch in Indonesia in the early days of World War II. One of those to be honored was Admiral Thomas Charles Hart, then retired, who had commanded the U.S. Asiatic Fleet in early 1942 at the time of the unsuccessful Allied defense of the Dutch East Indies. The islands were an important target for the Japanese because of their extensive oil reserves.

Although past mandatory retirement age in mid-1941, Admiral Hart was retained in command of the Asiatic Fleet because of his thorough understanding of the grave Far East situation. Shortly after the United States declared war, the Asiatic Fleet moved to the Dutch East Indies, where it defended the islands as part of a joint naval force including American, British, Dutch, and Australian units. Admiral Hart commanded the joint force, but the Dutch wanted to have a greater role in this operation.

Under pressure from the Dutch and possibly for additional reasons, Prime Minister Churchill and the president decided to give the joint force command to the Dutch. In February 1942, Admiral Hart was relieved by the Dutch admiral, Conrad Helfrich. Hart was piqued at having to give up command and felt that, but for the Dutch, he would not have been relieved.

At about 5:00 p.m. on the day before the investiture ceremony, I received a frantic call from my friend, Alexander Loudon, the Dutch ambassador. The conversation went something like this:

"A most serious matter has just arisen," said Aleck. "I am calling to ask the help of the president to prevent a serious affront to our queen. For some time, my government has had the intention to decorate Admiral Hart with the highest honor it can award a foreigner. This intention was made known to Admiral Hart via the Navy Department. My office contacted Admiral Hart late this afternoon to remind him of the ceremony tomorrow and advise him that the queen herself would make the presentation. To my amazement, Admiral Hart informed me that he had other plans. He said he is leaving for Connecticut tonight, and will not attend the ceremonies tomorrow morning.

"I can think of no more serious insult to my government and to our queen. The insult is all the greater because the queen is a guest in this country. Can anything be done to correct this unprecedented situation?"

As soon as I could get Aleck quieted down, I assured him that I would call him back as soon as I could come up with an answer. I briefly pondered the problem. Because time was of the essence, I decided to shortcut Navy Department channels and go directly to the president.

I tore over to the White House, and Grace Tully let me in to see the president at once. The president listened quietly to what I had to say and responded, "As you must be aware, Tommy Hart is a peppery individual. I'm not sure he thinks well of me. We had a tussle when I was assistant secretary of the navy, and it was not a pleasant experience for either of us. From everything I have heard, he is an outstanding officer, but his conduct here cannot be ignored."

The president continued, "I agree with the ambassador. The admiral's refusal to accept the decoration in these circumstances would be most embarrassing for us all. John, you get in touch with Tommy Hart and do what you can to get him to change his mind. Talk right up to him. Keep me out of this, if possible. But if he is adamant, as a last resort tell him that the commander in chief would esteem it a personal favor if he would appear at the Dutch Embassy tomorrow and receive the decoration from the hands of the queen."

I was not confident that my words would carry much weight with Admiral Hart. I was eighteen classes junior to him at the Naval Academy, and I had never served with him. However, our relations had always been cordial, and I had come to know him better in January 1941, when I brought the revised navy war plans to him in the Philippines and lived aboard his flagship for nearly two weeks. I hoped this would stand me in good stead in the encounter that was about to take place.

It was nearly 6:00 p.m. when I left the president's office. The next thing to do was to reach Admiral Hart. Fortunately, I got him on the telephone on my first try. We talked briefly about one thing and another, and then I plunged into the main purpose of the call.

"I've heard recently that Queen Wilhelmina intends to decorate you tomorrow with the Netherlands's highest decoration for your service in the defense of the Dutch East Indies. This is a high honor, and I congratulate you."

"Just a minute, my young friend," said he firmly. "I have other ideas. I'm returning to Connecticut tonight. Mrs. Hart and I have our tickets, and we leave Union Station at 10:00 p.m. The Dutch Embassy has already been informed that I shan't be present at tomorrow morning's investiture."

"But," said I, "the Dutch must feel they are deeply in your debt. Otherwise, it would never occur to them to give you their highest honor." The admiral replied that the Dutch did not seem to have such a high regard for his service when they pressed to have him relieved of command in the Dutch East Indies.

"But, Admiral," said I, "although the queen of the Netherlands is here in exile, she is essentially a guest of the United States. She has indicated her desire to give you this decoration, and your refusal to accept this honor would certainly lead to much embarrassment and international misunderstanding. Of course, I understand and sympathize if you feel that the Netherlands was responsible for your being brought home. I am sure you are better informed than I. But I assure you that I have never heard—at the White House or in the Navy Department—that you were relieved because of pressure from the Dutch."

"Well," said he, "I know other decorations are going to be handed out tomorrow, and I'm sure they won't miss me." And changing the subject, "I hope our paths will cross the next time I am in Washington. Thanks ever so much for taking the time out to call me." Of course, he was signing off.

"Admiral, may I continue for just a moment? I'm sure it may have occurred to you during this call that I was asked to ring you up. That is true. The president directed me to try to persuade you to accept the decoration. He said that if I couldn't persuade you to change your mind, as a last resort I should tell you that he, as commander in chief, would deem it a personal favor if you would present yourself at the embassy and accept the decoration from this country's distinguished guest, the queen of the Netherlands."

"What did you say about a favor?" said the admiral.

"I said that the commander in chief would deem it a personal favor if you would accept the decoration."

There was silence. I did not know what was going on. Suddenly there was a roar over the phone, "Tell him I'll go and accept the damn decoration." Admiral Hart slammed down the receiver with a resounding crash.

With relief, I hung up. In seconds, I called Ambassador Loudon and explained that Admiral Hart had found it possible to change his plans, and that he would be honored to be at the embassy as scheduled to receive the decoration. Aleck was pleased and relieved.

I then called the president and reported my conversation with the admiral. "It wasn't easy to change his mind, Mr. President," said I. "My powers of persuasion weren't up to it. I had to fall back on your argument of last resort." The president chuckled.

As the years passed, it was my privilege to see Admiral Hart on many occasions. Invariably he would refer to the decoration incident and remark that I had prevented him from "making a grave mistake." I would protest that it was the president's request for a personal favor that had saved him. Nevertheless, the admiral persisted in his point of view.

Chapter 10

Yarn: A Tour of Hyde Park

—⚉—

This yarn is about my visit to Hyde Park with the president in early June 1942. The president was in high good humor. In his book, *Off the Record with FDR,* Bill Hassett, the president's correspondence secretary, remarked about the therapeutic effect Hyde Park had on the president. He loved the Hudson Valley. His knowledge of its history from the earliest days to the present was remarkable. He enjoyed telling one yarn after another about its past, and would then bring things up to date with whimsies about the current crop of Hyde Park squires and their families. His commentary was all delivered most amusingly and with much enthusiasm.

The morning about which I write was perfect, weather-wise. We left our Washington train at Highland Falls, New York, on the west bank of the Hudson. As our caravan picked up speed and headed for Hyde Park in the bright morning sunshine, the president grew expansive.

"What do you know about this great valley, John?"

"Very little, sir," said I. "A few trips up and down the river on the New York Central Railroad are my only contact with the area."

"Well, my friend," said he, "I shall undertake to bring you up to date on the Hudson River Valley. As to this great part of our country, I can see that your education has been neglected. I'm going to give you a personally conducted tour this afternoon, and we'll top it off by stopping and having tea with Margaret Suckley." Margaret Suckley was the president's cousin, whom I had met on other occasions. "Of course, Margaret doesn't know that she is going to have tea with two distinguished gentlemen, nor do I think we should surprise her. When we get to the house, I'll ring her up and tell her the good news." And all this was said lightheartedly and with much exuberance.

I knew that the president had a Ford of not exactly current vintage that he liked to drive. I was told that he rarely used it, and when he did, it was more for a lark than for transportation. The president's infirmities prevented him from operating starters, foot brakes, and accelerators in the normal manner. His car was equipped with hand levers that enabled him to perform functions ordinarily controlled by the feet. The president didn't confide in me that he was going to drive his car on my "personally conducted tour," but that is exactly what happened.

The car was delivered to the front door about 3:00 p.m. The president and I climbed aboard. Charlie Fredericks, the president's Secret Service bodyguard, and Fala, the president's Scotty, got in the back seat and, with much clatter and grinding of gears, we were off. A Secret Service car preceded us, and another followed behind. As we approached the highway entrance, the president said, "Now, just where would you like to go?"

"I'll be pleased to go wherever you want to go, Mr. President," said I. "Remember that I have never been in this area before."

The lead Secret Service car stopped at the gate, and an agent came back to the president's car for instructions. "Do you want to go the Poughkeepsie way?" said the president to me.

"Any direction suits me, Mr. President," said I.

"Well, Poughkeepsie is a charming place, but it is not as interesting as the country to the north." To Mike Reilly, the Secret Service agent in charge of the White House detail, the president said,

"Have someone in that lead car keep an eye on us. I may very well want to turn off on some of the little-used roads to the right or left of the highway. I will indicate to you when and where I hope to turn. The car following can look out for itself. It should just follow us. We will drive slowly through Hyde Park and stop at the Vanderbilt place. John, you must see it, because I dare say that there will never again be another place like it built in the United States. It belongs to an age that is distinctly past."

Off we went at what I thought was a pretty good rate of speed, all things considered. As we approached Hyde Park, we slowed down perceptibly. "Now," said the president, "there is where I vote," pointing to a building on his left. "And over here is our Episcopal church. We'll stop there on the way back." And with a wave of his hand, he remarked, "There are a couple of old friends of mine standing on the corner. One of them, I'm sure, has voted for me ever since I entered politics. As for the other chap, I'm not sure he has ever voted for me, but we are good friends just the same."

On arrival at the Vanderbilt mansion, just a short distance north of the village of Hyde Park, the president thought I should go into the house. He said that, at the very least, I should look at the elegant ground floor. This I did.

The president decided that this was a good chance for Fala to have a run. From the high rate of speed at which the dog took off, he evidently thought well of the idea, too. On my return from a quick tour of the Vanderbilt mansion—indeed, it was a mansion—the president indicated that we should be getting on. He called to Fala. Charlie Fredericks called to Fala. But Fala either didn't hear or, hearing, thought little of returning to the car.

Finally, Charlie Fredericks took off after Fala. He cornered him under a low-branched pine tree, picked him up, and returned him to the car. Charlie, who was slightly on the stout side, was puffing. The Scottish Terrier was so little winded by the chase that the president gaily remarked, "You know, Charlie, I think Fala is in a lot better shape than you." The three of us had a good laugh. Fala, the silent one, only wore a pleased look.

The trip up and down the side roads was delightful. The president pointed out where he used to play as a young boy, warmly naming the playmates of his youth. We sat for a time on a bluff looking out over the Hudson, truly a beautiful sight on this pleasant June afternoon. The president, meanwhile, pointed out sights of interest on the opposite bank of the Hudson.

In due course, we arrived at Margaret Suckley's home. Her family was there as well. Tea was a fine occasion. There was much talk about Hyde Park and its residents, and many stories about various local characters. The president was greatly relaxed, and it was gratifying to see him look so well and enjoying himself to the utmost.

The return to Hyde Park was made at what I regarded as a rather high rate of speed. I was astonished at the dexterity with which the president manipulated the car's hand levers. As we neared the village of Hyde Park, the president slowed down. When we came abreast of the churchyard—I might add that he was a vestryman here—we turned in and came to a stop in front of the church. There was a neatly painted sign of black background on which appeared, in gold lettering, the hours of worship, the name of the pastor, etc. At the bottom was the caption, "The President's church."

"You know, John, one Saturday night, one of the local lads— he must have been a Republican—got a little high. The next morning, early Sunday worshippers were astonished to see under the caption, 'The President's church,' the words 'And God's church, too' in letters of equal size. Don't you love it? I've often wondered who did it. If I could find out, I would like to meet him. He must have a fine sense of humor." And with a hearty laugh, we were off for the great house at Hyde Park.

In a few minutes, we arrived. With difficulty, the president got out of the car and into his wheelchair, and we went inside. I thanked him for "the personal tour." "It was fun, wasn't it?" was his enthusiastic rejoinder. I thought then, and I think now, some thirty-six years after the event, that it was a glorious afternoon spent with a delightful companion.

Mind you, this was wartime. June 1942 was not one of our best wartime months. The responsibilities the president carried were many and varied. He urgently needed to take time to relax when he was able, yet he still found it possible to give me a personal tour of Hyde Park that day. Many politicians and many ordinary citizens seemed eager to fault him for almost anything. But I saw him on that occasion, and on so many others, as the good guy with whom it was always a pleasure to be.[28]

---

28 The events of June suggest the crushing weight the president carried with apparent ease. The month was a low point in the so-called Battle of the Atlantic, the Allied effort to wrest control of Atlantic shipping routes from the German U-boat. After the United States declared war, U-boats rushed to the American coast. U.S. merchantmen carrying war supplies were easy prey as they traveled alone, silhouetted against the brightly lit Atlantic coast. Only in late spring did Admiral Ernest King initiate the use of convoys with naval escorts, which resulted in an immediate decrease in losses. Orders for the blackout of seaboard cities were not issued until June. More merchantmen were sunk in June 1942 than in any other month of the entire war.

 Other Allied setbacks during the month included Japan's seizure of two of Alaska's Aleutian Islands (June 3–7), the loss of carrier *Yorktown* at the Battle of Midway (June 7), and the fall of British-held Tobruk, Libya, to General Rommel and his Afrika Korps (June 21). Tobruk's deep-water harbor and airport had great strategic importance in the desert war in North Africa.

Chapter 11

Special Jobs

After some weeks at the White House, when I had my regular duties in hand and the Map Room up and running, the president started to give me special jobs from time to time. Some of these details had some relation to the navy, albeit sometimes peripheral, but many did not. Some were purely ceremonial or logistical, while others required thought and resourcefulness. The variety of these tasks and the challenges they presented added considerable zest to my job as naval aide.

When Pa Watson showed me around the White House in January, he provided little guidance about the organization of White House operations. He remarked that everyone pretty much played things by ear. There was a good deal of truth in this. Usually the president would expressly assign tasks, but sometimes he did so in a most offhanded way, with little advance warning. Once I even learned about an assignment from a third person. On occasion, he would call at odd hours about jobs with exceedingly short deadlines. My approach in these situations was simply to "roll with the punches," in good navy fashion.

In my house I had two telephones with a direct line to the White House switchboard. It is amazing how often these telephones were used. Calls from the president were unpredictable, but I had many night calls. One woke me at a bit past midnight one night in the early spring of 1942. Mary Lambrecht, one of the White House switchboard operators, remarked, "Captain, the president wants to talk to you." In seconds, the president was on the line.

"John, I have just been informed that Major Randolph Church-ill, Winston's son, is someplace in New York. I have no idea where. I would like him to have luncheon with me today at 1:00 p.m. in my office. When I see you in the morning, you can let me know if you've had any luck locating him and whether he can come."

I thought the problem over for a minute or two and called Mary Lambrecht back. "Mary," said I, "please get the British con-sulate general's office in New York on the line. Say the call is from the White House, and let me speak to the duty officer." This was done. I introduced myself as the naval aide to the president and said I had been informed that Major Randolph Churchill was in New York. If this was true, could he tell me where the major was staying? After some delay, the duty officer indicated that the major might be staying at any one of six hotels, which he listed.

As a good bet, I started with the Waldorf-Astoria. After consid-erable negotiation with the assistant manager on duty, he reluc-tantly told me that the major was registered there. However, his suite did not answer, and the floor clerk reported that he had gone out for the evening. It was a start.

One of the desk clerks volunteered that he had overheard the major talking with a friend about going to the theater and a night-club that evening. The clerk did not know the name of the night-club, but he recalled the major saying he had been to the Stork Club the previous evening.

I wondered whether he would repeat the visit. It was worth a try. "Mary, get me the Stork Club." I worked my way past the tel-ephone operator at the Stork Club and found a cooperative per-son. I explained that I was looking for a gentleman named Major Randolph Churchill. I did not know whether he was at the club, but he would probably be in the uniform of a British Army officer. "Just a moment, please," said the voice on the line.

In a couple of minutes another voice said, "This is Major Randolph Churchill." Success, thought I. I identified myself and delivered the president's greetings and invitation to luncheon. After a discussion of transportation arrangements, the major accepted.

When I took the dispatches to the White House that morning, I told the president that he could expect Major Churchill for lunch. "How did you locate him, John?" he asked. When I told him, he commented that Alexander Graham Bell had certainly done quite a service when he invented the telephone. I realize that the foregoing yarn is trivial, hardly worth the time it takes to record it, but I include it to point up the variety of things I was called on to do.

On another occasion, the White House phone at my bedside rang at about 11:30 p.m. The president came on the line and said to the effect, "John, you know I am going on the air tomorrow night, and everyone here says my talk lacks color. Sam Rosenman and Bob Sherwood suggested that maybe you could come up with some story with drama and pathos in it." The president pronounced the word "drama" as "dray-ma." He wanted a story with dray-ma and pathos.

"Well," said I, "Mr. President, I'll do the best I can, but what's the deadline on this?"

The president turned away from the phone. I heard him say, "What's the deadline?" Then he came back and said, "About nine o'clock tomorrow morning."

"I'll do the best I can."

I called General George Marshall, the chief of staff of the army, and Lieutenant General Thomas Holcomb, the commandant of the marine corps, and told them what I was up against. I didn't know whom else to call.

When I got to the Navy Department early the next morning, I ran into Rear Admiral William C. Glassford, who had just returned from the Far East. He said he had a story about a navy medical doctor in the Dutch East Indies and what he had done to help people. Glassford said he could give me something in writing about four o'clock that afternoon. I told him I needed it in forty-five minutes. Glassford dictated his story and got it to me in time. In the end, I came up with four yarns that I considered to have dray-ma and pathos.

That evening, the president broadcast his fireside chat. He used three of my four yarns on the air.[29] From then on, whenever the president's writers wrote a piece, I was designated to come up with something. And I did, as best I could.

Another special job the president asked me to handle concerned the presidential retreat now known as Camp David. In late March or early April 1942, while the president was having his sinus treatment in Ross McIntire's office, he remarked about as follows, "Both of you"—referring to Ross and me—"know how much I like to go to Hyde Park for weekend breaks. With the war on, I know I cannot go as often as I have in the past. I would like to dodge the heat and humidity of the Washington summer as much as possible. Air conditioning is not the answer for me, as you both well know. I never had sinus trouble until I encountered air conditioning.

"Now, what I want you people to consider is, can't we find a place in easy reach of Washington where it would be possible to set up a modest camp that I could go to on weekends, or even overnight, to escape the Washington summer? This would be an alternative to the *Potomac.*" He was referring here to the USS *Potomac*,

---

29 In his fireside chat of April 28, 1942, the president used Admiral Glassford's story of how Dr. Corydon M. Wassell managed to evacuate about a dozen wounded U.S. naval officers from Java as the Japanese took over the Dutch East Indies in early 1942. Cecil B. DeMille, the Hollywood director, heard the president's talk, and made a movie based on the story. Released by Paramount in the spring of 1944, the movie was entitled *The Story of Dr. Wassell* and featured Gary Cooper as the doctor.

the presidential yacht. "The Secret Service is adamant that I use the *Potomac* only on rare occasions.[30]

"I know President Hoover had a camp on the Rapidan River in the Catoctin Mountains. I know nothing about it, but that might be a good area to investigate. At any rate, Ross, I want you and John and Steve Early to undertake to find a place that will suit my needs, and house the clerical staff that usually accompanies me to Hyde Park. Remember now, nothing elaborate—something most modest, functional, and within easy reach of the White House. Since proximity is so important, the place probably has to be in Virginia or Maryland. Summer is approaching, so we should get on this as soon as possible."

Ross, Steve, and I set up a date a couple of days later to visit Mr. Hoover's camp.[31] We decided to investigate that first, thinking that if was satisfactory for Mr. Hoover, it might suit President Roosevelt as well. In the end, I did not go with Ross and Steve, because the president gave me a job that took precedence over a pleasant afternoon in the Virginia countryside. I visited the camp some days later.

We quickly eliminated the Hoover camp. It was built alongside a stream and had little view of the surrounding countryside. President Hoover was fond of stream fishing, and while the camp was ideal for that, we didn't think President Roosevelt would like it.

Nearby, atop the Catoctin Mountains in Maryland, we found a simple camp built by the Works Progress Administration sometime around 1938 for use by federal agents and their families. The exact number of buildings escapes me at the moment, but it could not have been more than eight or ten. The buildings were small, save for a somewhat larger one that had a mess hall and a kitchen. We thought the larger cottage could be adapted for the president

---

30 After the United States entered the war, there was a marked increase in enemy submarine activity off the U.S. Atlantic Coast, and the Secret Service became concerned about the *Potomac*'s vulnerability to submarines.

31 Rapidan Camp in Virginia.

with a few minor alterations, and his staff could be accommodated in some of the adjoining buildings.

Rear Admiral Ben Moreell, Civil Engineer Corps and chief of the Navy Department's Bureau of Yards and Docks, was called in for consultation. Ben Moreell and action were no strangers, and action quickly followed. In a few short days, the larger of the cottages was altered to provide a combined living and dining room, a bedroom for the president, and three other small bedrooms. The small bedrooms had a common bath. The dining area was no larger than an ordinary residential dining room. At one end was a stone fireplace that contributed greatly to the comfort of the modest living/dining area on cooler days.

The president's bedroom was larger than the others, but it was not large. One wall was equipped with a hinged panel, which, when tripped, fell outward. It was designed to serve in an emergency as a ramp and escape route for the president and his wheelchair. A kitchen and pantry adjoined the dining/living room area. There was a screened porch, which was accessed through the dining area. From the porch, there was a spectacular view of the surrounding countryside.

The president quickly assigned me the responsibility of setting up and maintaining the camp. "John," said he, "since I shan't be using the *Potomac* except on rare occasions, in addition to your other duties, you are hereby appointed proprietor and landlord of the camp. And, by the way, shouldn't the camp have a name? I think I have a good one. Did you by any chance read James Hilton's *Lost Horizon*?"

"No, Mr. President."

"The novel tells of a mythical valley in the Himalayan Mountains. Some airplane passengers were forced to land there, and they found it much to their liking. Hilton named this valley Shangri-La. Of course, I haven't visited our retreat as yet, but I'm willing to call it Shangri-La, sight unseen." And so the camp got its name. In due course, a white sign with black lettering reading "Shangri-La" was nailed over the front entrance of the president's cabin.

Shangri-La remained the name of the camp for some ten or twelve years. Then President Eisenhower decided to scrap the name and call the place Camp David in honor of his young grandson. I prefer Shangri-La, because it reminds me of the following incident and President Roosevelt's sense of humor, which was always delightful.

The president used the name Shangri-La to play a little joke on the Japanese, to the amusement of all those who understood it. Sometime in early 1942, we received a dispatch from Churchill, expressing hope that the U.S. Navy would take some aggressive action against the Japanese in the Far East. The next day, Admiral King personally informed the president that the navy was setting up a plan to bomb Japan. The operation that eventuated was the air raid on Tokyo led by Lieutenant Colonel James Doolittle, U.S. Army Air Corps, with bombers launched from the carrier USS *Hornet*.[32]

President Roosevelt was at Hyde Park on 18 April 1942, the day of the Doolittle raid. I spoke to the president by phone the following morning.

"The most important item of the morning's report, Mr. President, is that U.S. planes made an air attack on Tokyo."

"Really?" said the president with a laugh. Of course, he was privy to the whole operation, and the raid was no surprise to him. "And where, John, do you suppose those planes came from?"

"That, Mr. President, is what the Japanese want to know. According to our intelligence sources, that question is on the lips of everyone in Tokyo." I moved on to the other items of my report.

---

32 On April 18, 1942, sixteen B-25 medium bombers took off from *Hornet* to bomb military targets in Tokyo and elsewhere on Honshu Island in Japan. The raid was planned and led by Lieutenant Colonel James Doolittle. The bombers had been modified for the mission and the crews specially trained to take off from a carrier. The planes, flying without fighter cover, were to drop their bombs and fly to bases in Free China. The raid's goal was to damage Japanese war production, boost American morale, and shake Japan's sense of invulnerability. Although little damage was done, the other goals were achieved.

About one o'clock that afternoon, the president called me. "I think I can answer the Japanese who are asking where the air raid came from. Ask Ernie King if he doesn't think it would be a good idea to say the raid came from Shangri-La. If we do, when this story reaches Japan, every Japanese will be busy looking at his or her equivalent of the *Rand-McNally Atlas* trying to find Shangri-La."

I called Admiral King and told him what the president had said. Admiral King laughed softly and said he thought rather well of the idea. Soon a press release was issued stating that it was "rumored" that the attack planes were from their base in Shangri-La. It was interesting to be around a guy as quick-witted as the president.

Although the name Shangri-la suggests a place of beauty, the furnishings in the president's cottage in the Catoctin Mountains in no way measured up to the camp's name. The president had instructed, "Remember, John, this is just a rustic retreat that must remain just that. Only the barest of necessities will be needed."

I visited the survey section of the Washington Navy Yard. Stored there were many household furnishings of other years, for the most part worn and outmoded. I found threadbare rugs in need of urgent repairs, but still usable. Beds of ancient vintage and unrelated pattern were also available. Knowing the size of the bed used by the president at the White House, I was on the lookout for something suitable for him. I finally found a formidable three-quarter-size brass bed from the 1890s or earlier, complete with springs and mattress. I had enough doubt about the suitability of this monstrosity that I asked the president's opinion, remarking that it seemed to me to be an awful lot of brass. "Why, of course, it will be just fine, John," said he, "just so long as the mattress is comfortable. And besides, aren't brass beds now in vogue?"

Outfitting the dining room was also problematic. Ultimately, I removed the dining table and twelve dining chairs from the presidential quarters on the *Potomac* and installed them at Shangri-La. A nondescript sideboard, bridge lamps, pictures, and bric-a-brac came from the survey section. The navy supplied all the table linen, bedding, towels, and things of that nature.

The president contributed two framed prints. One he particularly enjoyed. As I recall, the image had originally appeared in *Esquire* magazine. It depicted a young boy in a great state of perturbation reporting to a nearby female householder, "Johnny has written a dirty word on the sidewalk!" On the sidewalk in giant letters was the word "Roosevelt." The magazine contributed the original to the president, and he treasured it. We hung it in the hall directly opposite his bedroom door. It faced him each time he left the room, and he would stop and laugh at it.

The staff for the president's cottage came from the *Potomac*. The steward, the cook, and two messmen, all Filipino, were installed at Shangri-La, where they performed the duties of their rating exceptionally well. One of the messmen, an enthusiastic fisherman, often visited the Rapidan stream where Mr. Hoover used to fish. So it happened that Republican trout often graced the table of the Democratic president.

When all was in readiness, it was determined that Shangri-La would have a christening. On a pleasant Sunday afternoon in mid-May 1942, a picnic supper party was held at Shangri-La. The president and Mrs. Roosevelt; Malvina Thompson, Mrs. Roosevelt's secretary; Harry Hopkins; Ross McIntire; I; and a few others made the trip from Washington to the Catoctin retreat.

Although I had shown the president snapshots of what we were doing, this was the first time he had visited. He expressed approval of all that had been done, as did the others in the party. He was greatly pleased with the view from the screened porch. As the season progressed, it was evident that the screens kept out insects, but not the wind or rain, so the porch was glassed in. This contributed greatly to the president's comfort and enjoyment during the many hours he spent looking out over the Maryland countryside. The view was truly wonderful.

Of course, communication with the White House was important. The telephone people provided direct service to the White House switchboard. Four sparsely furnished cabins accommodated the staff members who ordinarily accompanied the president to Hyde Park. They messed with a small cadre of maintenance people and groundskeepers and the members of the *Potomac* crew. There was much competition among the crew for this choice duty.

I last visited Shangri-La on a beautiful fall day in November 1942. The autumn view from the porch was superb. The camp served an important purpose, providing an opportunity for the president to get away and escape the stresses of the presidency. There he could commune with nature for a few hours, and experience nature's rejuvenating effect.

With the passage of time and the influence of politics, FDR's rustic camp has grown into Camp David. Its growth parallels that of the Map Room into today's Situation Room. Again, I am reminded that great oaks from little acorns grow. My role in setting up these operations was largely improvisatory and rather amateurish.

The last of my yarns is about my participation in a series of events in the summer of 1942 that, for me personally, were among the most challenging and unnerving occurrences of the war. I refer to the case of eight German would-be saboteurs who were apprehended in this country. Eight Nazi agents were landed in the United States from German submarines, four on the coast of Long Island, and the rest in Florida.[33] All the agents had been schooled at a Nazi training center in the techniques of sabotage. All were equipped with explosives, primarily for use against U.S. transportation facilities. They all spoke English well, carried large sums of U.S. cash, and knew how to obtain additional explosives in this country. Their plan was to melt into the population and commit as many acts of sabotage as possible.

---

33 The Long Island landing occurred on June 13, 1942, near Amagansett, New York. The Florida landing occurred on June 17, 1941, at Ponte Vedra Beach near Jacksonville.

The landing on Long Island occurred in the dead of night, at about 2:00 a.m. The U.S. Coast Guard maintained foot patrols along the beaches of Long Island at points where enemy boat landings were considered possible. Shortly after the four saboteurs rowed themselves ashore from their submarine, a young coast guardsman on patrol came upon one of them. Oddly enough, the saboteur told the young man to take a good look at him and then disappeared into the night. Unnerved by the strange encounter, the young coast guardsman hastened to his headquarters to report the incident. He had no idea he had met a German agent.

Eventually, the saboteur who encountered the coast guardsman reached New York City and took up residence in a midtown hotel. After spending some days sampling the good life in Manhattan, he became convinced that he would be apprehended and regretted his involvement in the sabotage enterprise. He went to Washington, D.C., contacted the FBI, and disclosed all he knew about the plans of his co-saboteurs. Soon afterward, the other seven saboteurs were apprehended.

The eight saboteurs were brought to trial before a military commission sitting in Washington. All were convicted and sentenced to execution. This might seem to be harsh treatment, but this was wartime, and the saboteurs were landed in the U.S. specifically to do damage to the country.

One afternoon a few days after the completion of the trial, Grace Tully, the president's secretary, called me at my office in the Navy Department and told me the president wished to see me at once. On arrival in Miss Tully's office, I found Mr. Samuel I. Rosenman, formerly a justice of the Supreme Court of the State of New York, and currently counsel and assistant to the president. He greeted me with the remark, "John, it looks as though we are in for something."

The president wasted no time in telling us what he wanted. On the corner of his desk were two bound copies of the record of the proceedings in the trial of the saboteurs. He asked us to review the records and recommend final action to him as soon as possible. "The cabinet room is available to you for as long as you need it," said he.

There was no doubt about Sam Rosenman's qualifications for this job. As for me, I had a couple of law degrees, I was a member of two or three bars, and I had done three tours of duty in the Office of the Judge Advocate General. Nevertheless, I didn't regard myself as a lawyer, and I had no experience in work like this.

Sam was able to spend his entire time on the job. I put in many hours as well, but my efforts were interrupted because Queen Wilhelmina of the Netherlands was paying an official visit to Washington, and I sometimes had to be with the president in my capacity as naval aide.

The record of proceedings in the saboteur case was some 2,700 legal-size pages. It takes considerable time to read 2,700 pages. There were many late hours, and lots of coffee was consumed. In due course, Sam and I finished the job. In our judgment, the trial was a fair one. It was legal in all respects. The interests of the alleged saboteurs had been well-protected. The sentence of execution was a legal one. We prepared a memorandum to the president to that effect, pointing out, as well, that a degree of assistance had been rendered the prosecution by two of the co-conspirators.

A few days later, the president met with Sam and me, and took our memorandum under consideration. In the end, he let stand the commission's sentences as to six of the saboteurs. He mitigated the sentences of the two men who had assisted the prosecution, giving them each thirty years' imprisonment. I was glad that the ordeal was over. Or was it?

One Monday morning a couple of weeks after Sam and I finished our review, the president asked me to accompany him to his office so he could speak to me about a matter. Once settled in his office chair, he said, "John, you are familiar with the cases of the saboteurs. Six of them are under sentence of execution. Will you please see to it that the sentences in these cases are carried out by the end of the week?"

My answer was one that my thirty years of naval service had taught me, a simple, "Aye-aye, sir." Without further ado, I turned on my heel and left his office via the terrace door opening onto the White House gardens. The sun was shining brightly. A gentle breeze was blowing, and the gardens were in full bloom. Everything was serene, but I was disturbed. The question that bothered me was, how does one go about carrying into effect an approved sentence of execution of six human beings? Nothing in my naval training had prepared me for such a duty.

I knew that the saboteurs were in the custody of the provost marshal of the District of Columbia, a brigadier general in the national guard by the name of General Miller. I also knew that the saboteurs were confined in the District of Columbia jail. Beyond that, I was out of my depth. I called General Miller and asked him to come to the White House at once. For privacy's sake, I told him to meet me at the southeast gate of the White House grounds.

When General Miller arrived, I told him the problem, but omitted the time when the executions were to take place. I remarked only that the executions had to be carried out and plans should be made. The general replied, "This is a new one on me. But as it happens, before my executive officer was called to active reserve duty, he was second in command of the District of Columbia jail."

We called the general's executive officer and asked him to join us at the White House. We acquainted him with the facts, and he explained the details of an execution. The required procedures had a number of steps. The sentence had to be read to the condemned. He had to be given an opportunity to see his lawyer. He had to be made ready for the execution, with his head shaved. He had to be given an opportunity to see the prison chaplain, and other details. "In all, it requires about an hour per subject," said the executive.

"How much notice must be given regarding the time of an execution?" I asked.

"As much notice as possible, but at least six hours," was the reply.

I told the general and the colonel that I would give instructions later as to when the executions were to be carried out, and this information was not to be disclosed under any circumstances to anyone. The executions were to take place by the end of the week, and this was Monday.

On Friday evening, I went to bed reasonably early, at about 11:30 p.m. I called General Miller from the White House telephone at my bedside. I told him to carry out the sentences and to let me know when the operation had been completed. I said that after about 7:00 a.m., I would be available, in my Navy Department office or elsewhere, to receive his call. The general assured me that he would proceed promptly.

With that, I turned off my light. I did not sleep too well that night. How could I, burdened with the thought that I had set in motion the procedures to take six human lives, albeit legally? Even now, almost thirty years later, I still feel squeamish about it.

About 1:15 p.m. Saturday, I received a call from General Miller reporting that the executions had been carried out. I immediately called the president and reported this information to him. The president remarked, "John, get in touch with Steve Early so he can issue a press release about these proceedings."

It was Saturday afternoon, and I wondered if I would have difficulty reaching Steve. Even in wartime, the White House offices had a way of closing down on Saturday afternoon. I called Steve at his office, and got him. I told him the president wanted to issue a press release about an important event, and I would be there shortly to give him the details. "No, I can't tell you what it is about," and I was off.

When I arrived, Steve called in his assistant press secretary, Bill Hassett. I quickly related the facts, and Steve and Bill whipped up a short press release. When it was ready, Bill went to the pressroom, the hangout for the press covering the White House. Press releases were usually deposited there. Typically, the newsmen grabbed these handouts and dashed to an extensive battery of telephones nearby, calling their offices to get the news on the wire as fast as possible. When a release was important, near bedlam prevailed in the pressroom.

Bill found twenty or so reporters in the pressroom. He advised them that Steve would issue an important release in his office. They hustled in, while Bill remained outside. When all were inside, Bill quietly shut and locked the door, entering Steve's office through a side door. Bill nodded to Steve that "all were in."

Steve then remarked about as follows, "I've called you people in here in order to make an important announcement. When you hear the announcement, your first inclination will be to race for your telephone, but don't bother. You are locked in here, and you're not going to leave this office until I say you may do so."

At this, chatter erupted. "Keep quiet," said Steve. "You will recall that eight would-be saboteurs were recently tried by a military commission in the District of Columbia. All were convicted and sentenced to death. The proceedings in these cases were reviewed and approved by higher authority. I wish to announce that six of the eight saboteurs were executed today at the District of Columbia's jail." Their names followed. "The sentences of death in the cases of two of this group"—names given—"were commuted by the commander in chief to thirty years' imprisonment. That is all. Any questions?" There were none of importance.

Steve continued, "Copies of this release will be handed to you at the door as you leave. Let me suggest that you use restraint when you go, or someone will get hurt. Unlock the door, Bill." What a scramble! One chap slipped and slid the full length of the White House lobby on the marble floor. No one bothered to pick him up because all were in such haste to get to their respective telephones.

When the correspondents had cleared Steve's office, I called the president and reported that the press release had been issued. He thanked me and said he would see me in the morning.

Steve and I sat there for a few minutes discussing the events of the day. I told him how Sam Rosenman and I had reviewed the records of the military commission, and about the time and effort that had gone into that operation. We talked about many other things.

All of a sudden Steve remarked to me, "Skipper"—I was always "Skipper" to Steve—"you know, the Boss likes you." The president was always "the Boss" to Steve; he even called him that to his face. "Yes, Skipper," he repeated, "the Boss likes you."

"Well, that is fine," said I. "But when, may I ask, have you been discussing me with the president?"

"We have never spoken about you," said Steve.

"Then how do you know he likes me?" asked I.

"I know he likes you because he gives you the goddamnedest things to do."

Chapter 12

FDR

Sunday mornings were the best time for me to see the president. He was at leisure with no office to go to, and because of his immobility, he could hardly go elsewhere. I usually arrived around 9:00 a.m., shortly after Ross McIntire's morning visit to check on the president's health. I always found the president in bed. He had breakfasted and was surrounded with the Sunday papers. Invariably, he was in good spirits and eager to talk.

A word about the president's infirmity. He had been paralyzed below the waist from a polio attack in 1921. I suppose only the disabled could imagine what he endured as a result of his handicap. When he went to his office in the morning, he became a prisoner of his chair. He could never get up and stretch his legs. The patience with which he bore his affliction was remarkable. He never made reference to it.

To walk any distance, the president had to wear leg braces and have the support of a cane and another person. The braces were heavy and uncomfortable, so he wore them as little as possible. Without braces, he could take only a few steps using two canes. One of the qualifications for serving as naval aide was being tall and strong enough to support the president. At the many functions where I accompanied him, whenever he stood or walked, it was with the aid of a cane and my right arm.

The president had a keen interest in the navy. He told me that when he was twelve or thirteen years old, he had wanted to go to the Naval Academy. His mother had firmly dismissed this idea as a childish whim, telling him there were more important things in store for him than just being a naval officer. From 1913 to 1920, he served as assistant secretary of the navy, an experience he enjoyed greatly. In 1942, despite his many heavy burdens, his interest in the navy continued unabated.

The president asked that I keep him well informed about the Navy Department. To that end, I kept an eye out for papers relating to the administration of the department that I thought might interest him. These included such items as AlNavs, circular letters, and the like.[34] On Sunday mornings, I took my collection of administrative papers to the White House, along with any urgent dispatches that had come in overnight.

The president was always eager to see the administrative extras, and his interest was more than casual. A case in point was his response to an order issued by the under secretary of the navy, Mr. James V. Forrestal, just one of many papers I brought him one Sunday. The order indicated that the Office of the Judge Advocate General would no longer process ship construction contracts. Instead, they would be handled by a group of New York lawyers working under the direction of the under secretary.

The president wanted to know why the change was being made. He wondered if the order didn't take away an important

---

34　These documents include a variety of notifications and instructions about naval administration. AlNav is short for an "All Navy" message or dispatch issued by the CNO's Office to all naval commands. An example is officer promotion lists. Circular letters were issued by the bureaus of the Navy Department, naval districts, and the like to subordinate naval entities about such matters as regulations and regulation changes, instructions, procedures, and notices.

function of the Office of the Judge Advocate General. I said I thought it did. He folded the order and, without further comment, put it in his pocket.

A few days later, I discovered that the president had taken action. An annoyed Under Secretary Forrestal called me into his office. He wanted to know how the president had learned about his order. He told me the secretary had told him to withdraw it, and he hated like hell to do so. The order was withdrawn, and that was the end of the matter.

Once the president had reviewed the urgent dispatches and the weekly extras, he liked to talk. The navy was a favorite topic, and every so often he would begin his remarks by saying, "When I was in the navy," alluding to his days as assistant secretary.

He liked to discuss individuals. When he was "in the navy," Ernest J. King, Chester W. Nimitz, William F. "Bull" Halsey, and other current leaders were young and on the way up. He knew them all personally and took a great interest in their careers. He would often ask about their recent exploits. We would trade stories. When I brought him up to date, he would tell me tales of their activities in earlier days. We talked about many, many other navy topics, too many to mention. Suffice it to say, our navy discussions ranged widely.

Of course, our conversations were not limited to the navy, and there again we covered a lot of ground. The president liked to talk about things that were on his mind. He would start off, "Well, I've been thinking about so-and-so," and he would talk. He also asked me a lot of questions to try out ideas on me or see what I thought about something. Whether it was an event, a naval officer, a civilian, or something else, he was always asking what I thought. Often I would protest that I didn't know anything about the subject, but he would persist. It was startling to be quizzed on things I knew little about.

Fairly typical was a conversation about Al Smith, the Democratic politician and a presidential hopeful in 1932. This was one of the very rare occasions when the president brought up the topic of politics. "I'm going to ask you a question, John," he began. "Do you think Al Smith could have been elected to the presidency in 1932?"

"Why, Mr. President, I'm only a naval officer. I don't know anything about politics. All I know is what I read in the paper."

"Come on, now. You're begging the question, John. You're a citizen. You must have an idea about whether Al could have been elected."

"Well, Mr. President, I suppose almost any Democrat could have won in 1932. But Al Smith is a Catholic, and there may have been enough bigotry in the South and the Midwest Bible Belt to prevent him from being elected."

Without indicating whether he agreed or disagreed, the president said, "Al thinks he could have made it. He and I were good friends for years. My candidacy for the nomination was the start of all the misunderstanding that has developed between us since."

One Sunday, the president asked if I kept a diary. I told him I did not. "I just wondered," said he. "I've been very frank with you on occasion, and I trust you."

As you can see, Sunday mornings with the president were always interesting. He led our discussions, and he was never at a loss for things to talk about. We shared our enthusiasm for the navy, and I had the honor and pleasure of coming to know him on a personal basis.

Being naval aide was a seven-day-a-week job. Sundays were particularly busy because the White House staff would scatter, leaving the president pretty much on his own, and I would end up doing all kinds of things for him. On a couple of Sundays, I escorted him to church, and one of those services provided the occasion for some subsequent banter.

At the time of the offertory, the president asked if he could borrow two dollars because he didn't have any money. I dug out two dollars, and the president dropped them on the collection plate when it came our way.

About a week later, I was in his office, in the midst of discussing a navy matter, when all of a sudden he remarked: "John, what do you think of people who don't pay their debts?" I responded that I didn't have much experience in that area.

"Don't I owe you money?" he asked.

"Mr. President, if you are talking about that little transaction in church last Sunday, I would say that you do."

"This morning I said to myself, 'I owe John two dollars.' And here they are. We're all square now, aren't we?"

"Thank you, Mr. President, but I wasn't too worried about the money. Besides, very few people can say to themselves, 'The president of the United States owes me two dollars.'"

"John, you are a gentleman. If I'd borrowed two dollars from Hopkins, he would have hounded me daily until I repaid him."

All this was said in high good humor. Such moments defused the pressures of our workdays, and it was a joy to see the president relax.

The president had a sinus condition severe enough to require regular treatment. He once remarked to me, "John, you know I never knew what sinus trouble was until I became shipmates with air conditioning. Now, I can't shake it, and I blame it all on air conditioning."

In the afternoon from about 5:15 to 6:00 p.m., the president often went to Ross McIntire's office in the White House basement for sinus treatments and massage therapy. I'm sure he looked forward to these visits. They were a fine escape from his strenuous workday, and they brought him physical relief. He sat in a dental-type chair while Ross packed his sinuses. Afterward, Lieutenant (first class) George A. Fox, Hospital Corps, U.S. Navy, a physiotherapist, massaged his legs and feet.

During these sessions, the president relaxed completely. He would scan the evening papers and remark lightly about the happenings of the day. His asides about certain callers of his were always pointed and amusing. More often than not, he also fed his

Scotty, Fala. The president's valet, Arthur Prettyman, a retired U.S. Navy steward, would bring the dog's rations to the president. He would in turn place the bowl before the anxiously waiting Fala, thereby impressing him as to who was, in fact, his master.

As the officer in charge of the Map Room, I was acutely aware of the war-related pressures on the president. Seeing how fatigued he was when he arrived at Ross's office, I made it a priority to conserve his time and energy and protect him from unnecessary distractions. I started to do as much of my afternoon briefing as I could in Ross's office so the president could go to his quarters as soon as Ross and Lieutenant Fox were finished. When he wanted something done, I didn't waste his time asking him how or why or anything else. I just said, "Aye-aye," and went and did it. When I had urgent war news, I never awakened him at night. Once or twice I was tempted to do so, but I felt he needed uninterrupted rest more than news, good or bad.

On one occasion, I found myself fending off a distraction from the top of the Navy Department. I was usually the first in the office of the secretary of the navy for his daily conference. I used the time before the conferences to go over the "secret" and "confidential" dispatches that I would show the president later. On this particular day, Admiral King was next to arrive. He was soon engaged in conversation with the secretary. I paid no attention to them.

Suddenly, I heard the secretary remark in an angry tone, "Admiral King, that matter has been settled. I don't want you to raise it again."

I glanced up. The secretary was livid, and there was complete silence in the room. In a moment or so, the rest of the conferees began arriving. I was glad to see them because they broke the tension.

The next morning, as I was leaving the secretary's conference, Admiral King intercepted me and asked that I go to his office.

"Certainly, sir," said I, and I fell in on his left as we headed upstairs. Not a word was said by either of us.

Once inside his office, he went to the windows, turned his back on them, and remained standing as he faced me across his desk.

"You were at the secretary's conference yesterday morning, were you not?" he asked.

"I was, sir."

"You heard what the secretary said to me?" he asked.

"I did, sir."

"I want to inform you that I am going to make an issue of his remark. I have not been spoken to like that since I can remember. I just want to make sure that you heard what was said."

I collected my wits for a second and remarked, "Admiral King, I don't know why you called me in. I know you haven't asked my opinion, and what I am about to say comes right off the top of my head, without opportunity for reflection.

"The navy is a military organization, and the secretary is your superior. I suppose he has a right to speak firmly to you if he thinks it in order. What disturbs me is the position of our commander in chief." I was referring, of course, to the president. "He has plenty on his mind, and he carries a heavy load. I think he would be greatly distressed and further burdened by a row between the secretary of the navy and the chief of naval operations."

Admiral King's face flushed. Clearly angry, he wheeled around and looked out on Constitution Avenue. The full import of what I had said suddenly hit me. I know that my knees knocked. It may well be that the knocking sound—it must have been audible—reminded Admiral King that I was still there.

He turned around and looked me dead in the eye with that gimlet glare at which he was so expert. I would not have been surprised if he had lit into me, if he had said, "I didn't ask you here to give me an unsolicited opinion, and I don't like your brashness." All he said was, "Good day," biting off his words in typical King fashion.

I concluded the interview was over. I replied with a cheerful, "Good morning, sir," and got the hell out of his office as fast as I could. He never referred to the incident with the secretary again. If the president ever became aware of it, he didn't hear of it from me. In retrospect, I still think I gave Admiral King good advice.

The president liked people, and he was typically in buoyant spirits, lighthearted and gay. When he went to his office in the morning, Howell Crim, the White House's chief usher, usually pushed his chair. Along the way, the president always exchanged pleasantries with the members of the White House staff—cooks, gardeners, maintenance men, and the like. They found it convenient to be on his route to wish him good morning and receive a cheery salutation in return. He knew most of them by name and asked about their personal concerns and activities. "How's your little fellow after his appendicitis operation?" he'd ask a Filipino cook. And to a gardener, "How are the roses doing this spring?" With the weight of a country at war on his shoulders, he still took the time to be cordial to the little people, and they loved him for it. I was assured by long-time White House employees that this sort of cordiality was not present in other administrations.

President Roosevelt was a kindly person who enjoyed doing little things for others. Time and again I saw him go to great lengths to be thoughtful, and on many, many occasions he was kind and generous to my family and me. The birthday present he thought up for my daughter Meredith is just one example. On Meredith's sixteenth birthday, I took her to the White House, and Grace Tully maneuvered her in to meet the president. When informed it was her sixteenth birthday, the president remarked, "Sweet Sixteen, and I bet that she has never been kissed," whereupon he pulled her head down and bussed her on the cheek. "Your father should have told me this is your birthday. Right now I haven't a present for you, but I'll have one soon." A few days later, when the president was shoving off for Hyde Park, he told me what the present was: a long weekend at Shangri-La for Meredith and her sister, mother, and father.

The president delighted in private jokes, in saying or doing something puzzling and watching others figure out his point. He concocted one of these jokes for Wendell Willkie, his Republican opponent in the 1940 presidential campaign, and managed to fool Ross McIntire as well. The president told me this yarn.

In 1940, Willkie put on a driving campaign. He was going night and day, up and down the country, inveighing against the president and all that he stood for. However, one day in Portland, Oregon, Mr. Willkie lost his voice, and his campaign came to a virtual standstill.

On the morning the press carried the story that Willkie had lost his voice, Ross McIntire made his usual bedside call on the president. The president asked Ross if he had seen the Willkie story. When Ross said no, the president read it aloud.

"Now, Ross," said the president, "you know that cough syrup you prescribe for me, and that gargle that's a favorite of yours, and the spray and the APC capsules[35] that the navy gives out? Also those throat lozenges that you give me an hour or so before I make a radio talk? I want you to make up a package of all of those items with directions on how to use them, and send the package this morning, airmail special delivery, to Wendell in Portland. And Ross, put in a card reading, 'Best wishes for a speedy recovery, FDR.'"

The president told me, "John, you know Ross is ordinarily pretty quick. But this time, he just stood there and stared at me as if he couldn't trust his ears. He opened his mouth as if to say something, but nothing came out. Finally, a light came over his face. He said, 'I suppose, Mr. President, the idea is to get Wendell talking again as soon as possible.' And I said, 'Ross, how did you ever guess?'" The president never told me if Mr. Willkie got the joke.

I liked the lightness of the president's humor and the gentle way he did so many things. He may have used a lot of force on other people. One day I heard him blister one of his closest associates, but he never directed anything like that towards me.

---

35 All-purpose capsules for pain relief.

I recall only one incident when the president gave a hint that his spirit might not be equal to the task at hand. One evening about 6:00 p.m., when I was sitting at the corner of the president's desk, the door opened, and Grace Tully came in a bit breathlessly.

"Mr. President," said she. "Mrs. Roosevelt is on the telephone. She wants to know when you are coming over to pour cocktails for her guests, as you promised." The president smiled faintly and said, "Grace, ask her who she is having for cocktails."

In a couple of moments Grace returned with a paper in her hand, and started reading. "Mrs. Roosevelt says her guests are Dean Landis,[36] Alexander Woollcott—"

"That's enough, Grace. Tell her I'll be over in ten minutes."

Turning to me, he said, "Alex is always good for a laugh, and I think I need a laugh tonight. I just thought I would inquire who would be there. You know my missus can show up with odd ones every once in a while."

While most of my extended conversations with the president took place on Sunday mornings, on a few rare occasions we talked together over a nightcap in the small first-floor den at Hyde Park. He, quite naturally, led our conversations, launching into topics as they occurred to him. I confess I greatly enjoyed these little before-bed talks. Every so often he would reminisce, and his remarks were awfully interesting. I always enjoyed hearing what was on his mind.

Quite naturally, the progress of the war and the prospects for peace were matters of great concern to the president. He frequently referred to World War I and the fact that so little was accomplished in creating a lasting peace. He thought the victorious Allied powers had missed an opportunity to create a foundation upon which continuing peace could be built.

---

36 In 1942, James M. Landis was dean of Harvard Law School and regional director of the U.S. Office of Civilian Defense, an organization to coordinate the protection of civilians during the war. Mrs. Roosevelt was active in the organization until February 1942.

One evening over a nightcap, he spoke about the attitude of the country towards the League of Nations after World War I. He remarked about the country's relief when the war finally wound down. He recalled that many in the United States counseled a complete withdrawal from European affairs. George Harvey, the publisher of *Harvey's Weekly*, had mounted a continual barrage of protest against U.S. involvement in the League of Nations. Harvey conceded that such an organization might be useful for Europe, but thought the United States should have no part of it.

"I must confess," said the president, "that, along with many others in public life, I could work up little enthusiasm for the League. On the other hand, I did not actively oppose it. In 1920, when James Cox and I became the Democratic nominees for president and vice president, we called on President Wilson. No doubt you recall President Wilson's commitment to the League, and his physical collapse during a nationwide tour in support of it. He was bedridden for months. Indeed, he was bedridden when we called on him.

"Mr. Wilson talked earnestly to us about the League and his hopes for it, not sparing those who opposed him. Mr. Cox and I were impressed. When we left his room and made our way out of the White House, with hardly more than a word about the League, we shook hands. From then on, the League was an issue with us. Obviously, the country was unimpressed. I think the country was just not ready for so far-reaching a commitment. However, when this war ends, and we have created a United Nations organization dedicated to keeping the peace, I think the country will be ready to accept it."

It is tragic that FDR did not live to see the United Nations set up and in operation. He died two weeks before the start of the San Francisco conference that drafted the organization's charter.

Chapter 13

Sea Duty and War Production

———∞∞∞———

In January 1942, I was not pleased to receive orders to serve as the president's naval aide. For about a year and a half, I had been hoping for a ship command. In September 1940, I was expecting assignment to a light cruiser, when I was sent to the Office of the Chief of Naval Operations instead. In 1941, I was asked if I would like command of a heavy cruiser. "Of course I would," said I, loud and clear. Then came the attack on Pearl Harbor, and I found myself on my way to the White House. The cruiser command went to another, and this was a disappointment.

Why did I want to go to sea? I enjoyed sea duty. I liked being part of a ship. Shipboard discipline appealed to me, and I enjoyed the association with the men, both officers and enlisted personnel. To my mind, in a ship there is law and order and comradeship at its best. Command was also important to me. During my last year at the Naval Academy, I discovered I enjoyed command. I liked the process of whipping my men into shape, of getting them to work as a team and take pride in their performance and their unit. Of course, once the war started, I felt I should be in it. Many of my friends were in combat, and a number had been killed early in the war. Out of loyalty, I felt I should be out there fighting, not serving in a protected shore billet.

When I became naval aide, I was afraid that the job might be a long-term assignment unless I was unacceptable to the president, something I hoped would not eventuate. I knew admirals Stark and King wanted me at the White House, and it was important not to disappoint them. Accordingly, I decided to do the best job I could as naval aide, and let the future take care of itself.

Vice Admiral Randall Jacobs became chief of the Bureau of Navigation in late December 1941. His office was directly across the corridor from the naval aide's Navy Department office, and as a result, I saw a great deal of him. He knew of my disappointment in not getting a heavy cruiser command. "I'll keep you in mind for a big ship command if you can be available in the spring of 1943," said he. With this in mind, starting in April, after the president and I had come to know each other better through our Sunday morning sessions, I began to drop hints, ever so gently, about my hopes for a ship command.

Initially, whenever I gently hinted about going to sea, the president invariably changed the subject. Sometimes he would remark that since he had "been in the navy," he understood my position perfectly and sympathized with it, "but this is war time, and we all must serve where we can best help the war effort." Sometime later, he said that I could probably leave after I had been on the job for a year or thereabouts, but he would make a final decision when the time came. In other words, I had no firm commitment about when I could go. Meanwhile, I kept in touch with Rear Admiral Jacobs.

In early summer 1942, the president said to me, "John, my missus tells me that the battleship *Iowa*, now under construction at the Brooklyn navy yard, is due to be launched 27 August 1942. Mrs. Wallace, the vice president's wife, is from Iowa, and she is to be the ship's sponsor. Malvina Thompson, my missus's secretary, has never seen a ship christened, and she wants to go. My missus wants to go, too. Do you suppose you could arrange to escort them to the ceremonies? In addition, Ambassador Joseph Grew is en route to the U.S. upon being repatriated from Japan.[37] He is coming to Washington the day before the *Iowa* christening. I am planning to have a small state dinner that evening, and I think you should attend. See if you can work all these things in."

I attended the dinner and took the midnight train to New York. I breakfasted with Mrs. Roosevelt and Miss Thompson at Mrs. Roosevelt's apartment. A navy car at my disposal arrived at the apartment, and at 9:30 a.m. we were en route to the navy yard. The commandant, Rear Admiral Edward J. Marquart, received Mrs. Roosevelt and Miss Thompson, and he and his wife proceeded to look out for them.

I was impressed with *Iowa*. Poised on the launching platform, so trim and sleek, she was a beautiful sight to behold. As I stood there, the thought crossed my mind that she should be ready for commissioning about 1 April 1943, and why shouldn't I make a "try" for her as her first captain? On my return to Washington, I dared to bare my thoughts about *Iowa* to Admiral Jacobs. Would I have enough rank? "By next April," said he, "we ought to be well below you in rank for commanding officers of battleships." Subsequently, rumors reached me that another was being considered for the job, but I remained hopeful.

From 17 September to 1 October 1942, I accompanied the president on a two-week tour of the country's war materiel factories and troop training facilities. The president made the trip to get a firsthand look at, and feel for, our war production and training effort, and he wanted the tour to be completely "nonpolitical." I recall that time and again I heard the president say, "The best poli-

---

37 Joseph C. Grew, the U.S. ambassador to Japan, was in Tokyo at the time of the Pearl Harbor attack. He was interned briefly by the Japanese government, but returned to the United States under a U.S.–Japan plan for the repatriation of diplomats.

tics are no politics." I suppose this trip was about as nonpolitical as any trip by a sitting president could be.

The president's itinerary took him in a circle around the country. His train departed Washington, proceeded northwest to Michigan, and then west to Washington State across the northern plains. From the Seattle area, the train went south to San Diego, California, east through Texas to South Carolina, and back to Washington, D.C.

The president's party included a number of White House associates: Steve Early, Ross McIntire, secretaries Grace Tully and Dorothy Brady, the president's physiotherapist, Secret Service men, Fala, and myself.[38] Misses Laura Delano and Margaret Suckley, the president's cousins, and Henry Hooker, a longtime friend, rode the train for the duration of the journey. Many dignitaries and politicians joined us for short stays. To document the trip, there were three members of the press and four navy photographers aboard.

The president's schedule was formidable. He inspected over twenty-five facilities, and visited up to five sites a day. But there was much about trip that was pleasant and relaxing for him. He genuinely liked to ride the rails. His hangout was the modest lounge space at the end of the rear car. He liked company, and enjoyed having his cousins and Henry Hooker aboard. The trip also gave him an opportunity to see three of his children. His daughter, Anna Boettinger, rode the train for several days, and he dined at Anna's home in the Seattle area. He visited his son John at his home in Coronado, California, and his son Elliott at his ranch near Fort Worth, Texas.

The president also found some quiet time for contemplation, something he enjoyed. He worked with his stamp collection, which accompanied him on absences from the White House of more than a few days. He also played solitaire, occasionally with two decks of cards. He told me that some of his best thinking took place while playing solitaire.

---

38 Mrs. Roosevelt was present at the beginning of the trip, but left after a couple of days' travel.

The president's inspection stops followed a pattern. At each site, he would detrain into a car, where typically he was joined by that state's governor and the commanders or officers of the facility in question. After the inspection, he would reboard the train for the next leg of the journey. For security reasons, the trip was not publicized. The governors and those in charge of the inspection sites knew in advance of the president's visit, but lower-level personnel did not. As a result, we were greeted by many astonished faces wherever we went.

Although it was not yet nine months since the Pearl Harbor attack, we were impressed with the scale of military training and the level of military efficiency and preparedness. At the Naval Training Station Great Lakes in Illinois, sixty-three thousand men were in training, and the station received about ten thousand new recruits every week. In California, at the recently built Oakland Naval Supply Base and Army Port of Embarkation nearby, we saw thousands of tons of war supplies assembled for transshipment to the Pacific War Zone. In San Diego, the naval training station was organized to easily feed thirty-five thousand men in forty-five minutes, and had on occasion fed fifty thousand men in the space of an hour.

The president reviewed large numbers of trainees: soldiers at some four army facilities, marines in San Diego, and army air personnel at Kelly and Randolph Fields in Texas. The changing face of the military was evident. At Randolph Field, known as "the West Point of the Air," we observed many groups of black cadets. At Camp Jackson in South Carolina, we also saw units of black troops, and barracks under construction in anticipation of the arrival of a considerable number of WAACs.[39]

---

39 The Women's Army Auxiliary Corps (WAAC) was created in May 1942 to allow women to serve the army in non-combatant jobs at lower rank and pay than their male, regular army counterparts. The corps was so successful that, in July 1943, it was converted into the Women's Army Corps (WAC) and became part of the regular army. Members of the WAC had the same ranks and pay as their regular army counterparts.

We were also impressed by the country's war production. The speed at which industry had mobilized to manufacture war materiel was remarkable. The Ford Motor Company's Willow Run plant near Ypsilanti, Michigan, was manufacturing heavy bombers—B-24s. The plant was located on what had been farmland about a year before, and it employed approximately forty thousand persons, including some five thousand women. The first bomber had come off the assembly line about a week before. To our surprise, the plant had a large number of midget employees. We were informed that they generally "bucked" rivets in wing sections and other areas where persons of normal size could not work because of the limited space. The pace of production at the Kaiser Shipbuilding Company in Portland, Oregon, was similar. Kaiser built cargo ships on production lines. The company was breaking world records in shipbuilding almost daily, launching ships ten days after their keels were laid.

In Washington State, the president, Ross McIntire, and I drove about fifty miles to Bremerton to inspect the Puget Sound navy yard. We drove along the dock where we saw many, many ships that had been damaged at Pearl Harbor being overhauled. We also saw much new construction.

In no time, the president's presence became known, much to the surprise of all. His car took him into the very midst of a huge throng of navy yard workmen, civilian employees, and service personnel. As they closed in on him, he stopped the car and made an impromptu speech over the public address system:

> I can only say a word or two to you. The first is that I am not really here, because I am making this trip under navy orders, and that means that my cruise is not published in the papers. So just remember that for about ten days, you haven't seen me.

This was said with a good chuckle, and prompted much applause.

I have been looking things over, coming across the country, and I can tell you that I am more than convinced that the people of this whole nation are in this war to win it, and win it just as fast as we can. I am very proud of what I have seen. I am proud of the officers and the men and the workmen here in this old navy yard, which I used to know in the good old days. The golf course that I played on during World War I is now covered with machine shops and other build-ings. I am glad to see Bremerton again, and I am happy in knowing all that you are doing. I have seen wounded ships and wounded men, and we are putting them back together and making them new.

I am on my way almost immediately, going to take in other places and other yards and other camps, and when I get back to Washington, maybe if they let me talk, I will say something about what I have seen here and how fine the effort of all of you is throughout this great nation of ours. I thank you.

There was thunderous applause for the president's remarks.

In Long Beach, California, we toured the Douglas Aircraft Corporation plant. Donald W. Douglas, president of the company, had been at the Naval Academy two classes ahead of me, and it was a pleasure to see him again. He did not graduate from the academy. We midshipmen thought he spent most of his time making card-board airplanes to fly from the balcony of the armory. That activity had evidently paid off.

The Douglas facility was largely an assembly plant. It produced light and heavy bombers, fighters, reconnaissance planes, and other aircraft from parts manufactured by other companies. At the time of our visit, it was churning out about four hundred planes a month and soon expected to double that rate.

In San Diego, we visited the U.S. Naval Hospital. Hundreds of bluejackets lined the approach to the hospital on the president's arrival. Driving to the patio of the hospital, the president came abreast of some 150 wounded officers and men seated in chairs and wheelchairs. Most of the 2,700 patients had been wounded at Pearl Harbor, Dutch Harbor, Alaska, or aboard the *Yorktown* and the *Wasp*. The president shook hands with as many as he could. He was greatly moved by this experience.

At a plant in San Diego, Ensign Charles Berry, our communications expert, ran me down. "A dispatch for you, Captain," said he. I tore open the envelope. The dispatch was from Captain William M. Fechteler, the officer in charge of captains' details in the navy personnel office. It read:

> *Iowa* goes in commission on 18 January 1943. Are you interested?
> Fechteler

My reply to him was:

> Of course I'm interested. Will see you in Washington.

I wanted a major ship command. When I had talked to the president about releasing me if such an opportunity arose, he had always deferred any decision. It appeared that the time for decision was fast approaching.

About noon on 27 September 1942, we were scheduled to pass east through Uvalde, Texas, the hometown of John Nance Garner, the president's vice president during his first two terms. When the president announced his intention to run for a third term, Mr. Garner's nose got out of joint. He had hoped to run for the presidency in 1940, and he opposed the president's nomination. When the president was nominated, Mr. Garner retired to his Uvalde ranch to sulk.

When the president learned he would pass through Uvalde on his tour, he asked Steve Early to telephone Garner and say that the president would be pleased if Garner were inclined to visit with him on his train. Garner agreed to come.

We pulled into Uvalde a few minutes ahead of schedule. Ross McIntire, Steve Early, and I disembarked and stood on the platform in the warm Texas sunshine to await Mr. Garner's arrival. On the dot of the appointed hour, around the corner came a Ford of ancient vintage. It pulled up to the platform, and its white-haired driver, cigar in hand, greeted Ross and Steve enthusiastically. I was presented to Mr. Garner.

We walked to the rear platform of the president's car. The president was seated in the observation section. Steve escorted Mr. Garner on board and returned to the platform. From the peals of laughter that came through the open door from time to time, it was evident that the president and his ex-vice president were having a good time.

The visit lasted about a half hour. When Mr. Garner reappeared, Ross, Steve, and I escorted him to his car. He remarked about the president's evident good health and how he appreciated the opportunity to see him again. When we reached his car, Mr. Garner turned to Ross, and with his hand on Ross's shoulder, said, "Ross, a great man is in your hands. Take good care of him, because this country needs him badly." At the time, I knew nothing of the depth of the political breach between the president and Mr. Garner, but I was impressed with the earnestness of his charge to Ross.

With a great deal of clatter, Mr. Garner got his Ford under way and departed. Ross, Steve, and I returned to the president's car. "You know," said the president, "it was fine to see John Garner again. He is a great, great American and a great friend." To this day, that morning's events are pleasant to think upon.

In Mississippi, we stopped to inspect Camp Shelby, an army basic training facility near Hattiesburg, with a population of about thirty-four thousand. I rode in the president's car. At one point on our tour, we picked up a lieutenant colonel who had been on the faculty of Brown University in civilian life. At Camp Shelby, he had been placed in command of illiterate trainees. We drove by his battalion of about six hundred men, a fine-looking group.

This photo taken at Casablanca was McCrea's favorite of FDR and himself. McCrea's protective stance at FDR's side suggests the role he undertook as naval aide: shielding the president as much as possible from unnecessary burdens and distractions in order to lighten his heavy load.

At the Naval Academy during the summer of 1911, McCrea was one of a group of midshipmen selected to help launch the navy's third airplane, the Wright B-1 Flyer. Here the midshipmen wait in front of the plane before the launch operation. They were to run full tilt down the parade ground pulling the aircraft with lines until it achieved enough momentum for liftoff.

John McCrea during his final year at the Naval Academy in 1915. The three stripes on his sleeves indicate his rank, commander of his company in the student military organization.

Admiral Harold R. "Betty" Stark was Chief of Naval Operations from August 1939 to March 1942. In September 1940, he reluctantly accepted McCrea for the job of compiling a study of the navy's preparedness for war, but he quickly grew to appreciate McCrea's abilities. [NH 61816 courtesy of Naval History and Heritage Command.]

Admiral Ernest J. King and Secretary of the Navy Frank Knox in September 1941. Both offered McCrea advice after he first reported to the president as naval aide. As part of McCrea's duties as naval aide, he attended the secretary's daily morning conferences and acted as liaison between the Navy Department and the president. [NH 56978 courtesy of Naval History and Heritage Command.]

McCrea's first project at the White House was to set up the Map Room, where top-secret war communications were stored and maps of the theaters of war were displayed for the president's convenience. This is a rare photo of the interior of the Map Room with a watch officer at work. [Courtesy of the Franklin D. Roosevelt Presidential Library and Museum.]

The president invited Prime Minister Winston Churchill to a meeting of the Pacific War Council held on June 25, 1942. Those in attendance were (seated L to R) Mr. Churchill; the president; and (standing L to R) Dr. Eelco van Kleffens, foreign minister of the Netherlands; Sir Owen Dixon, Australian minister to the United States; Leighton McCarthy, Canadian minister to the United States; W. L. Mackenzie King, the prime minister of Canada; Viscount Halifax, British ambassador to the United States; T. V. Soong, Chinese minister of foreign affairs; Manuel Quezon, president of the Philippine Commonwealth; and Walter Nash, New Zealand minister to the United States. Also present but not photographed were Harry Hopkins and McCrea.

President Roosevelt was unable to walk or stand without uncomfortable heavy leg braces. Whenever McCrea accompanied him, FDR maneuvered on foot with the aid of a cane and McCrea's right arm. [Courtesy of the Franklin D. Roosevelt Presidential Library and Museum.]

In early August 1942, Queen Wilhelmina of the Netherlands came to Washington for a full day of activities organized in her honor by the White House and other events at the Dutch embassy. Here Eleanor Roosevelt, the queen, the president, and McCrea pose for photographers on the night of the queen's arrival.

At President Roosevelt's request, McCrea escorted Mrs. Roosevelt to the christening and launch of the USS *Iowa* on 27 August 1942. Impressed by the ship's trim, sleek lines, McCrea dared to wonder that day if he might be able to become her first commanding officer.

The president greets a wounded bluejacket at the San Diego Naval Hospital in CA. McCrea observed that FDR was greatly moved by his encounters with the wounded.

On Veterans Day 1942, the president spoke at Arlington National Cemetery. Seated is FDR's guest, General John J. Pershing, commander of American forces in Europe in World War I. Standing behind the president (R to L) are McCrea and Charles Fredericks, Secret Service. Riding with FDR and McCrea to the ceremony, Pershing expressed confidence in Lt. General Dwight D. Eisenhower, remarks that McCrea conveyed to Eisenhower when they met at the Casablanca Conference.

Aboard the president's C-54 in North Africa are: (seated, 1st row) FDR conferring with Harry Hopkins; (seated, 2nd row) Lt. George A. Fox and Rear Adm. Ross T. McIntire, the president's physiotherapist and physician, respectively; Guy Spaman (back turned), Secret Service; and McCrea. Standing (L to R) are an unidentified man; Arthur Prettyman, the president's valet; Charles Fredericks, Secret Service; E. R. Hipsley, Secret Service; W. K. Deckard, Secret Service; and Captain Otis Bryan, pilot of the plane.

After McCrea delivered the president's dinner invitation to the Sultan of Morocco, he joined the president's party as FDR reviewed army troops north of Rabat. Seated in one of the jeeps behind the president, McCrea was able to observe the astonishment of the troops when they realized the reviewing officer was their commander in chief, the president of the United States.

On 22 January 1943, the president hosted a dinner party for the Sultan of Morocco. Shown here are those who attended. Seated (L to R): the sultan, the president, and Prime Minister Churchill. Standing (L to R): Maj. General George S. Patton, Jr., commander of U.S. forces in French Morocco; Robert D. Murphy, the president's representative in North Africa; Harry Hopkins; the Crown Prince of Morocco; General Charles A. Noguès, resident general of Morocco; the Grand Vizier to the sultan; the Chief of Protocol of Morocco; Lt. Col. Elliott Roosevelt; and McCrea. At McCrea's suggestion, the president altered his seating plan to place the crown prince next to General Patton because of the prince's great admiration for the general.

At Casablanca Roosevelt and Churchill (seated) hoped French generals Henri Giraud (standing L) and Charles de Gaulle (standing R) would agree to work together to lead free French forces. Here, at FDR's urging, the generals shake hands for the press although they agreed on nothing except their wish to liberate France. McCrea, who was present at some meetings with the generals, thought de Gaulle was the more difficult.

On 27 January 1943, during his return trip from the Casablanca Conference, President Roosevelt visited the president of Liberia in Monrovia, the capital. Here FDR greets well-wishers on his arrival, while McCrea in a white uniform circulates in the crowd behind him.

On 30 January 1942, President Roosevelt celebrated his 61st birthday on the final air leg of his trip home from Casablanca. Observing him cut his cake are (L to R) Adm. William D. Leahy, the president's chief of staff; Harry Hopkins, the president's advisor and close friend; and Lt. Cohen, pilot of their Pan American Airways Clipper.

On 22 February 1943, *Iowa's* ship's company, guests, and distinguished speakers assembled on *Iowa's* quarterdeck at the stern for the ship's commissioning ceremonies. McCrea, the final speaker, addressed much of his speech to *Iowa's* ship's company. [80-G-K-825 courtesy of Naval History and Heritage Command.]

McCrea on *Iowa's* bridge on a chilly day during the ship's early shakedown activities in 1943. [80-G-K-6119 courtesy of Naval History and Heritage Command.]

McCrea insisted that *Iowa's* crew wear proper dress because he believed that the self-discipline necessary to appear in correct uniform was the first step toward battle readiness. Here McCrea, accompanied by other officers, inspects the uniforms of a line of *Iowa* bluejackets.

Inside the conning tower McCrea supervises the activities of a helmsman. As commanding officer of *Iowa*, McCrea had in his charge many sailors as young and inexperienced as this one.

On *Iowa's* voyage to North Africa with President Roosevelt and the Joint Chiefs of Staff, McCrea poses with Victory, known as Vickie, who was to become *Iowa's* mascot. Vickie always slept at the foot of McCrea's bed, and when the president took over the captain's cabin for the trip, he shared the cabin with Vickie.

President Roosevelt bids farewell to *Iowa's* crew upon returning from North Africa. Standing behind him are McCrea and *Iowa's* executive officer, Commander Thomas J. Casey. The structure over Casey's right shoulder is one of the masts of USS *Potomac*, the president's yacht, which was waiting to take him to Washington.

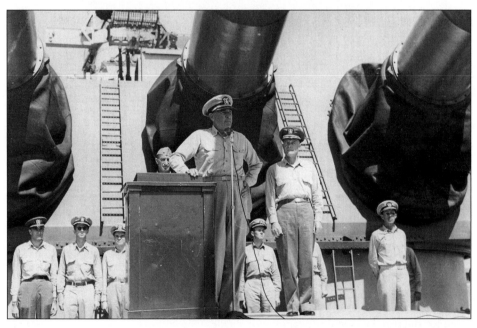

McCrea speaking under the 16-inch guns of turret three at an award ceremony in March 1944 honoring Rear Admiral Olaf M. Hustvedt. The admiral is standing to McCrea's left.

Iowa fires the 16-inch guns of turrets one and two during a battle drill in the Pacific. [Courtesy of the National Archives.]

Rear Admiral McCrea stands on a snowy landing strip on Attu, the Aleutian Islands. He is wearing the heavy overcoat issued to him with the comment, "Out where you're going, you'll be glad you have that." [Courtesy of the National Archives.]

After FDR's death, McCrea was abruptly recalled to Washington. On 25 April 1945 he bid farewell to the men of his task force flagship, USS *Richmond* (CL-9). McCrea is standing behind the desk at the center of the first elevated row of men. [Courtesy of the National Archives.]

The colonel stated that the men who joined his battalion were almost all completely illiterate. None could read. A very few could write their names, but nothing more. At Shelby, the illiterate troops attended small classes where they were taught ABCs and writing. One requirement for graduation from the illiterate battalion to the general service was the ability to write a letter to one's family. When a man learned to write a letter, his great pride in this achievement was shared by the instructors in the teaching operation. His accomplishment was an inspiration to all.

All this was amazing to the president. He told me he was astonished that such a large group of grown men could not write their own names. My reply was that on my first midshipmen cruise in the summer of 1912, I had witnessed the distribution of paychecks to numbers of men who couldn't write their names. They acknowledged receipt with "their mark," an "X." One is left to wonder about the effectiveness of our public school education when some six hundred out of thirty-four thousand men were completely illiterate.

The colonel continued, "I assure you, Mr. President, it was a shock to be uprooted from my secure position at Brown and put in uniform. I was satisfied with my work at Brown. But I assure you, Mr. President, the satisfaction I felt at Brown cannot compare with what I feel here, contributing to the well-being of so many unfortunate young men in need of the basics of education." The president thanked the colonel, wished him continued success in combating illiteracy, and we were off to see less interesting activities. For me, seeing what was being done with the illiterate battalion at Camp Shelby was the highlight of our whole trip.

We arrived back in Washington on 1 October 1942. The president had had a profitable journey. Strenuous as it was—fourteen successive nights on a train—he had seen much of the country and gotten the feel of the country's war effort. He was pleased with what he had seen. He had also found time to relax, enjoy some beautiful fall weather, and visit with his children in the West.

During those two weeks, I had seen a great deal of him, both on and off the train. As in our Sunday morning sessions at the White House, we had discussed naval matters at length, and the trip had strengthened our relationship.

The day after our return, I got in touch with William Fechteler in the Bureau of Personnel to discuss command of *Iowa*. He assured me that Admiral King and Admiral Jacobs, chief of the Bureau of Personnel, approved of my having this assignment. However, I would have to negotiate my release from the White House with the president. In addition, I would have to discuss with him who my relief should be. Personnel gave me the names of three possible relief candidates. I knew the men and would have been glad to turn over the job to any of them.

Fechteler pressed me for a date when I could notify him if the president would release me. I told him, "This is early October. You don't need a commanding officer for *Iowa* until 18 January. I promise I will talk with the president and get this matter resolved as soon as possible, but don't expect me to run over to the White House this afternoon and come back with an answer. I must pick my time to talk to him. Sunday mornings are our best times together. When I think the time right, I'll broach this subject with him."

One Sunday morning in late October, I maneuvered my conversation with the president into the matter of my leaving. We had been talking about odds and ends, and I sensed it was time to make my move. I told him that when I came to the White House, I had been scheduled to get command of a heavy cruiser at an early date, and that I could have command of *Iowa* on its commissioning in January. I said that I was not insensible to the honor of being the naval aide to the commander in chief, especially in wartime, and while I realized that much of importance regarding the war was taking place in Washington, I nevertheless felt I should be out there somewhere in a ship. I had to live with myself, and I could take no comfort in a shore assignment.

"Many of my friends are out there," said I. "Many have had trouble, grave trouble, and somehow I feel I must get there, too. I might add that both my wife and my mother think I am crazy to want to leave this assignment for sea duty. But after all, Mr. President, I must live with my conscience, and I really think I ought to go." Then I came forward with the clincher. "After all, Mr. President, your four sons are out there. Two of them have already seen combat duty."

"Couldn't you get a comparable job later?" was his reply.

"I might, Mr. President," said I. "But I'm not too sure."

"Very well, John," said he. "I'll release you in time to get the *Iowa*.

"And now for your relief. I suppose you have someone in mind, but so have I. Where is old Wilson Brown? He served as my naval aide before, and we got along well. He knows me, and I know him. If I get a stranger here, no matter how capable he might be, I will have to go through the process of getting used to him. I have many pressures on me, and I want to avoid taking on more pressures than necessary."

"To answer your question, Mr. President, I can say that Wilson is a vice admiral and has recently been ordered from sea duty to duty as commandant of the First Naval District in Boston."

"John," said the president, "tell those chaps in the Navy Department that I want Wilson Brown as your relief."

I thanked the president, and we moved on to other subjects.

After leaving the president, I encountered Admiral Leahy and told him that the president had agreed to release me to take command of *Iowa*.

"Ah," said Admiral Leahy, "I have just the chap for your relief." He mentioned the name of an officer a few classes junior to me at the Naval Academy. Under no circumstances would I have wanted this officer to relieve me. I knew full well I would not make flag rank without a major ship command. But rather than surrender my job to the chap Admiral Leahy had in mind, I would have gone to the president, told him I had reappraised the situation, and said that I would prefer to continue as his naval aide. I am convinced the president would have approved that unusual request. My relations with him were excellent.

"But, Admiral Leahy," said I, "the president has already resolved the matter of my relief. He wants Vice Admiral Wilson Brown."

The admiral hesitated a moment and then said, "Well, I'll be damned." I sensed the president's choice did not meet with Admiral Leahy's approval. As for myself, I was pleased.

The next morning, I promptly reported to Captain Fechteler that I was released. I also told him that the president wanted Vice Admiral Brown as my relief. On 7 November 1942, the Bureau of Personnel issued orders detaching me from duty as naval aide, effective on or about 20 January 1943.

Chapter 14

The Invasion of North Africa and Preparations for the Casablanca Conference

———⌗———

The most significant event of the fall of 1942 was the first commitment of U.S. troops in the Afro-European Theater of the war, an assault known as Operation Torch. On 8 November, a combined American-British force under the command of Lieutenant General Dwight D. Eisenhower invaded Morocco and Algeria in French North Africa. The commitment of U.S. troops against the European Axis powers had been eagerly awaited by the American public, and the country's response to the invasion was most favorable.

On 26 October, shortly before the invasion, Wendell Willkie made a national radio broadcast during prime time. Willkie was the Republican candidate defeated by President Roosevelt in the 1940 presidential election. He had recently returned from a worldwide tour, undertaken with the approval and support of the president, during which he had held discussions with foreign leaders and peoples about the world situation. The president endorsed Willkie's endeavor because he thought it would benefit the Allied cause. Abroad, it would be viewed as a sign of how democracy works in the United States where a defeated presidential candidate could go on a mission with the support of the man who defeated him.

Willkie's broadcast was to report to the American people about his discussions abroad. The broadcast was well-publicized and had the full cooperation of the White House, although no one at the White House knew what direction the report would take. The president had encouraged Willkie to be critical if he thought criticism was indicated.

The president invited Admiral Leahy, Harry Hopkins, Steve Early, Bill Hassett, Ross McIntire, and myself to the oval room to listen to the broadcast. Mr. Willkie complained bitterly that United States troops had not yet engaged the enemy. He thought this should be done at once. Of course, Mr. Willkie was not aware—nor were any in the oval room save the president, Harry Hopkins, Admiral Leahy, and myself—that the first massive convoy of our troops would land in North Africa within the next two weeks. Later, as our little audience withdrew, the president quietly remarked to me, "By a week from next Sunday, we will have met Wendell's main criticism." And so it was.[40]

---

40 During Operation Torch, November 8–10, 1942, Allied troops landed on the Atlantic coast of Morocco and in the Mediterranean near Oran and Algiers in Algeria. Morocco and Algeria were French territories, and under the Nazi-Vichy armistice of June 1940, the Vichy French Government controlled them and the French military forces there, subject to Nazi approval.

After the 1940 armistice, to maintain contact with Vichy and its territories, the United States promptly recognized the Vichy government and sent Admiral William D. Leahy as U.S. ambassador to Vichy. With an eye towards future military action, Roosevelt dispatched diplomat Robert D. Murphy to Algeria to feel out the sympathies of French military leaders there. Murphy found a number who favored the Allies, and during Operation Torch, opposition to Allied landings in Algiers was minor. By contrast, the forces commanded by General George S. Patton that landed near Casablanca met stiff Vichy resistance. After the Torch landings, the Allies quickly consolidated control of the area. Many of the Vichy forces that opposed the invasion subsequently agreed to work with the Allies.

A day or so after the landing of Allied troops, the president told me he knew little about French North Africa. "See if you can help me correct that deficiency," said he. "I would like to know more about the area where our troops are committed. While the North African operations were in the planning and preparatory stages, I couldn't ask for that sort of information. But now the troops are committed, that restraint is removed."

I got in touch with the Office of Naval Intelligence. Some friends over there produced the sort of information I was looking for. The president was pleased. "Just the sort of information I want."

Late one afternoon in early December, the president sent for me and sat me down at the corner of his desk. "John, I want to talk to you in great confidence. The matter I want to talk about is to be known to no one except those who need to know." This was the first time the president had ever spoken thus to me, and I was naturally most curious.

He continued, "Since you are the custodian of all dispatches passed between Winston and me, you know, for the most part, what we are thinking. Since the landing of our troops in North Africa, I have been in touch with Winston by letter. I feel we should meet soon to resolve some items, and our meeting should take place in Africa. Winston agrees and has suggested Khartoum [Sudan] as the location. I'm not too keen on that suggestion. Marrakech and Rabat have been suggested. I'm inclined to rule those areas out as well and settle for Casablanca." And then, to my amazement, the president asked, "What do you think of this whole idea?"

I gathered my wits as quickly as possible. "Right off the top of my head, Mr. President, I do not think well of the idea. I think there is too much risk involved for you."

"Our men in that area are taking risks," said the president. "Why shouldn't their commander in chief share that risk with them?"

I continued, "The Atlantic can be boisterous in the winter months, and a most uncomfortable passage across the Atlantic is a good possibility."

"Oh, we wouldn't go by ship," said the president. "We would fly."

This was a big surprise, because I knew the president was not enthusiastic about flying. I quickly saw I was getting nowhere. "Mr. President," said I, "you have taken me quite by surprise. I would like to give your proposal a little thought. Again, I say I wouldn't recommend it, but I'd like to think about it tonight, if I may."

"Good," said he.[41]

The following morning, after we finished going over the dispatches, I told him that I had given considerable thought to the North African proposal. While I thought the risks great, I had concluded that he had already made up his mind to go through with the trip. Otherwise, he would not have told me about it the way he did.

He laughed and remarked that I was about right. "Winston is all for it," he added.

"I still think that the risk is great, Mr. President. From what I have read in the dispatches and the press, the area is in turmoil. I would suppose that North Africa is full of people who would be willing to take you out for ten dollars." Why I said that, I'll never know, but I did say it, and I felt it. The president laughed heartily.

---

41 The risks of a presidential trip to Casablanca at this time were substantial. Passenger planes were unpressurized and flew at low altitude. The Atlantic abounded with U-boats, and transport planes being ferried across the Atlantic had been shot down by the anti-aircraft guns of Nazi subs. Allied troops were fighting the Germans in nearby Tunisia, and Casablanca was easily within range of Nazi bombers. In December, the Luftwaffe bombed the native quarter of Casablanca and killed hundreds. Moreover, the area was full of German agents who had active spy networks. Keeping the presence of the president and prime minister a secret would be challenging indeed.

"But since you intend to go," I continued, "it will be up to us who are to arrange the details to do everything possible to minimize the risk to you."

About ten days later, Admiral François Darlan was gunned down in North Africa by an assassin.[42] To me, this unfortunate murder highlighted the potential for violence in the area. The president typically took bad news in stride with no visible emotional reaction, and so it was in this case. When I read the dispatch about Darlan's death from our people in North Africa, his only response was a single word, "Unfortunate." I was tempted to remind him of my concern about the possibility of violence against him, but I kept my mouth shut.

The president renewed the conversation about his trip. "By the way, John, you are to accompany me on this trip to North Africa, and we will not be back in time for the commissioning of the *Iowa* on 18 January." I remarked that I hoped that the Navy Department wouldn't take the ship away from me. With a twinkle in his eye, the president responded, "Under the circumstances, John, I don't think they would do that." His remark was most reassuring.

The president asked that I take charge of the travel arrangements for the trip to Casablanca and return. Again he emphasized that the trip was top secret, and no one should know about it who did not need to know. The president said he could not leave Washington until after he had addressed the Congress on Saturday,

---

42 By chance, Admiral Darlan, commander in chief of all Vichy armed forces, was in Algiers at the time of Operation Torch. With the approval of FDR and Churchill, General Eisenhower reached an agreement with Darlan that he could serve as commander in chief of the French North African forces and high commissioner of West and North Africa in exchange for help with Vichy resistance in West Africa and Tunisia, the next Allied objective. Darlan issued a cease-fire order in the name of Marshal Pétain, and all resistance ended. Despite Darlan's willingness to work for the Allies, many considered him an opportunistic Nazi sympathizer and criticized Eisenhower's dealings with him. Darlan was assassinated by a French monarchist, apparently acting alone.

9 January 1943. He would go by train to Miami. From Miami, he would proceed by chartered Pan American Clipper in easy steps to Bathurst, Gambia, West Africa, and thence by army air corps plane to Casablanca. Once I knew what the president wanted, I got busy. There were many details to be worked out.[43]

Early in the planning, the president told me that Pa Watson would not make the trip. "You will recall, John," said he, "that Pa had a heart attack last spring. And while he is now back on active duty, Ross feels he is in no condition to stand the stress and strain of a long air trip across the Atlantic and on to Casablanca. I dread telling Pa I have decided he should not go with us. I'll let you know when I have told him. Meanwhile, he must be kept ignorant of what is up."

A number of persons were detailed to make travel arrangements under my supervision. The White House transportation specialist made most of the train arrangements. Admiral King assigned an officer to arrange over-water transportation. He chartered two Pan American Boeing seaplanes for service between Miami and Bathurst. They had a cruising speed of about 130 knots, and each carried a crew of eleven. General George Marshall directed an army signal corps officer to report to me about communications matters and another officer to arrange air transportation in Africa. For overland flights in Africa, the army supplied two C-54 Army planes manufactured by Douglas Aircraft Corporation. They had a cruising speed of around 180 miles per hour. None of the planes had pressurized cabins.

Much happened during the strenuous days of preparations to go abroad. I consulted with Supervising Agent Michael F. Reilly of

---

43 The Casablanca Conference was scheduled for January 14–23, 1943. The president and the prime minister wanted to confer in person about diplomatic and military matters. Joseph Stalin, premier of the U.S.S.R., was invited, but he declined because of the press of war on the Eastern front. Also to attend were the Combined Chiefs of Staff of the United States and Britain, and their advisors. They were to meet to plan the next stages of the war.

the Secret Service detail about Secret Service coverage. He concluded that the Secret Service detail should be divided into two parts: one group to accompany the president, and the other, headed by Reilly himself, to go to Casablanca before the president's arrival.

I discussed the details of the trip with Ross McIntire. He felt that the itinerary must include stops to give the president travel breaks, but a planned overnight stop at Bathurst caused him concern. "That is tsetse fly country," said Ross. "The bite of the tsetse fly can carry sleeping sickness. The Bathurst stop would be fine if the president could be quartered in a ship." I went directly to Admiral King and told him of Ross's concern. Admiral King's terse reply, so very typical of him, was a single sentence. "There will be a ship at Bathurst to house the president." With that assurance, I was gone. Ross also insisted we take one thousand pounds of bottled water, because he would take no chances with the health of the president's party on account of foreign drinking water.

Concerns about secrecy stood out. Personal identification for civilians without passports was an issue. I worried that if civilians became separated from the president's party on foreign soil, they would be unable to identify themselves. I knew Harry Hopkins well enough to know that he was a wanderer. He would take off in any direction at any time if the mood hit him, and he did not have a passport.

Ultimately, I decided not to obtain any passports. There might be difficulties getting special passports, and any attempt to get them would mean many would know what the White House was contemplating. To meet the identification problem, I drew up a card that stated that the bearer was a member of the president's party. The president signed all the cards, and I handed them out to the civilians.

Also, for secrecy's sake, the crew of the train to Miami was specially selected. The engineer, the fireman, and a trainman were the only regular railroad employees on board. The rest of the crew were replaced by Filipino messmen from the president's yacht, who had been instructed on how to make up berths and operate the galley.

During the trip preparations, we had a scare about a serious breach of security. One afternoon, Colonel Starling, the chief of the White House Secret Service detail, called me, saying it was urgent that he see me at once. Over he came to the Map Room, and we went out into the corridor out of earshot of the Map Room personnel.

"Captain, is there anything going on here involving travel by the president that I should be aware of?"

"I don't understand what you're driving at, Colonel. Could you be more specific?"

The colonel responded, "A taxi driver here in Washington called the White House today and told the telephone operator he wanted to talk to someone in authority who had to do with the movements of the president. He was put through to me. He said he wanted to come see me. He left a few moments ago.

"He told me he had answered a call from the British Embassy this morning. There he had picked up a couple of ladies and driven them to the Woodward & Lothrop department store. On the way, one lady said to the other that the president was going soon to North Africa where he would meet with Mr. Churchill. They talked about the subject at some length. The taxi driver said he had no way of knowing whether this was true, but he thought it wasn't something that should be talked about. I told the taxi driver that I agreed with him, but as far as I knew, there was nothing to it. I thanked him, and he departed. Captain, how do you suppose such a rumor could get started?"

"I have no reply," said I, quickly coming to the conclusion that the colonel was not one of those who "needed to know." Needless to say, I was perturbed. How could that have gotten out? The origin appeared to be the British Embassy. I told Harry Hopkins and the president about the incident, and it was decided that the less said, the better.

The president was scheduled to address the Congress at noon on 9 January 1943, the day of his departure for Casablanca. The previous evening, the president told me he wanted to enter the House on my arm. When I arrived at the White House the next morning, the Map Room watch officer told me the president wished to see me as soon as practicable. I was due to see him anyway at 9:00 a.m., so I was curious. I went directly to the president's bedroom and was announced by his valet. The conversation went something like this:

"You will recall, John, that I told you that I would undertake to tell Pa Watson about our upcoming trip and inform you when I had done so. I intentionally put off telling Pa as long as possible. When he brought the appointment list to me this morning, I broke the news to him. I told him that, on Ross's advice, because of the amount of flying involved and his recent heart attack, I was not taking him on this trip. Pa was shocked. He slumped in his chair and broke into tears. He said that maybe his usefulness around the White House was about at an end. I comforted him as best I could, to little avail. After a bit, he recovered his composure and withdrew.

"Now, John, I told you last evening that I would enter the House chamber this noon on your arm. If I do that, I think it would be a further shock to Pa. Will you please run Pa down at once and tell him that I neglected to tell him that I would enter the House chamber this noon on his arm, as usual? That might soften the blow a bit of his not going to North Africa with us."

As soon as I caught up with Pa, we went to his private office, and I gave him the president's message. Pa erupted. He thought the president was badly advised to make this trip. The risk was too great. He asked why I hadn't informed him about the plan. "I've always taken you into my confidence, John," said he, "and in this important instance, you have not taken me into yours."

I calmed Pa down as best I could. I explained that the president had told me, in no uncertain terms, that no one, absolutely no one, was to know about the trip except those who needed to know. I explained that the president had said that he himself would tell Pa that he would not be going. This was of little comfort. Pa was deeply hurt.

Pa was also worried about the president. He repeated over and over that the president had been badly advised to make the trip. "I hope you didn't encourage him," he said. I told Pa I had done everything I could to dissuade the president, without success. Insofar as I knew, a deal had been made with Mr. Churchill, and that was it.

Then Pa exclaimed emphatically, "There's only one so-and-so around here who is crazy enough to promote such a thing, and his name is Hopkins." I note here that "so-and-so" is not an exact quote.

Chapter 15

The Casablanca Conference

———∞∞∞———

Shortly before 10:30 p.m. on 9 January 1943, the president and his entourage left the White House as inconspicuously as possible for the trip to Casablanca. The presidential train, fully packed with baggage, food, and supplies, was parked in the underground station at the Bureau of Engraving. Departing Washington, the train traveled to Miami, arriving before dawn on 11 January. At 5:45 a.m. the president and his party detrained and left for the Pan American base, where two seaplanes were waiting to fly them to Trinidad.[44]

Plane number one took on the president, Harry Hopkins, Admiral William Leahy, Ross McIntire, three Secret Service agents, Arthur Prettyman, the president's valet, and myself. One of the Secret Service agents was Elmer R. Hipsley, an Olympic swimmer, who had been selected to ride the president's seaplane "just in

---

44 The president's air itinerary from Miami to West Africa took him south to the island of Trinidad and Belém, Brazil, and then east across the South Atlantic to Bathurst in the British colony of Gambia. This route to Africa was essentially that used by the U.S. Army Air Transport Command to fly supplies from the United States to the Allies in Africa. The route had been adopted in part because it offered the aircraft of the day the shortest passage across the Atlantic.

case."[45] Plane number one took off promptly, and flying with favorable winds at about 150 miles per hour at an altitude of about nine thousand feet, we reached Trinidad in the late afternoon. The presidential party spent the night at the delightful navy-operated hotel at Macqueripe Beach.

For a number of days, Admiral Leahy, chief of the Joint Chiefs of Staff, had suffered with a heavy cold, and the trip had not improved his condition. On the advice of Ross McIntire and over Leahy's vigorous objections, the president decided to leave the admiral to recuperate at the hotel.

At 6:00 a.m. on 12 January, the rest of the presidential party took off for Belém, Brazil, arriving in mid-afternoon. The president went ashore to attend a short reception at the U.S. Air Transport Command. Meanwhile, the two seaplanes took on maximum loads of gas and provisions for the night flight across the Atlantic.

At 6:00 p.m., we departed for Africa. We arrived at Bathurst the next afternoon after a nineteen-hour flight. The transatlantic crossing had not been pleasant. We encountered rough air and got little rest. The president's plane found comparatively acceptable air at an altitude of about four thousand feet, while plane number two flew at about one thousand feet. Waiting in the harbor at Bathurst was the USS *Memphis*, the ship promised by Admiral King to house the president. The president was obviously weary, but he went on a short boat tour of the harbor and hosted a few of us at dinner in the admiral's cabin.

The following morning, 14 January 1943, the presidential party departed at dawn for Yundum Field and our flight to Casablanca. We drove through Bathurst. The natives appeared to be struggling to get up enthusiasm to face another day. We were told that unskilled labor there was paid about a shilling nine pence per

---

45 Plane number two carried a communications specialist, support staff, and two additional Secret Service agents.

day, plus half a cup of rice. Due to the poor living conditions, life expectancy was said to be about twenty-six years.[46]

At Yundum Field, two C-54 army planes were waiting. Once airborne, we briefly swung seaward to give the president an aerial view of Dakar and Saint-Louis in Senegal, French West Africa.[47] Then we turned inland and headed for Casablanca.

As we approached the Atlas Mountains, the president was seated amidships, I was directly across the aisle, and Ross was in front of me. Because the plane was not pressurized, Ross and I became aware that we were gradually rising above our cruising altitude of eight thousand feet. At Ross's request, I found out that the pilot expected to reach about twelve thousand feet. After I returned to my seat, Ross addressed me in a low tone of voice over his shoulder, "John, how about putting on your oxygen mask? I want the president to put his on, but if I suggest it, he will probably make a fuss. If he sees you put on your mask, he will probably follow." I reached for my mask and adjusted it. Sure enough, when the president saw me putting on my mask, he started to fumble with his. I promptly moved across the aisle and adjusted it for him. Ross put his mask on, too, and we were all set when we reached twelve thousand feet.

After crossing the Atlas Mountains, we lowered down gradually and landed in Casablanca at 6:30 p.m. At the airport to meet us were Mike Reilly, the leader of the Secret Service advance party, and representatives of the U.S. Army. The president's son, Lieutenant Colonel Elliott Roosevelt, was also there. Somehow he had found out about the president's arrival and proceeded on his own to meet the plane.[48]

---

46 According to Elliott Roosevelt, FDR's son, the president was horrified by the poverty in Bathurst. The experience reinforced his commitment to develop local economies and encourage self-government in colonial areas.

47 At this time, Senegal was a French colony.

48 Elliott Roosevelt was a pilot and officer in the army air forces. He was to serve as his father's military aide at the conference.

The U.S. Army had made the arrangements for the conference and done an impressive job. To house the meetings and the participants, they had commandeered the Hotel Anfa and a good-sized area around it, including some fourteen private villas. The entire area was surrounded by barbed-wire fence, and there was a heavy guard of troops, planes, and artillery. The president and Harry Hopkins were installed in a most spacious villa. Prime Minister Churchill was housed nearby in a villa of similar size. Ross McIntire and I were assigned a villa across the street from the president.

The army provided the president's villa with a staff so well-organized that on his first evening in Casablanca, he was able to host a dinner for the prime minister, the American and British Joint Chiefs, plus Harry Hopkins, Lieutenant Colonel Roosevelt, and W. Averell Harriman[49]—some twelve persons in all.

After dinner, the president's guests stayed on, renewing old acquaintances and talking shop. It was a pleasure for me to see the heads of the British Royal Navy and Air Force, Admiral of the Fleet Sir Dudley Pound, and Air Chief Marshal Sir Charles Portal. I had worked with them when I served as the navy's secretary at the meetings of the British and U.S. Chiefs of Staff in early January 1942. It was well past midnight when the group broke up. The president had had a most strenuous day, and Ross was anxious that he retire as early as possible.

At the conference, the president kept me busy with assignments of one sort or another. He had a steady stream of visitors, including the prime minister, diplomatic personnel, and American, British, French, and French North African military leaders and field commanders. He held many meetings at his villa. I attended some, but not all, of these conferences. The president had

---

49 W. Averell Harriman was an American businessman and diplomat. Beginning in 1941, Roosevelt sent him as a special envoy to Europe and the Soviet Union to negotiate Lend-Lease arrangements. Harriman became the U.S. ambassador to the Soviet Union from 1943 to 1946.

a look that he gave me when he wanted me to stay. If I didn't get the look, I withdrew. On a number of occasions, he asked me to attend meetings to make notes for his file. I was also present for many of the president's private talks with the prime minister, Admiral King, General Marshall, General Arnold, and others.

I did not sit in on any the formal military conferences of the Combined Chiefs of Staff. The military was in charge of those. However, on one occasion the president presided over a meeting of the Combined Chiefs of Staff, military advisors, the prime minister, and Harry Hopkins. Those at this meeting represented the military brains of the war effort of Great Britain and the United States, and they were a most impressive group.[50] And then there was McCrea, like a fly on the wall, without a word to say, to make a memorandum for the president's file.

During the conference, the prime minister was in and out of the president's villa two or three times a day for dinners, lunches, or anything else that was going on. I was fond of Mr. Churchill, who was most outspoken and often had something memorable to say. I asked the marine guard to discreetly keep an eye on his villa. When they saw Mr. Churchill coming down the street, they were to let me know so I could welcome him at the president's door.

At the conference, the president and the prime minister hoped to create a French military command that could take charge of

---

50 The group consisted of Field Marshal Sir John Dill, British Army, chief of the Joint Staff Mission in Washington, D.C., a diplomatic position; General Sir Alan F. Brooke, chief of the Imperial General Staff, British Army; Admiral of the Fleet Sir Dudley Pound, first sea lord, Royal Navy; Air Chief Marshal Sir Charles Portal, chief of the Air Staff, Royal Air Force; Lieutenant General Lord Hastings L. Ismay, Office of the Minister of Defense; Vice Admiral Lord Louis Mountbatten, chief of Combined Operations, Royal Navy; Lieutenant General Sir Ian C. Jacob, military assistant secretary to the British War Cabinet; General George C. Marshall, chief of staff of the U.S. Army; Admiral Ernest J. King, chief of naval operations and commander in chief of the U.S. Fleet; Lieutenant General H. H. Arnold, deputy chief of staff for Air and chief of the U.S. Army Air Forces; and Brigadier General John R. Deane, U.S. Army.

French forces in North Africa and work for the liberation of France. They wanted to persuade generals Charles de Gaulle and Henri Giraud, two proud and opinionated men, to work together. De Gaulle, the self-appointed leader of the Free French Movement, had fled France after the German invasion and was living in England. Giraud had been captured, but he escaped from a German prison camp and made his way to Morocco. At the time of the conference, he was commander in chief of French troops in North Africa.[51]

At their first meeting in Casablanca, the prime minister informed the president that he had invited de Gaulle to attend the conference, but the general had decided not to come. This annoyed the PM greatly, and the president as well.

The president told the prime minister—rather sternly, I thought—that it was up to the prime minister to get de Gaulle here. At this, the prime minister let fly a blast on de Gaulle: "I tell you, Mr. President, General de Gaulle is most difficult to deal with. We house him. We feed him. We pay him. We pamper him, and as best we can, we put up with his truculence and insults, but he refuses to raise a finger in support of our war efforts. He insists that he is entitled to a military command. I ask you, Mr. President, what sort of a military command could either of us give him?"

The president acknowledged that de Gaulle was difficult, but referring to the hoped-for collaboration between de Gaulle and Giraud, he said: "Winston, this is a shotgun marriage. We have our party here"—referring to Giraud—"and I feel it's up to you to get your party here." I inwardly squirmed a bit at the bluntness of the

---

51 Before Torch, the United States had hoped that Giraud could lead the Vichy French troops in North Africa after the invasion, but Giraud refused unless he could lead the invasion itself. After the invasion and a change of heart, Giraud was brought to North Africa, but the Vichy troops wouldn't follow his orders, so the Allies turned to Admiral Darlan. Giraud became commander in chief after Darlan's assassination.

president's remarks, but he put a light touch on the proceedings with a hearty laugh. That felt easier.

Churchill was as outspoken about the Russians as he was about de Gaulle. During another discussion with the president, he thoroughly took them to task. Finally, he said, "Mr. President, it is my considered opinion, sir, that the Kremlin has been, and is now, populated with *wicked men*." The PM spoke the words "wicked men" with great emphasis. The president was quiet for a second, and then, with a twinkle, he said, "Winston, do you realize that you are talking about one of our allies?" The PM responded, "I have considered that as well."

On our first full day in Casablanca, I made inquiries about a division of U.S. destroyers that had arrived in Casablanca the day before. The division was under the control of an old friend, Rear Admiral John L. "Jimmy" Hall, commander of our naval forces in North Africa. I hoped that Jimmy's destroyers could supply much-needed laundry service for our party. I learned that one of the destroyers was the USS *Mayrant*, the ship to which Franklin D. Roosevelt Jr. was assigned. I sent a note to Jimmy asking him to send Lieutenant FDR Jr. to my villa without telling him whom he was to visit.

In a couple of hours, FDR Jr. arrived. He sighted me and burst out, "My God, Captain! Is Pa here?" I told him his suspicion was correct and took him across the street to see his father. On the way, I told Franklin that his father was unaware of *Mayrant*'s presence in Casablanca, and he should be prepared for a surprised parent. The president was surprised indeed, and father and son indulged in a fond embrace. The president quickly issued an invitation to stay for dinner, and, of course, young Franklin accepted.

The same afternoon, Lieutenant General Dwight D. Eisenhower called on the president. Eisenhower was then commander in chief of the Allied Expeditionary Force in North Africa. When I had the opportunity, I told General Eisenhower about a conversation that General Pershing had with the president on Armistice

Day 1942, and Pershing's comment that General Marshall had assured him that Eisenhower would do all right. General Eisenhower smiled and remarked to the effect that, before this war was over, he would probably need all the friends he could muster.

The next evening, 16 January, the president gave an unusual dinner party. He asked the army to invite some officers of the Women's Army Auxiliary Corps to dine with him at his villa as a symbolic tribute to women serving in the army. Lieutenant Colonel Elliott Roosevelt, Lieutenant FDR Jr., and Harry Hopkins joined the president, and Prime Minister Churchill made an unexpected visit later. I think it can safely be said that never in their wildest dreams did these five army captains ever imagine that one evening, in a country far from their native land, they would be dining in such company. It was typical of the president to come up with something so memorable to honor his guests.

On 19 January, the president gave me a handwritten note to the sultan of Morocco inviting the sultan to dinner at his villa on 22 January. The president asked that I hand deliver the note in Rabat, and we discussed how I might get there. That night the president and I attended a dinner at General Patton's villa. On our way back, the president told me that General Patton had promised a car and escort at my villa at 8:00 a.m. to take me to Rabat on 21 January.

The morning of 21 January arrived, and at 7:30, thirty minutes ahead of schedule, an army car and escort appeared at the door. My escort turned out to be Brigadier General William H. Wilbur of General Patton's staff. The general told me that General Patton had contacted General Charles Noguès, the French resident general, who would make arrangements for my reception at the sultan's palace.[52]

---

52 During Operation Torch, General Noguès ordered French troops to oppose the landings of General Patton's troops on the Atlantic coast of Morocco. After Darlan's order to cease resistance, he provided invaluable service to the Allies.

Rabat was some eighty-five miles away, and our motorcycle escort saw to it that we made a rapid trip. On the way, General Wilbur and I conversed, principally about the war to date in North Africa. He wanted to know my class at the Naval Academy. When I told him it was 1915, he wondered if I had known his brother John, of the class of 1912. I acknowledged that I did, as well as any plebe gets to know an upperclassman. Of course I'd known John. He was a four-striper of our battalion, one of the highest-ranking student officers.

This opened up a new line of conversation that was most unexpected. When we were about fifteen or twenty minutes distant from our destination, General Wilbur remarked, "Captain McCrea, I suppose you have the note that the president wishes delivered to the sultan."

"Of course, General. It's right here in my pocket."

"When are you going to give it to me?"

"I don't understand, General. What you are suggesting?"

"I take it that the delivery of this note is a joint operation, and since I am senior to you, I propose to deliver the note."

"General Wilbur, of course you are senior to me, but I am the naval aide to the president of the United States. The president charged me with delivery of this note on his behalf, and that is what I propose to do."

No rejoinder from the general. I was astonished at his suggestion, and the general did not pursue the matter. When we returned to Casablanca that afternoon, I told the president about the incident. "You handled it correctly," said he with a chuckle. "A rather odd point of view."

At General Noguès's residence, we freshened up a bit, and took off for the sultan's palace with the general. I shall long remember our reception at the palace. No Hollywood director could have put on a more dazzling spectacle. The courtyard was ankle-deep in white sand. The walls of the courtyard and the palace were also white. A unit of cavalry was drawn up at attention, dressed in colorful costumes. The color red predominated. Every horse was white with a red blanket. The sounding of trumpets contributed to the lavishness of the scene.

We were escorted into a waiting room. I was introduced to the *chef de protocol* and the grand vizier. I told the *chef de protocol* of my mission. He informed me that I should give him the note when he called for it.

We were then escorted into a throne room. I was given a seat in the center of the room behind a small table. The grand vizier and the *chef de protocol* were seated behind their desks on slightly raised platforms on either side of the room.

In a few moments, there was a blare of trumpets, and all rose. The curtains parted, and the sultan, dressed in the robes of his office, entered and seated himself in an elaborate chair. The *chef de protocol* announced my presence in Arabic, French, and English. He stated that he was informed that I bore a message from the president of the United States addressed to His Majesty the sultan. I handed him the president's note, and he read it in English, Arabic, and French. The sultan and the *chef de protocol* conferred, and finally the *chef de protocol* said that His Majesty accepted with great pleasure the invitation of the president of the United States to have dinner with him at Casablanca on 22 January. The *chef de protocol* added that His Majesty wondered if it would be appropriate for his son, the crown prince, to accompany him. I replied that the president would be pleased to have the crown prince as his dinner guest, and the *chef de protocol* so informed His Majesty.

This interlude at an end, all stood while His Majesty withdrew. The *chef de protocol* joined me. He said that His Majesty's desire to include the crown prince had caught him by surprise. He remarked that the prince, a boy of some twelve years, was a great admirer of General Patton.

After the ceremonies at the palace, General Wilbur and I proceeded a few miles north of Rabat to join the president and his party. The president was preparing to review the U.S. Army's

2nd Armored Division and 3rd and 9th Infantry Divisions. These divisions had served under General Patton during the Allied assault on the Atlantic coast of Morocco. For the inspections, the president transferred to an army jeep. As his jeep passed down the line, it was interesting to see the surprise of the GIs when they realized that the inspecting officer was none other than their commander in chief, the president of the United States.

During a break in the inspections, the president's party proceeded to an area near an army field kitchen, where tables had been set up for the noonday meal. The group lunched there, and the president received a group of fifty officers and men who had distinguished themselves during Torch at the landings in heavy surf at Fedala, Safi, and Mehdia-Port Lyautey.

Following the inspections, the presidential party proceeded to the area where the Battle of Mehdia-Port Lyautey was fought on 8–11 November 1942. At Port Lyautey, there were several partially sunken ships in the harbor, reminders of the November landings. Near Fort Mehdia, there was a new military cemetery, where American and French casualties were interred. On behalf of the president, I helped place wreaths in the American and French sections of the cemetery. During these proceedings, a high wind developed, and it was all we could do to get the heavy, lead-backed wreaths to their appointed positions.

Afterward, we withdrew to a sheltered spot, where an army colonel explained the phases of the battle with the aid of an exceedingly large-scale chart. The weather took a turn for the worse, and to the relief of all, the president announced he was "ready to go home."

Twenty-two January was an important day. Much excitement ensued when General Charles de Gaulle arrived about noon. "I thought he wasn't coming," said FDR to the PM. "I persuaded him otherwise," was the PM's rejoinder.[53]

---

53 The PM threatened to cut off the salary the British were paying de Gaulle, and he arrived the next day.

Shortly afterward, the president awarded the Medal of Honor to General Wilbur, my escort to Rabat. At the award ceremony, General Patton pulled me aside and remarked: "General Wilbur received this well-deserved decoration some ten weeks after his outstanding exploit. This sort of delay should not be tolerated. Have you any influence with the president?"

"I see the president at least twice daily and more often than that, sometimes."

"The next time you see him," said General Patton, "I wish you would tell him that I believe the commanding general should have the authority to confer the Medal of Honor on the field of battle. That's the way it should be done."

Past experience in the Navy Department had led me to conclude that decorations, especially those for bravery, should not be awarded hastily. A case in point flashed across my mind. An officer had been highly and hastily recommended for a distinguished decoration. When the facts were known, it was determined that the officer had done a conspicuous deed, but his conduct was such that he was fortunate to escape disciplinary action. I told General Patton that I did not share his opinion, but I would convey his point of view to the president. The president said he'd think about it, but I never heard the matter mentioned again.

The event of the day was the president's dinner in honor of the sultan of Morocco. The sultan, accompanied by the crown prince, the *chef de protocol*, and the grand vizier, arrived at the president's villa at about 7:45 p.m. The sultan and his entourage were magnificently attired in white silk robes. They came bearing gifts: a gold-mounted dagger for the president, displayed beautifully in a hardwood and handcrafted teak wood case; and two golden bracelets and a high golden tiara for Mrs. Roosevelt. The president presented the sultan with a personally inscribed photograph of himself in a heavy silver frame, engraved at the top with the seal of the president of the United States.

The PM arrived almost simultaneously with the sultan. In addition to the sultan's party, the dinner guests included General Charles Noguès, General Patton, Robert Murphy,[54] Harry Hopkins, Lieutenant Colonel Elliott Roosevelt, and myself, twelve in all.

No alcoholic beverages were served before, during, or after the dinner, nor any pork or pork products, because these items are forbidden to Mohammedans.[55] The fact that no alcoholic beverages were being served appeared to take the PM by surprise. He started to glower, and the glower was particularly pronounced during the small talk that preceded the dinner.

When we went in to dinner, the sultan was seated on the president's right and the PM on his left. Because of the crown prince's admiration for General Patton, I arranged to have the prince seated next to the general.

An amusing incident took place shortly after we were seated. I was informed that a Royal Marine, the PM's orderly, wanted to speak to me. I asked that the marine come to the dining area. The marine stomped his way in with such vigor as to virtually monopolize the attention of those of us at the foot of the table. He informed me that the PM had received an important message requiring immediate attention. Pointing out the PM, I told the marine to speak to him. He stomped his way the length of the table, saluted the PM, delivered his message, and stomped his way out of the dining area.

After a word with the president, the PM retreated. He returned about twenty minutes later. I have no doubt that his message had been urgent. However, when he reappeared, it was evident that the

54 Murphy was an American diplomat. Starting in late 1940, he served as Roosevelt's envoy in French North Africa, where he did reconnaissance and gathered intelligence about members of the Vichy regime and armed forces who harbored pro-Allied sentiments. It was as a result of his work that there was relatively little opposition to the Allied landings in Algeria.
55 Mohammedan was the word used in the West at that time for a Muslim.

PM had taken time out to have a quick drink or two while handling his urgent dispatch.

The dinner party broke up shortly before 10:00 p.m. After the guests departed, the president and I had a good laugh about the PM and his message. The president had been amused by the PM's disgruntlement over the absence of alcoholic beverages. He wondered if he could have arranged the message as an excuse to get a drink. I didn't think that was possible. To this day, I regard the dispatch as a coincidence, and the PM made the most of it.

Saturday, 23 January was a busy day. Everyone was getting ready to leave. After dinner, the president dictated at length some "background material" for an announcement to the press the following day. About midnight, the president and the PM collaborated on a cable to Stalin about the conference and a joint communiqué to be issued to the press the next day, with the understanding that the press would not release the information for three days. The president was lucky to get to bed at 2:30 a.m.

By 24 January, the last day of the conference, it was clear that the negotiations between General Giraud and General de Gaulle had not gone well. Their respective senses of honor apparently would not let them cooperate. Having sat in on the generals' meetings with the president, I thought de Gaulle was the stickier of the two.[56]

On the final morning, the president, the PM, and the two generals repaired to the lawn behind the president's villa to pose for pictures. A photographer called out, "Generals, shake hands." That appeared to be the last thing the generals wished to do. The president called out, "Why not shake hands? You two Frenchmen are loyal to your country, and that warrants a cordial handshake anytime." The generals reluctantly shook hands, and the photogra-

---

56 McCrea took notes of some of the president's meetings with Giraud and de Gaulle.

phers caught them in the act. The picture went all over the world, and I suppose it contributed to French unity.[57]

At noon, the president, accompanied by the prime minister, invited the assembled newsmen to seat themselves on the lawn for a news conference. It was a beautiful day with brilliant sunshine. With the two heads of state seated before them, the correspondents heard a presentation about the conference, the reasons for it, and what had been accomplished.

In the course of the president's talk, which was largely off the cuff, he made reference to the Civil War and the great Northern general, Ulysses S. Grant. He noted Grant's initials, and how he came to be known as "Unconditional Surrender Grant." Then he remarked that, like Grant, the Allies would continue the war effort until the enemy unconditionally surrendered.

When the president made this statement, I saw the PM's head snap around towards him, giving me the impression that the phrase came as a surprise. I subsequently learned that the PM and the president were in complete agreement on this point. Of course, the world press made much of the remark. Many thought it would provoke the enemy to greater efforts and close the doors to a negotiated peace.

In due course, the news conference ended, and good-byes and good wishes were exchanged. Shortly afterward, a motorcade carrying the president, the PM, and their parties departed Casablanca, heading south.

---

57 Although the generals shook hands, they did not agree at Casablanca to work together to lead the Free French forces, as the president and the prime minister had hoped. Giraud was willing to work with, but not under, de Gaulle, but de Gaulle insisted that he be in overall command. They did not work together until June 1943, when they temporarily became co-presidents of the French Committee of National Liberation.

Chapter 16

Return to the White House
and Detachment

—— ∞∞ ——

The motorcade carrying the president and the PM headed for Marrakech, some 150 miles south of Casablanca near the Atlas Mountains. The day was pleasant, and we proceeded at a lively clip. In mid-afternoon, we stopped briefly for a roadside bag lunch. During lunch, Mr. Churchill held forth at length in praise of the Atlas Mountains as an artist's paradise. "Atlas Mountain sunsets are superb," said he.

At about 5:30 p.m., we arrived at Marrakech, an old Berber and Arab town. We went directly to the large villa of the United States vice consul at Marrakech, Mr. Kenneth Pendar. Both the villa and its setting were most beautiful.

The villa had a sixty-foot tower, and the PM highly recommended the view of the mountains from the top. Despite the president's infirmities and the narrowness of the stairway, he decided he wanted to go up. "Where are my horses?" said he, referring to the stalwart Secret Service officers who would pick him up, chair and all, and carry him when necessary. Getting the president up the stairway was not easy, but it was done.

The platform at the top was small and could barely accommodate the president and a chair for Mr. Churchill. Since this was the president's only foreseeable opportunity to witness an Atlas Mountains sunset, he proposed to the PM that they do just that. Mr. Pendar suggested they might like a drink or two to while away the time till sunset. That was evidently a good thought, and highballs were ordered.

Harry Hopkins, Ross McIntire, and I climbed the tower, took a quick look at the view, and decided we were in the way. We departed for a quick sightseeing tour of the Marrakech marketplace. We left the PM holding forth about Marrakech, the Berbers, and the glories of the Atlas Mountains.

At seven-thirty the next morning, 25 January, the president's party was preparing to depart for the airport for our flight to Bathurst. Just as we were loading into the car, who should appear to bid farewell to the president but the PM, dressed in his pajamas, slippers, and bathrobe.

"Good-bye, Mr. President," said the PM.

"Good-bye, sir," the president responded.

"Safe home, Mr. President. This is a great struggle in which we are engaged, Mr. President, but we shall prevail no matter how long nor how bitter the struggle may be. We shall prevail, Mr. President, because God in heaven must be on our side. What a comfort, Mr. President, that thought is."

Here the PM hesitated. Then his face lit up. Some thought must be crossing his mind, thought I.

"Can you think, Mr. President, of any good reason why I should not accompany you to the airport? I am told it is only twelve miles away."

"Not at all, Winston. I should be honored if you came," said the president.

Quick as a flash, the PM turned and shouted to his bodyguard, Walter H. Thompson of Scotland Yard. "Thompson, my hat, please. My stick and a cigar, Thompson, and hurry. We mustn't keep the president waiting." Hat, stick, and cigar were quickly forthcoming.

Seating was quickly rearranged. I sat on the left jump seat, Ross McIntire was directly behind me, and the PM sat between Ross and the president. On the way to the airport, the events of the past week were discussed. The president and the PM agreed that more such meetings should be held.

At the airport, our car drove up to the boarding ramp. The Secret Service chaps assisted the president into his wheelchair, carried him up the ramp, and deposited him in his seat in the plane. The PM, who had come on board, remarked, "God bless you, Mr. President. Safe home. I trust we shall meet sometime this summer." They clasped hands, and the president thanked the PM for coming to the airport with him.

I accompanied the PM to the door of the plane, and he bade me good-bye. At the foot of the ramp was Black, the navy photographer who had accompanied us from Washington. His camera was trained on the PM. Suddenly, the PM saw Black and his camera. He let out a roar, really a roar. "Don't you dare, young man! You with that camera, don't you dare. Do you hear me?"

There was no chance that Black had not heard the PM, nor could he have missed the PM's threatening gestures with his stick. I waved Black aside. But what a picture was missed: His Majesty's prime minister leaving the president's plane attired in bathrobe and slippers with his bowler, stick, and cigar.

We reached Yundum Field, Bathurst, in mid-afternoon. After a long, dusty ride from the airport, it was a delight to see the boat from *Memphis* waiting for us at the dock. On boarding *Memphis*, the president told me that, if possible, he wished to fly his personal flag while the vessel was at anchor in Bathurst.[58] I immediately told Captain McCown about the president's wish. Captain McCown

---

58 Senior naval officers of the rank of rear admiral or higher, known as flag officers, have personal flags denoting their rank, which they may fly in ships under their command. By navy regulation, the president, as commander in chief of the navy, also has a personal flag to signal his presence on board a ship. At this time, the design of the presidential flag featured a central eagle, like that in the presidential seal, with four large stars, one in each corner.

responded that personal flags and ceremonial bunting had been turned in for the duration of the war on orders from the Navy Department, something I already knew.

"Henry," said I, "the man has spoken, and despite the many obstacles to be overcome, I am certain that *Memphis* is resourceful enough to come up with something in the way of a presidential flag. The president wants to fly his flag in African waters because no president has ever done so before. Let us see what can be done to gratify that whim." I might add that whenever I sought to satisfy a presidential request and encountered opposition, the phrase "the man has spoken" invariably got results. So it was in this case.

Memphis's signal corps did the seemingly impossible in an all-night effort. They produced a beautiful presidential flag with nothing more to go on than a colored photograph. They had none of the colored bunting normally used to make flags. Instead, they used paint and crayons with the hope that it would not rain. All the pieces were stitched together by sewing machine. The president was pleased. Later, before the assembled crew of the *Memphis*, he thanked them for the flag and the effort that produced it.

During the president's last two days in Africa, he did a bit of sightseeing. On 26 January, Viscount Swinton, the minister resident of British West Africa, joined the president for a three-hour trip up the Gambia River.[59] On 27 January, the presidential party made a day trip to the Republic of Liberia, some seven hundred miles to the south.[60] We flew to Roberts Field, Monrovia, where

---

59 British West Africa was the collective name for the British colonies Gambia, Sierra Leone, the Gold Coast, and Nigeria, controlled by the British until well after WWII.

60 Although Liberia was an independent and nominally neutral country, by January 1943 it had become crucial to the Allied war effort. Roberts Field in Monrovia, the capital, was an important stop on the U.S. South Atlantic air supply route to Africa and the Near East. The country was also a vital source of natural rubber, particularly after December 1941, when the Japanese invaded Malaya, Asia's prime rubber-producing area. The president visited Liberia to recognize the country's importance to the Allies. At the urging of the United States, Liberia eventually declared war on Germany in 1944.

the president lunched with Edwin J. Barclay, president of Liberia, and his secretary of state, Clarence L. Simpson.

After luncheon, presidents Roosevelt and Barclay reviewed some troops. An excellent band rendered "The Star-Spangled Banner" with a decidedly unusual flourish. The president asked me to find out where they got that arrangement. I was informed that some fifteen members of the band had been members of Cab Calloway's Harlem orchestra. "They certainly put swing into it," said the president, "but I think I'm a purist when it comes to 'The Star-Spangled Banner.'"

Later, the general manager of the nearby Firestone Tire and Rubber Company's rubber plantation joined our party. He took us on a tour of his installation. Our motorcade wound through the trees, giving us a view of the rubber plant in every stage of growth, from young shoot to latex-producing tree in the seventh year of cultivation.

Following the Firestone tour, we flew back to Bathurst. That evening, around 11:30 p.m., we boarded our two Pan American Clippers for our return to the United States. On our way back, we flew in easy stages, making overnight stops at Natal, Brazil, and Trinidad before reaching our final destination, Miami.

The thirtieth of January 1943, the day of our flight from Trinidad to Miami, was the president's sixty-first birthday. When we were outward bound, I thought it might be in order to recognize the event and give the president a little memento of the occasion. I talked the matter over with Harry Hopkins, Admiral Leahy, Ross McIntire, and Rear Admiral Jesse V. Oldendorf, the commandant of Naval Operating Base Trinidad. We agreed that a print or two of Trinidad would be appropriate. Admiral Oldendorf undertook to acquire the gift.

When the president reached plane number one that morning, it was flying international signal flags that read, "For the commander in chief, Birthday Greetings." At 12:30 p.m., the passengers on plane number two toasted the president, and I delivered a message from them wishing him many happy returns of the day. Then the president was presented with a gift from the entire group in both planes, a bound collection of old prints from Trinidad.

That afternoon, we landed in the beautiful waters of Biscayne Bay at Miami. On the president's precedent-shattering round trip to Africa, he had flown in excess of fourteen thousand miles over land and sea.[61] The presidential train was parked a few blocks away. Our baggage was soon stowed on board, and we departed for Washington. When we arrived on 31 January, we were greeted with snow flurries, a stark contrast to the equatorial conditions of a few days earlier. The trip had been interesting but strenuous, and it was good to be home again.

The next item of business for me was to get detached from my duties as naval aide and report to the commandant of the Third Naval District in New York, as the prospective commanding officer of USS *Iowa*. My relief, Vice Admiral Wilson Brown, had already reported to the White House. Since he had served as naval aide before, he was familiar with many aspects of his job, but not the Map Room. By the time of my return, he had been thoroughly briefed by Lieutenant Commander William C. Mott, my able, number one assistant.

I was anxious to get to New York to catch up with *Iowa*. I was detached from my duties as naval aide on 3 February 1943. Grace Tully brought my orders to the president for his signature. After he had signed them, he remarked about as follows: "John, I want you to know that we are going to miss you around here. I'm sure Grace agrees with that. You have been of much assistance to me and have

---

61 President Roosevelt's trip was precedent-shattering in a number of ways. In addition to being the first sitting president to fly his personal flag in an African port and celebrate his birthday on a plane, he was the first to visit the continent of Africa, to leave the United States during wartime, to fly a plane on official business, and the first since Lincoln to visit an active theater of war.

taken on many onerous tasks on my behalf to my complete satisfaction. As you are aware, the war has subjected me to many pressures, and you have helped me to bear those pressures. We are
going to miss you, and I have an idea that you are going to miss
Grace and me as well. Good luck to you, and I want you to know
that one day I hope to ride *Iowa* with you."

At that, I was a bit overcome. I admit there were tears in my
eyes. Suddenly it occurred to me that I was running off and leaving
this fine person with many, many problems, some of which I could
have helped to resolve. After all, what was *Iowa*? A battleship command—and I had long hoped to have one—but at this moment, I
felt selfish indeed to leave my respected commander in chief and
friend to satisfy my own personal whim.

The president more or less put me at ease by remarking, "Grace,
where is that little gift I have for John?" Miss Tully produced a fine
photograph of the president, which he then inscribed to me. The
inscription reads: "For Captain John L. McCrea, with affectionate
regards, Franklin D. Roosevelt, 3 February 1943."

"Now, John, you're due in the Map Room in a few minutes.
I'm supposed to be there, too." And off we went. Again, the president made a few complimentary remarks and presented to me, on
behalf of the Map Room watch group, an album containing a picture of every ship in which I had served to date.

At this point, I hope I will be pardoned if I quote the remarks
written by President Roosevelt in his own hand in my fitness report:

15 January 1942 to 31 March 1942. Captain McCrea has
given me every satisfaction as naval aide. He has shown tact
and ability in conference work with foreign naval and staff
missions, and also marked speed and efficiency in keeping and
getting current naval information to the commander in chief.

1 April 1942 to 3 February 1943. I am sorry to lose his
services as naval aide. His duties, especially in time of war,
are varied and difficult. He has shown real ability in his staff

work for me, in the position of secretary of the Pacific War Council, in his handling of the recent trip to North Africa, and in his coordination of war information.

I have greatly enjoyed having him with me.

My feelings on leaving the president were complex, a mixture of sadness, guilt, and a desire to be off. The president and I felt we understood each other. He knew I had done my very best for him and his staff. We both felt I had managed to lighten, in a small way, the heavy burdens that he carried. Although he might have preferred that I stay on, as someone who had been "in the navy," I think he understood my desire to go to sea to fight. He also knew that I was most grateful to have had the opportunity to be of service to him.

Chapter 17

Iowa Goes into Commission

—∞∞∞—

The work of preparing *Iowa* for commissioning began well before I left the White House. A first priority was the selection of *Iowa's* officers and crew. The Navy Department's Bureau of Personnel regarded the assignment of personnel to a new ship as its prerogative, so I had little say in the matter. The bureau's choice for *Iowa's* executive officer, my second in command, was Commander Thomas J. Casey. When his name was mentioned to me as a possible executive, I knew nothing about him, personally or officially. However, when I learned that a friend whose judgment I trusted had once requested Casey as executive for his heavy cruiser command, I informed the detail officer that Casey was acceptable to me.

The bureau's insistence on controlling personnel assignments gave rise to some friction, because I wanted certain people in *Iowa* with whom I had served in the past. In 1934–35, when I was the navigator of the heavy cruiser *Astoria*, I had come to know a young junior lieutenant by the name of Lynne C. Quiggle, Naval Academy class of 1930. Quiggle was a perfectionist in everything he did. He had command of one of *Astoria's* broadside divisions,[62]

---

62   A broadside division operates guns that fire outward from one side of the ship.

and I regarded his division as outstanding in every respect. I made up my mind that if I ever got a worthwhile command, I would use my best efforts to get him in my ship.

I contacted Quiggle, by then a commander, about his coming to *Iowa* as gunnery officer.[63] He was reluctant because he had recently been given a destroyer command. Quiggle and I had dinner one night to discuss the matter. I said I did not want him in *Iowa* if he didn't want to be there. However, I told him that as gunnery officer of *Iowa*, he could do more damage to the enemy with one salvo than could be inflicted by thirty destroyers. He stuck out his hand and said, "I want to go to *Iowa* with you."

I requested that the bureau appoint Quiggle as gunnery officer. He was an ordnance postgraduate and fully qualified for the job. The bureau flatly refused my request, on grounds that Quiggle was four years too junior for the assignment. After tempers had cooled a bit, I told the detail officer, a friend of many years' standing, that the bureau had appointed some 125 officers of its own choosing, and I thought it only fair that I have at least one officer whom I had specifically requested. In the end, I prevailed.

I also persuaded the Bureau of Personnel to permit me to have three enlisted men whose performance had impressed me in other ships. All of them did an outstanding job in *Iowa*. William T. McMahon ultimately became *Iowa*'s first lieutenant,[64] and Frank Duncan became *Iowa*'s chief police petty officer.[65] Jacob Prendergast

---

63 The job of gunnery officer was a key position in a battleship at war. The gunnery officer was in charge of the ship's gunnery department, which operated and maintained armament and cared for ammunition.

64 The job of the first lieutenant was to direct the deck department, responsible for the maintenance of the ship and its boats and for damage control. In a large ship like *Iowa*, the position was usually held by a commissioned officer.

65 The chief police petty officer, sometimes referred to as chief master-at-arms, was the ship's chief petty officer in charge of policing and internal security.

came to *Iowa* as the chief gunner.[66] In short order, he was given command of turret number three, relieving a young junior lieutenant reserve officer, a commissioned officer who outranked him. While earnest, the junior lieutenant had no experience managing a division of some one hundred men, or commanding a turret. I hated to remove his command, but *Iowa* was in the midst of a war, and to measure up, she had to effectively meet the war's demands.

The rest of *Iowa's* crew was assembled from here, there, and all over. If memory serves, the day we went in commission, we had roughly 130 officers and 2,500 enlisted men, including marines. Later, the ship had about 150 officers and around 2,650 enlisted men.

I reported to the commandant of the Third Naval District for duty as prospective commanding officer of the *Iowa* on 8 February 1943. The ship was at the New York Navy Yard in Brooklyn. The ship's commissioning had been postponed until late February, and pre-commission work for the ship had been proceeding in my absence under the supervision of Commander Casey, *Iowa's* prospective executive officer.

The pre-commission work for *Iowa* involved setting up and organizing all of the ship's departments. The work was substantial because *Iowa* was the first ship of her class, and all the departments had to be organized from scratch. Our only guideline was experience in ships of similar type. Our task was to organize and to develop effective ways to delegate and supervise. Commander Casey already had much of this work in hand by the time I arrived in New York.

While the organizational work was going on, *Iowa* made much use of the many schools established by the Navy Department to instruct crew members and others in such matters as the fundamentals of going to sea, fire and damage control procedures, and

---

66 In WWII, the chief gunner provided technical expertise concerning the ship's guns and the fire control devices used for aiming.

the like. Hundreds of men were sent to every one of the schools prior to the ship's commissioning.

Iowa's commissioning took place on Washington's birthday, 22 February 1943. The ceremonies were held on the quarterdeck of the ship, where the ship's company and guests had been assembled. The heads of the ship's departments, Commander Casey and I, together with Frank Knox, the secretary of the navy, and other high ranking navy and civilian officials, were under the guns of the after turret, facing aft. The weather was pretty good for February in New York.

There were a number of speakers, of which I was the last. After some preliminary remarks, I addressed fully half of my speech to *Iowa*'s officers and men. I spoke of the challenges we faced in properly commissioning a ship of *Iowa*'s size during wartime, the work left to be done, and the limited time to accomplish it. Most important, I stated my goals for the ship:

> I expect a clean ship.
> I expect a smart ship.
> Above all, I expect a fighting ship.

In conclusion, I remarked,

> As you all know, much remains to be done. The tremendous amount of work thus far accomplished augurs well for the future which you and I face together . . . with determination and confidence. Our commander in chief, our secretary, and our brothers in arms will expect much of us. We cannot and must not fail them.

A word of explanation is in order about my expectations for *Iowa*, which were already well known to the ship's company as a result of training. Obviously, a "clean ship" is one that is well maintained. Cleanliness is a prerequisite for an effective war ship. Smartness is harder to define. A "smart ship" is outstanding in literally hundreds of things, especially officer and petty officer control, seamanship, compliance with regulations, pride in performance, personal dignity, and self-discipline. A smart ship is always ready to do the job and do it well, whether the job is routine or otherwise.

As the term implies, a "fighting ship" is one that is battle-ready. Its men demonstrate two essential characteristics: battle discipline and mastery of their ship and its equipment. Battle discipline is achieved when all orders are carried out instinctively, instantaneously, and expertly while under stress and in adverse conditions. In training, cleanliness and smartness are stressed because they contribute significantly to battle discipline. Mastery is the product of rigorous training. Every officer and man must learn every detail of his job. The men must know the capabilities and limitations of their equipment and become expert in its use. And everyone must learn to be battle-minded, resourceful, and enterprising. These goals would be the object of intensive training in the months ahead.

After my speech came the commissioning ceremony. It was short and to the point. I commanded my executive to break the commissioning flag, set the watch, and then break the flag of the secretary of the navy. When these orders were carried out, I announced, "The USS *Iowa* is now officially a ship of the United States Navy and in the service of this country."

Following the ceremonies, a midday meal was served to the crew, and a luncheon for guests was served in the officers' mess. I hosted a small luncheon in my cabin. My seventy-seven-year-old mother and Secretary Knox hit it off during lunch. Mr. Knox told me later that she had said I was too young to have command of such a large ship. I was then approaching my fifty-second birthday, but I suppose we all remain children to our mothers. All in all, *Iowa*'s commissioning was a fine occasion.

Picking up the New York papers the next day, I was disturbed to note a detailed spread, datelined Washington, D.C., about the commissioning and the ship. For security reasons, the commissioning of men-of-war during wartime was supposed to be done with a minimum of press coverage. The press had to agree not to disclose the name of the ship, its size, arms, speed, and other details. I soon learned that after luncheon, Secretary Knox had dashed back to Washington and, bubbling with enthusiasm, he had called a press conference at which he had revealed much more about the commissioning than he should have. I don't believe that he identified *Iowa* by name, but he told so much about the ship that anyone with any curiosity would have been able to identify her.

Shortly afterward, I received a letter of caution signed by Admiral Frederick J. Horne, the vice chief of naval operations, inviting the attention of the commanding officer of *Iowa* to the fact that information supplied to the press about his command had to be within the limits set in Navy Department letter number so-and-so, and this procedure had not been followed in the commissioning of *Iowa*. Long ago I had learned that arguing with seniors on matters of little importance was useless, so *Iowa* merely acknowledged receipt of the letter of caution.

The next week I was in Washington and took the opportunity to discuss the caution with Admiral Horne, a good friend. I pointed out that all the offending press reports on the commissioning had Washington datelines, and that I had been informed that the news release came from Secretary Knox. I added that I would appreciate being told how I, a laborer in the fields, could control an exuberant secretary of the navy if he wished to hold a news conference about the activities of his day. Admiral Horne and I had a good laugh, and that was that.

Although *Iowa* was in commission, she was not yet ready to go to sea. Having participated in the commissioning of the cruiser *Astoria,* I knew that a newly commissioned ship requires much work before it is ready for sea trials. At the same time, I believed it important that *Iowa* clear away from the yard as soon as possible. A ship must be self-contained. It must acquire the ability to identify and solve its own problems with its own resources, if possible. With this in mind, I made every effort to leave the yard promptly.

Iowa remained at the navy yard for about a month. All sorts of problems in operations cropped up, some foreseen, some not, and all had to be resolved. In addition, last-minute construction details were completed, stores and equipment were loaded, and there was an intensive effort to train the ship's company in their new duties. Instruction, drills, and inspections were routine.

One of the first deficiencies I addressed was the matter of dress among the crew. I had noticed a tendency in some ships at the navy yard to relax uniform regulations to the point that the men wore pretty much what they pleased. As far as I was concerned, that would not happen in *Iowa*. I realize that correct uniform may seem trivial to some, but I believe that everything that goes on in a ship, including adherence to dress regulations, has a bearing on battle discipline.

As a nation, we do not regiment easily, and this is particularly true with the young. Appearing in correct uniform for the occasion requires a certain amount of self-discipline. Self-discipline in time becomes a habit, and good habits contribute significantly to discipline under stress. A sloppily dressed, unkempt crew cannot be expected to turn in an acceptable performance during battle.

My approach to obtaining compliance with dress regulations was one I had used in other ships. I made it my business to wear the correct uniform at all times, setting an example for both officers and men. It wasn't long before all hands caught on.

There was much interest in *Iowa* among those who knew of the ship. One person I knew would have an interest was my old friend, Rear Admiral Husband E. Kimmel. Following the attack on Pearl Harbor, he had been quickly relieved of command of the Pacific Fleet, and he had retired from the navy. At the time *Iowa* was at the navy yard, he was in the employ of a New York engineering firm headed by an Annapolis classmate. I could not leave the ship, but Tom Casey, my executive, agreed to deliver to the admiral my invitation to lunch in *Iowa* with Casey, Commander Quiggle (*Iowa*'s gunnery officer), and myself. I limited the group to assure Admiral Kimmel that his visit to the ship would be a quiet affair.

After the luncheon, we made an extensive tour of the ship. Kimmel took a great interest in everything. When he left the ship, I saw a tear in his eye as he bade me good-bye. He remarked, "Thank you, John. This is the nicest and kindest thing that has come my way since the Pearl Harbor attack."

On the morning of 24 March 1943, *Iowa* cast off her mooring lines and headed down the East River. We passed under the Manhattan and Brooklyn Bridges and into New York Harbor. That afternoon, the ship went into dry dock in Bayonne, New Jersey, for inspection of her hull. A few days later, we moved to an anchorage at Gravesend Bay, adjacent to the Narrows at the entrance of New York Harbor. There the ship could operate independently, but the yard was nearby in case problems arose that were beyond the ship's capacity to solve.

At the anchorage, we loaded ammunition and prepared for the first test fire of the ship's main battery, the sixteen-inch turret guns, and the secondary battery of five-inch guns. When all arrangements were made, *Iowa* went to sea and fired one round per gun. Everything went well.

Chapter 18

Shakedown

—∞∞∞—

In mid-April 1943, *Iowa* left the New York area. With three escorting destroyers, she traveled to Chesapeake Bay, where she was to spend five weeks on her "shakedown cruise."[67] During shakedown, the crew is supposed to get acquainted with operating its new ship under sea conditions, but *Iowa*'s cruise was significantly hampered by the locale selected and *Iowa*'s size.

At the time, German submarines dominated the Atlantic. U.S. destroyers were urgently needed to screen vessels and convoys on war missions, and none could be spared to do screening duty on a shakedown cruise. Accordingly, it was decided that *Iowa* would shake down in Chesapeake Bay, a protected area where screening vessels would not be required.

While the Chesapeake is protected, it is a shallow body of water. *Iowa* was the first of the forty-five-thousand-ton battleships. Her length overall was 887 feet, 3 inches, and her beam was 108 feet, 2 inches. Normally she drew in the neighborhood of forty

---

67 A shakedown cruise is a sea trial for a new ship. The vessel's systems and seaworthiness are tested, and the crew learns to operate the ship while under way. Such trials are generally performed in open water.

feet. To operate in the bay, *Iowa* had to make a number of adjustments. To reduce her draft, she could carry no more than a quarter of her fuel capacity. Her speed could not exceed twelve knots, so that a minimum of bottom sand would find its way into her condensers. Even with these adjustments, she could operate only in certain areas of the bay.

Obviously, maneuvering was greatly curtailed during shakedown. Maneuvering machinery could not be tested as it would have been had *Iowa* been operating on the high seas at speeds limited only by design. Thus, the engineering department could accomplish little.[68]

Of course, shallow water and limited space did not affect numerous other activities, which were performed in the usual manner. General upkeep and gunnery drills were unaffected. There were day and night firing drills, and searchlight and airplane exercises. Other activities included lecture courses with notebook assignments for officers, educational films, and first aid training. Although *Iowa*'s shakedown lacked thoroughness in many, many ways, it was about as good as conditions would permit.

When *Iowa* arrived in the Chesapeake Bay area, many people wanted to see the ship. We spent weekends at anchor off Annapolis Roads, a convenient time and place for visitors, and visitors of high and low rank descended upon us. We received all sorts of naval personnel and many members of Congress, especially members of the House and Senate Naval Affairs Committees.

One fine day *Iowa* received a dispatch from Admiral Ernest J. King, the chief of naval operations, indicating that he would visit the following morning. His visit was to be completely informal— no shifting of the flags, side honors only, no formal inspection, and no interruption of routine training.

---

68 The engineering department is responsible for operating, maintaining, and repairing the ship's propulsion systems, including engines, boilers, and electrical equipment.

I knew Admiral King to be a man of few words and hard as nails. I cautioned the ship's people about this, advising complete and frank answers to his questions. In preparation for the admiral's visit, we had the ship's plans laid out in my cabin, where he could inspect them should he care to.

The next morning, the admiral arrived accompanied by a couple of members of his staff. The heads of departments and I showed him about the ship. We started on the upper conning platform and worked our way down.[69] In addition to answering questions, we remarked on areas where improvement could and should be made. In particular, I noted that the charthouse working space, where the navigation charts were laid out, was a substantial distance—some thirty-six paces—from the normal conning position of the commanding officer. After the forenoon's activities, I had luncheon in my cabin for Admiral King, his staff members, and the heads of *Iowa*'s departments.

After lunch, the tour of the ship resumed. Admiral King was a keen observer and greatly interested in the progress that had been made in whipping the ship into shape. His inspection was thorough. He carefully examined one of the sixteen-inch turrets from gun chamber to magazine. He also inspected a five-inch mount, a forty-millimeter mount, and a twenty-millimeter mount, together with their respective ammunition supplies. The turret was manned at the time of inspection, as were the other guns. There was no interruption in the ship's work as we went about the ship.

The admiral was greatly interested in the crew's living and berthing facilities and was pleased with what he saw. I was pleased as well. The admiral could not help but notice that the crew was in appropriate uniform for the work at hand. As the afternoon inspection continued, I felt we had given him a pretty good show,

69 To conn means to control the steering of a ship or the place where conning is done.

but the admiral had not uttered a word suggesting how he felt in the matter.

Shortly after 4:00 p.m., the admiral decided to leave the ship. We walked to the gangway. The eight side boys were drawn up at attention.[70] The bugler sounded attention on the bugle. Then, and only then, did Admiral King indicate to me his reaction to his visit. We shook hands, and he remarked firmly, "Captain McCrea, I have enjoyed my visit to *Iowa* this day. I sense that the seeds of discipline have been planted in this ship. Good day."

Admiral King stepped on the outer grating, saluted the colors, descended the accommodation ladder, and boarded *Iowa's* gig, which set out for Annapolis's inner harbor. Of course, I was pleased with what he had said, and I thought that the ship's company should know about it. On the way to my cabin, I stopped at the quartermaster's desk and wrote: "Admiral King, on leaving the ship a few minutes ago, remarked that he was pleased by what he saw on *Iowa* today." I handed the memo to the officer of the deck, remarking, "When the gig is out of earshot, have this word passed." It had been a good day indeed for *Iowa*.

Towards the end of the shakedown cruise, I thought it appropriate to address the ship's company to take stock of what we had accomplished in training and what remained to be done before we were battle-ready. At the outset, I acknowledged that we had made considerable progress. I told them that under ordinary circumstances, I would not ask for more, but these were unusual times.

I knew many of the men were young and new to the navy, and I doubted they had a clear idea of what we would face in battle. To

---

70 Side boys are the seamen who line up on either side of the gangway when a dignitary boards or leaves a navy ship. The number of side boys is determined by the rank of the dignitary—the higher the rank, the greater the number of side boys. The practice originated in the days of sail, when dignitaries were hoisted aboard in a boatswain's chair. Since dignitaries of high rank were usually older and heavier, they required larger numbers of side boys to assist them.

impress on them why their training must be thorough, I commenced the heart of my remarks with an assessment of the war and our adversaries.

> Every one of us must realize that this country is engaged in a worldwide war with ruthless enemies who are bent on destroying us and our government. . . . [T]he outcome of this war is still in doubt. . . . From our earliest days at school, we have been told of the invincibility of American arms. . . . Well, that just isn't so.

I said that every previous war our country had fought, including World War I, was a street corner brawl compared to this one. I likened the U.S. conflict with Japan to two undefeated champs in a ring, fighting to the death. There are no rules. The winner will be the one that gets in the most solid and timely blows.

Next, I discussed the fighting abilities of our three possible adversaries, the navies of Italy, Germany, and Japan, focusing primarily on the Japanese. I described my visit to a Japanese destroyer in Tsingtao, China, twenty years before, and my impression of the Japanese sailors. They drilled all day, every day. I marveled at their precision and endurance. They lived in primitive conditions on meager rations, yet I was struck by their ruggedness and physical hardihood. I noted that this ruggedness and hardihood, coupled with the fanaticism with which the Japanese go about the business of war, has made them difficult to beat. They show an utter disregard of human life and the rules of civilized warfare.

Completing my analysis of our potential foes, I asked, "Are we ready to meet the enemy?" and answered my own question. "You and I know we are not." I described what was necessary to achieve readiness. Every officer and man must know every detail of his job. Everyone must be "battle-minded," and each man must know the capabilities and limitations of the equipment he operates. Above all, every man must acquire "battle discipline" through prompt and instant obedience to all orders and through self-discipline.

Noting that some men might not think their battle stations important, I stated that "the ship has urgent need for every one of you men in your assigned station." I described how each man's individual performance was crucial to the performance and safety of the ship as a whole:

> Instinctively, you all expect that when the ship is in danger and your lives are at stake, the necessary action to protect you and the ship will by ordered by the commanding officer. But such orders will be of little effect if the chain of transmission is broken because some officer or man has not disciplined himself sufficiently in small things to the point that he obeys instinctively in the heat of battle. Let me suggest to you fire-men standing before your boiler fronts, you men in the mag-azines, you lookouts in the tops, there must be no more lonely feeling on this earth than to occupy those stations in battle without full confidence that the ship organization is working as a whole—that you are not fighting a one-man battle.

I acknowledged the size and complexity of the challenges we faced in putting our ship together to get the most out of her. "Mistakes will be made, but we will recognize and correct them." I also acknowledged that the demands of the service might be difficult for some to accept.

> You men have been brought up in an atmosphere of liberal-ism which emphasized the importance of the individual, but you must—and the older men will bear me out in this—for-get a good bit of that in the navy. Individuals in this ship count for nothing compared to the demands of the ship and the service, and that goes for me as well as everyone else in the ship's company.

I observed that many men new to the service might find service ways unreasonable. I noted that service ways were the outgrowth of many years of experience. Nevertheless, I indicated that

> [i]f any of you have suggestions as to how things can better be done, remember that your suggestions, honestly and frankly put, will always receive full consideration by your division officer, and the executive officer, and by myself.

In concluding, I restated my three goals for *Iowa* that I had set in my commissioning speech—a clean ship, a smart ship, and a fighting ship—and I summarized what remained to be done to achieve them. Finally, I remarked that when we had achieved these things, we would

> have the sort of ship in which you and I will be proud to serve. It will then be the sort of ship on which our country and our commander in chief can count. It will be the sort of ship that when our moment comes, the enemy will have reason to believe she is truly the largest and most powerful ship in the world.[71]

Iowa completed her shakedown cruise in late May. We departed Chesapeake Bay and proceeded north to Bayonne, New Jersey, where the ship entered dry dock for an exchange of her propellers. In late June, we headed north to Casco Bay, Maine, for a second phase of shakedown activities off the Maine coast.

---

71 The complexity of *Iowa*'s equipment and the teamwork required to operate it is evident in a 1955 navy training film on the operation of an *Iowa*-class gun turret with its three independent sixteen-inch guns (https://www.youtube.com/watch?v=_wT1xkRpCKk). A single turret employed seventy-nine men doing specialized tasks on different levels within the turret.

Chapter 19

Aground

———❦———

At this point, *Iowa*'s story reaches an unanticipated low. It would be easy to play down this incident and my part in it. Nevertheless, I shall tell the yarn as I see it. In July 1943, *Iowa* traveled from New York to Casco Bay, Maine. In mid-afternoon on 16 July, *Iowa* made her approach to Casco. The tide was low. I, of course, was at the conn. A bit belatedly, I started to turn to starboard to enter the gate, and in the midst of the turn, *Iowa* hit a rock about amidships on the port side. The impact damaged the hull some twenty feet below the waterline, creating a gash about fifty feet in length. *Iowa*'s entrance to the harbor was not slowed, and the ship proceeded to its assigned anchorage. A diver was called, and he gave a cursory report on the damage.

I immediately drafted a dispatch to the commander in chief of the Atlantic Fleet, with the chief of naval operations as an information addressee. The dispatch read about as follows: "At such-and-such time, *Iowa*, entering Casco Bay, captain at the conn, struck a submerged rock and did undetermined damage to the hull on the port side from about amidships and aft."

I called in a group of senior officers: Tom Casey; the navigator, Commander William J. Whiteside; the first lieutenant and damage control officer, George A. Leahey; and Lynne Quiggle. I read the draft dispatch to them and asked for comment. All recommended that the words "captain at the conn" be eliminated. I thanked them for their counsel, but I flatly overruled them. The dispatch was sent.

As it turned out, that dispatch produced the only positive repercussion of this incident. Some years afterward, a brother naval officer stopped me in the front corridor of the Navy Department. He was my senior, and I knew him only slightly. He remarked, "John, for some time I've had it on my mind to say something to you about your dispatch reporting *Iowa*'s Casco Bay casualty to higher authority. Whether you know it or not, you earned credit for character in the Navy Department for including the words 'captain at the conn.' I just thought you'd like to know the reaction here."

I return to July 1943 and that fateful day. Of course, I regretted the damage to the ship, but I knew it could be repaired. The greatest damage was to my pride. I had always been a good shiphandler. I had had command of three ships prior to *Iowa*, two destroyers and a large minesweeper, and I had also handled the heavy cruiser *Astoria,* and the battleship *Pennsylvania*. I had managed all of them without mishap and, for the most part, in close quarters. And now here, with the largest and newest ship in the navy under my command, I had pulled a cropper.

As noted earlier, I had complained about the distance between the charthouse and the normal conning area, forward of the conning tower. In fact, that very morning I had shown the problem to the assistant chief of Construction and Repair, never imagining I would demonstrate the gravity of the problem later that afternoon. But the responsibility was mine, pure and simple. We had negotiated the entrance to Casco Bay before, and there was enough water for the ship. My judgment as to when to put the rudder over was in error. But I can tell you I was crushed.

Earlier in the day, I had signaled one of our escorting destroyers and invited the captain, William R. Smedberg, to dine with me that evening. I was immensely fond of "Smeddy." We had worked together for Admiral Stark when he was chief of naval operations. After the accident, I did not withdraw the invitation, but Smeddy's company, while charming, didn't improve my mood.

After Smeddy had gone, I sat for some time feeling very much alone. I pondered the day's happenings. Until the moment I felt the impact of *Iowa* on the rock, I had held a good opinion of myself as a shiphandler. I was reminded that "pride goeth before a fall." I was aware that in those few fateful seconds, I had disappointed many, and confirmed the suspicion of many others that I was not much of a naval officer after all. I was distressed and depressed.

I wrote a hurried note to my wife. I was sure she would sympathize with me. And then I wrote a short personal note to Admiral King. It read about as follows: "Dear Admiral King, by now you have heard of *Iowa*'s misfortune this afternoon. I know you will do what you think is best for the navy, but I would hope I would not lose command of *Iowa*. Sincerely." Admiral King never replied to my note, nor did he ever refer to it in subsequent years. No doubt he realized that I had written in haste and under strain, and chose to ignore it.

Higher authority ordered an investigation into the incident a few days later. The senior of the investigative group was Rear Admiral Morton L. Deyo, whom I knew well. *Iowa*'s navigator and I were the defendants.

When the proceedings commenced, I asked permission to read a statement of events, and began to read. I hadn't gotten far when Admiral Deyo remarked that it was 9:30 a.m., the hour for his morning coffee, and he was declaring a recess. He invited me to have coffee with him.

As soon as we were in his cabin, he said, "John, do you realize what you are doing? Every word of your remarks can be used against you in this proceeding."

"Admiral Deyo," I responded, "Thank you for your interest in me and my situation. However, I have done three tours of duty in the Office of the Judge Advocate General and passed judgment on many boards of investigation and courts of inquiry involving damage to ships. As a result of those experiences, I came to feel that the navy, as owner of the ships, should be entitled to know about the events that affected its property. Therefore, I decided that if I ever became a defendant in such a proceeding, I would not avail myself of the defendant's right to have the navy establish the facts against me.

"I am aware that I am entitled to sit back and let the Judge Advocate General prove its case. I choose not to do this. As *Iowa*'s commanding officer, I feel I owe it to the navy to voluntarily make available every bit of information I have about the incident, no matter how involved I might be. That is the way I feel about it, Admiral, and after this recess, that is what I plan to do.

"Again, I thank you for your interest, and for the coffee, too. Of course, I expect to be questioned by you and other members of the investigating panel, and I assure you that my answers will be as full and complete as possible."

Well, that is the way the proceeding went. In the end, I was given a letter of reprimand, which I certainly deserved, and *Iowa* was sent to the Boston navy yard for repairs.

Later, Ross McIntire told me that at the time of the *Iowa* inquiry, he had asked the president if there was anything that could be done to help me. According to Ross, the president replied, "The worst thing that could happen to John in his career would be for me to interfere with the naval process." However, the president did send me a box of Cuban cigars. President Batista of Cuba used to send him small lockers of Cuban cigars, but he never smoked them. I was a cigar smoker then, and while I was at the White House, I was well supplied. The note accompanying the president's gift merely stated, "I know you like good cigars. FDR." What a gentleman, and what a nice touch.

Chapter 20

Plans for a Secret Mission

———— ⊙⊛⊙ ————

In August 1943, upon completion of *Iowa*'s hull repairs, the ship was sent to the U.S. naval base in Argentia, Newfoundland,[72] for more training and her first operational assignment, a watch for the German battleship *Tirpitz*. *Tirpitz* was based in a northern Norwegian fjord, and the Allies feared she would raid convoys bound for the Soviet Union. Argentia was on the route taken by the convoys and a natural base for countering any such raids.

Argentia was rugged and inhospitable. It had frequent storms with high winds, there was no holding ground at the anchorage, and there were treacherous currents in the passage from the harbor to Placentia Bay. One bright spot during our time there was the

---

72 Naval Station Argentia was established in early 1941 in what was then the British Dominion of Newfoundland, now Canada. The anchorage at the base was the site of the Atlantic Conference, held August 9–12, 1941, where President Roosevelt, Prime Minister Churchill, and their military leaders met on naval vessels to discuss the geopolitical situation in Europe and their war aims. The joint declaration issued by Roosevelt and Churchill at the end of the conference, known as the Atlantic Charter, set forth their vision for the post-war world and was the first in a series of policy statements and agreements that led to the formation of the United Nations in 1945.

arrival in the mail of a large box addressed to me from the White House. Inside was a beautiful afghan, hand-knit by Mrs. Roosevelt, with a note reading, "The president and I trust that this will keep you warm in your new ship." My wife told me that when I left the White House, Mrs. Roosevelt had asked her whether I needed anything. Estelle told her she had just thrown out my old afghan, and this was the result. I was deeply touched.

After some eight uncomfortable weeks in and around Argentia, we were supposed to participate in a few days' operations at sea. The day of our departure was surprisingly pleasant, with bright sunshine and gentle winds. *Iowa* had just slipped her mooring and was proceeding to sea when the communication messenger came to the bridge with an envelope marked "Secret." I opened the envelope. The message was from the commander in chief of the U.S. Fleet:

> *Iowa*, proceed to Hampton Roads. On arrival, report to Commander in Chief Atlantic for duty as may be assigned. Advise as to estimated time of arrival.

I handed the dispatch to Tom Casey, saying, "As soon as you have digested this, Tom, please have the word passed on the loudspeaker that *Iowa* is en route to Hampton Roads, Virginia." The word passed. In seconds, there were cheers from nearly three thousand throats throughout the ship. What a pleasure to be bound for Hampton Roads!

We anchored at Hampton Roads on a Sunday afternoon in late October 1943. I proceeded immediately to USS *Vixen*, the administrative flagship of the commander in chief of the Atlantic Fleet, which was flying the four-star flag of Admiral Royal E. Ingersoll. Admiral Ingersoll and I were friends, having both served with Admiral Harold Stark when he was chief of naval operations.

After an exchange of pleasantries, Admiral Ingersoll remarked, "I suppose you know why you are here."

"No, sir, I do not."

"You are going to take the president and the Joint Chiefs of Staff in *Iowa* to the Mediterranean.[73] You are to go to Washington and report to Admiral King tomorrow morning. He wants to talk with you about the details of the trip. Secrecy is imperative.

"Of course, *Iowa* will have to be readied to receive the president. His physical condition requires special arrangements. From the ship's plans, it seems that the captain's cabin will accommodate him better than the admiral's cabin, and it has more deck space available to him outside.

"One thing that will take a few days is the installation of a bathtub in the captain's bath space. The tub will fit in the area occupied by your shower. We want *Iowa* to dock at the naval operating base at 6:30 a.m. tomorrow so work can get started." I should note that the president needed a square bathtub with the basin set diagonally. The sides of such a tub were wide and afforded solid support for his arms when he maneuvered himself in and out of the tub.

The admiral and I agreed that I would fly to Washington in his plane the following morning and return by boat in the afternoon. He cautioned me again about the secrecy of the arrangements, and I departed.

On my return to *Iowa*, I told Commander Casey what was in the wind. "The bath installation cannot be secret. To stop the ques-

---

73 The president and the Joint Chiefs were to attend three conferences abroad. At the First Cairo Conference (November 22–26, 1943), they were to meet with Prime Minister Churchill, his top military leaders, and Generalissimo Chiang Kai-shek of China to discuss problems in the war with Japan in Asia. Then the president, the prime minister, and their military entourage were to attend the Tehran Conference (November 28–December 1) to meet with Stalin to discuss strategy in the war against Germany, and particularly the opening of a second front in Europe. Finally, the American–British group returned to Cairo for a Second Cairo Conference (December 2–7) with Turkish leaders to discuss Turkey's possible entrance into the war.

tions about it, Tom, drop the word that I have evidently gone a bit soft and have arranged to remove my shower and install a tub in its place. Word will spread fast, I assure you."

The next morning I arrived at Admiral King's office in the Navy Department about nine o'clock. Here I digress a moment to say that, in my book, Admiral King was everything a naval officer should be. He was ramrod straight and carried himself with dignity. He was strictly business and a man of few words. While his manner was cold and forbidding, and he had a service reputation for being quick-tempered, I always found it a pleasure to work with him. He was a no-fooling guy, and I preferred a no-fooling officer to the wishy-washy type. In my view, there were many others who could have performed well as commander in chief of the U.S. Fleet in time of war, but the country was fortunate to have a man of King's stature.

While waiting for Admiral King, I talked to Admiral Richard S. Edwards, King's deputy, about the upcoming operation. When I got in to see King, he remarked on the importance of the mission, the secrecy required, and the problem of *Iowa's* coming up with bunks for forty or more additional people. He added, "Your destination in the Mediterranean has not yet been decided, but we will determine that soon. What causes me some concern is where *Iowa* should remain while the conferences at Cairo and Tehran are going on."

I remarked that Admiral Edwards had told me that *Iowa* would return to the United States, and the group would be given westward passage in a heavy cruiser. There was a moment of ominous silence. When Admiral King spoke, his manner made me almost sorry I had said anything. "I shall not permit the president to make a December crossing of the Atlantic in a heavy cruiser. *Iowa* will remain available for that duty."

The admiral outlined the plans for the president's departure from Washington. On 11 November 1943, the president would attend the ceremonies at the Tomb of the Unknown Soldier at

Arlington Cemetery. That afternoon he would board his yacht *Potomac* at the navy yard and proceed to the marine base at Quantico, Virginia. There he would take a special train to Newport News, Virginia, and board *Iowa* during daylight hours on 12 November 1943, the day of departure. As part of the effort to maintain secrecy, the *Potomac* would proceed to Chesapeake Bay and remain there while the president was abroad. Our talk at an end, Admiral King informed me that the president wished to see me.

I repaired to the White House. Except for a brief conversation at a news correspondents' dinner, I had not seen the president since my detachment from the White House in February. He was in fine fettle and looked to be in good health. His zest for living was enormous.

"I suppose Ernie has told you about this upcoming trip," said he. "I am looking forward to it greatly. There is nothing so wonderful as a sea voyage by way of relaxation." And on and on. "I must be here for the Arlington Cemetery ceremonies on 11 November. The appearance of the president at these ceremonies is too well-established to be avoided." The president emphasized the importance of secrecy and "supposed that all necessary details would be worked out with Ernie."

I reported back to Admiral King about my talk with the president and left Washington about 6:30 p.m. on a Norfolk-bound boat. After dining, I retired to my stateroom to write a memorandum about things to be done in connection with *Iowa*'s upcoming assignment. One item stood out: secrecy. I was dubious about the arrangements described to me. It seemed unlikely the president could travel by special train without his movements becoming known all over Tidewater Virginia. Wasn't there a better solution? Couldn't *Iowa* contribute?

I spent an hour on deck pondering these questions. The experience of maneuvering *Iowa* in shallow water during her Chesapeake shakedown gave me an idea so simple that I was annoyed I hadn't thought of it sooner. Essentially, my plan was this: While *Iowa* was at the Norfolk naval base, 80 percent of her fuel would be pumped out to reduce her draft. *Iowa* would then move to Hampton Roads and upload the special equipment required for the president. This included extra handrails, a couple of small elevators, and other items. Thereafter *Iowa* would proceed to the mouth of the Potomac River, anchor, and install the special equipment. The presidential party on *Potomac* would travel down the river at night and board *Iowa* after first light on the day of departure, 12 November. Afterward, *Iowa* would return to Hampton Roads, receive two naval tankers—one on either side—and fuel to capacity. Once fueled, she could sail for the Mediterranean any time the tides would serve.

The more I thought about this plan, the better I liked it. In fact, I felt pretty much what Jack Horner must have felt when he pulled the plum out of that pie. The next thing was to sleep on it. If I still thought well of my proposal in the morning, I would take action.

My boat arrived at Norfolk about 6:30 a.m. Proceeding directly to *Iowa*, I talked briefly with Commander Casey and the navigator about my plan, and consulted a Chesapeake Bay chart, not available to me the night before. Armed with the probable depth of high water slack at about 11:15 p.m. on the night of 12 November, I went to see Admiral Ingersoll. He listened to my proposal and approved. He told me to return to Washington to present my idea to Admiral King, and made his plane available for the round trip.

Back in Admiral King's office for the second time in twenty-four hours, I explained my plan. King listened patiently, looked at the chart, and asked about the time required to refuel *Iowa*. When I assured him that two tankers could do it in about four and a half hours, he said, "I approve of your proposal. It contributes substantially to secrecy and reduces wear and tear on the president." He directed me to go immediately to discuss the plan with the president.

The president liked my idea. "Tell Ernie I approve the change. It will be pleasant going down the Potomac at night."

When I delivered the president's message, Admiral King indicated he would ride his flagship USS *Dauntless* to meet *Iowa* in the Potomac on the afternoon of 11 November, and he would invite generals Marshall and Arnold to accompany him. *Dauntless* would also give passage to the Joint Chiefs of Staff personnel who were going to the conferences. These included generals and flag officers down to enlisted clerical workers.

The bathtub installation was completed in a few days, and *Iowa* commenced preparations to receive our guests. The secretary to the Joint Chiefs furnished me with a list of our passengers. While the president's special equipment was installed, we made plans for the smooth embarkation and quartering of our guests. Having served as executive officer of the *Pennsylvania* when she was the flagship of the U.S. Fleet, I was not unacquainted with the problem of looking out for distinguished visitors.

We assigned quarters and messing arrangements. The president would occupy the captain's quarters and mess there as well. The president's personal staff—Admiral Leahy; Harry Hopkins; Vice Admiral Wilson Brown, the president's naval aide; Admiral Ross McIntire; and General Watson—would take meals with the president. General Marshall, General Arnold, and Admiral King were to dine at a mess set up in the flag quarters for officers of the rank of army colonel, navy captain, and above. Officers of lesser rank and members of the Secret Service were messed in the wardroom.

We assigned to each visiting officer an officer escort to show the visitor to his quarters, see that his personal effects were delivered, and put the visitor at his ease throughout the trip. We also prepared a small brochure that listed facts about the ship and other useful information.

On the morning of 11 November, *Iowa* got under way into the Potomac. At this point, the ship's company would have no further contact with the shore, so it was possible to make an announcement over the loudspeaker system about the nature of the upcoming trip. Quite naturally, the announcement caused a stir of excitement.

About mid-afternoon, *Dauntless*, flying the flag of Admiral King, was sighted standing down the Potomac. On board were Admiral King, generals Marshall and Arnold, Lieutenant General Brehon B. Somervell, and staff officers. *Iowa's* executive officer and I greeted our passengers and introduced them to their escorts. The army and the air forces officers went on tours of the ship. Later I had tea in my cabin for senior officers.

Since *Iowa* was at anchor, I undertook to be Admiral King's escort. After tea, he asked about the arrangements made by *Iowa* for the trip. I showed him our brochure and the assignment of passengers' quarters, and he expressed his approval. Next he asked to look about the ship. On concluding his tour, he said to me exactly what he had said when he inspected *Iowa* at Annapolis in April 1943: "The seeds of discipline seem to have been planted in this ship."

Early the next morning, 12 November, the president and his party boarded *Iowa* in the lower Potomac off Point Lookout. Directly after the party was transferred, *Iowa* weighed anchor and proceeded to Hampton Roads for refueling.

That evening the president invited me to have dinner "in *my* mess," as he put it—lately the captain's mess. Present were Harry Hopkins, Admiral Leahy, Admiral Wilson Brown, and Pa Watson. During dinner, the president inquired when I proposed to get *Iowa* under way. "We should complete fueling about ten-thirty tonight, sir," said I. "High-water slack will be at eleven-thirty and, subject to your approval, I would recommend that we get under way at that time."

"You know, John, today is Friday," said the president. "We are about to start on an important mission. Before it is over, many important decisions must be made. I'm just sailor enough to share the sailor's superstition that Friday is an unlucky day. Do you suppose that you could delay departure until Saturday? This, of course, without affecting your plans too much." My reply was in the affirmative.

Fueling completed, the tankers shoved off, and *Iowa* made preparations for departure. The sea details went to their stations at 11:45 p.m. The anchor was brought to short stay, and on Saturday, 13 November at 0001 hours—12:01 a.m. landlubber time— orders were given to heave up. Four minutes later, the *Iowa* was under way for the Mediterranean, escorted by three destroyers. As a security precaution at sea, strict radio silence was to be observed, and the ships were to be darkened at night.

Chapter 21

Voyage to Algeria

—∞∞∞—

Iowa's destination in the Mediterranean was Mers-el-Kébir, the seaport of the city of Oran in northwestern Algeria. For simplicity's sake, I shall refer to it as Oran. According to plan, once *Iowa* cleared the Virginia Capes en route for the Strait of Gibraltar, she would cruise at a standard speed of 25 knots, though she was capable of 32.5 knots at full speed. *Iowa* would use zigzag plan steering, an antisubmarine tactic. Because of zigzagging, she would advance along a straight-line base course at a rate of about 85 to 90 percent of her standard speed, or between 21.5 and 23.5 knots along the established course.

Throughout the trip, *Iowa* was to be accompanied by at least three destroyers acting as escort and antisubmarine screen. To perform this duty, Admiral Ingersoll designated a squadron of nine late-class destroyers capable of speeds of about forty knots. The squadron was divided into three divisions of three. The first division was to escort from Virginia to somewhat beyond Bermuda; the second division, from Bermuda to the Azores; and the third division, from the Azores into the Mediterranean. Some twelve hours before *Iowa* reached the Strait of Gibraltar, our escort was to be beefed up with six Royal Navy destroyers.

No information was given to the American destroyer squadron commander as to the purpose of *Iowa*'s trip. The operation was top secret, and the destroyer escort command had "no need to know." No personal flags were flown by *Iowa*, so insofar as the destroyers could tell, *Iowa* had no flag officer on board.

The destroyer squadron commander had been told to prepare his ships for distant service, to have them deployed at certain points and times along the course to Gibraltar, and, when on station, to take orders from the commander of a capital ship of the Atlantic Fleet that would be making an Atlantic passage. The order to prepare for distant service went out to each destroyer in the squadron. As I was informed later, one of the destroyers, the *William D. Porter*, took extraordinary steps in response to this order. And thereby hangs a tale.

On Sunday, 14 November 1943, our second day at sea, the weather was good with a brisk breeze blowing. The sea was choppy, and whitecaps were evident everywhere. It was decided that at 2:00 p.m., *Iowa* would exercise her forty-millimeter antiaircraft batteries against weather balloons to demonstrate to the president and other distinguished passengers the efficacy of this segment of *Iowa*'s antiaircraft defenses.

Iowa's escorting destroyers were informed of *Iowa*'s intention, and the drill got under way as scheduled.[74] The ship's company went to battle stations at 2:00 p.m. When all reports were in and communications had been tested, permission was given to secure such stations as were not immediately concerned with the forty-millimeter exercise. This included *Iowa*'s twenty-millimeter and five-inch batteries, which did not participate.

---

74 Commander Charles F. Pick Jr., USNR, was observing the drill on *Iowa*'s navigation bridge. He saw the president seated on the captain's veranda on the port (left) side of the first superstructure deck. He was in his wheelchair, propelled by his valet, Arthur Prettyman. Around him, standing in a semicircle, were Admiral Leahy, Admiral King, generals Marshall and Arnold, Harry Hopkins, and others.

The forty-millimeter batteries shot down a number of weather balloons and, all in all, gave a creditable performance. The demonstration was quite an eye-opener, I am sure, for those of the army air forces, who were witnessing a battleship's air defenses for the first time. Of course, only a portion of *Iowa's* defensive capability was demonstrated.

The drill had been in progress for about twenty minutes when over the TBS—that is, "talk between ships" radio phone—came a message in an urgent tone of voice: "Lion, Lion!"—*Iowa's* code name was Lion—"Torpedo headed your way!" This message came from the *William D. Porter*, the center ship in our screen, which at that moment was about 45 degrees on *Iowa's* starboard (right) bow, some 3,500 yards distant.

Had there been a leak about the trip? Had we been ambushed? All this raced through my mind in seconds. I immediately rang up full speed, and directed that battle stations be sounded. A general alarm gong clanged the alarm. The boatswain's mate piped the crew to battle stations and announced, "This is *not*, repeat *not*, a drill."[75]

Seconds later, another message came over the TBS from the *Porter*. "The torpedo may be ours." This was a bit of comfort, to be sure, but still, there was a torpedo headed our way.

After *Porter's* first message, I started to swing the ship to port, thinking to outrun the torpedo. After the second message, I immediately turned the ship sharply to starboard to head directly towards the *Porter*. I did so to present as narrow a target as possible for the torpedo. *Iowa's* beam was only about 108 feet, while her length–a little over 887 feet—presented a substantial target. No trace of the

---

75 According to Pick, the ship's loudspeakers blared repeatedly, "Torpedo! Torpedo on the starboard beam!" The presidential party leaped into action. A Secret Service agent pulled his pistol as if to shoot the torpedo. Prettyman propelled the president's chair rapidly to the starboard side of the ship. Pick learned later that the president had ordered the move so he could see the torpedo.

torpedo was visible to us in *Iowa*. In a relatively calm sea, we probably could have seen it, but on this day, whitecaps were everywhere.

Just about the time that we hit full speed, there was a tremendous underwater explosion on our starboard side near the stern. The ship shuddered mildly, enough to prompt me to ask *Iowa*'s executive, "Tom, do you think we have been hit?"

His reply: "No, I don't think so, Captain, because had we been hit, I think we would have felt it much more than we did." It is my belief that the turbulence caused by *Iowa*'s making a sharp turn at full speed was sufficient to detonate the torpedo's firing mechanism.

About this time, when my attention was focused ahead, there was purred into my ear in a low tone of voice, "Captain McCrea, what is the interlude?" It was Admiral King. I told him briefly, and as thoroughly as I could, what had occurred. "I shall keep you informed as events unfold, Admiral," said I. He left the bridge and returned to the captain's veranda.

Gradually, things calmed down. Further shooting was called off, the formation reformed, and things returned to normal. Visual dispatches were exchanged with the *Porter*. We learned that the torpedo had come from the *Porter*, and that it had been fired accidentally during a drill where *Iowa* had been used as the point of aim. I sent a signal to our destroyer escort that henceforth *Iowa* was not to be used as a point of aim in drills.

On *Porter*'s return to port, the commander in chief of the Atlantic Fleet ordered a full-fledged investigation into the incident. In the spring of 1944, I learned about the findings from a friend. The proceedings determined that *Porter*'s chief torpedoman, as part of his preparation for distant service, had inserted primers[76] into the firing locks of the torpedo launching mechanism "as a

---

76 A primer is a small explosive device that provides the impetus to launch a torpedo from its tube.

precaution to see that they fitted." This strikes me as entirely unnecessary, but no doubt, the exercise was done in good faith. Inadvertently, one primer was not removed, leaving one torpedo primed and ready to fire during Porter's torpedo drill on 14 November. Although no damage resulted during the torpedo incident, it was deeply embarrassing for the U.S. Navy that one of its ships fired a live torpedo at another, and doubly embarrassing because the president of the United States was embarked in the target ship.[77]

The rest of *Iowa*'s voyage to the Mediterranean went off without incident. I was on the bridge or within a few steps of the conning platform at all times. My sea cabin, on the same level as the conning platform, was small, but equipped with all the necessary amenities. As always, all my meals were served there while we were under way.

On the passage across the Atlantic, I saw a good bit of Admiral King. He spent many hours on the bridge, from choice I suppose. On the other hand, there was hardly any other place for him to go. Since Admiral King was greatly interested in our operation, and the charts were available in the charthouse, he found it convenient to spend a good bit of time on the bridge.

I think it was the second night out that Admiral King heard the officer of the deck give an order to the helm, changing course in accordance with the zigzag plan. "May I see you in your cabin?" said Admiral King. There he remarked, "It is dark, and I note *Iowa* is zigzagging, which is unusual during dark hours. Why?" His question, uttered in an icy tone, suggested rebuke, displeasure, almost anything bad.

I replied, "When I was in Washington recently, I discussed this trip with Rear Admiral Francis Stuart Low, your submarine fellow,

---

77 The torpedo incident was not reported in the popular press until the late 1950s. However, word of it circulated in the navy, and U.S. warships were known to greet the *Porter* with the signal, "Don't shoot! We're Republicans."

and he informed me that the enemy had made significant developments in radar periscopes. With that in mind, he suggested that I zigzag at night. The suggestion made sense to me, and that is what I am doing."

"Thank you," said he. That ended that.

Admiral King was austere and unapproachable. No one in his right mind would have ever clapped him on the back as a friendly gesture. I wonder if anyone ever had the courage to greet him with an, "Ernie, old boy, how goes everything today?" Certainly no one his junior, or even near his time at the Naval Academy, would have done so. But despite his manner, I found him quite human and surprisingly companionable. It was a pleasure to talk with him. He was a knowledgeable, no-foolishness guy.

One evening, we were in my sea cabin. He occupied the only chair, while I perched on the side of my bed. We fell to discussing Admiral Alfred T. Mahan, the author, naval historian, and critic, and some of his writing. One of Mahan's great efforts was his *Types of Naval Officers*, in which he analyzed some of the great officers of all countries and all times. Leading the conversation, of course, Admiral King got around to making observations about some of our own naval officers. He had served with many of them and had firm views about most.

The admiral did not like Admiral Hugh Rodman, with whom I had served on three occasions. Although he gave Rodman credit for being quick-witted, he regarded him as superficial in the extreme. Although Rodman had done well in command of a division of United States battleships that served in the British Grand Fleet during World War I, and subsequently became the first commander in chief of the Pacific Fleet, King stated that Rodman was "lacking in many aspects that I regard as essential in a flag officer."

Since Admiral King knew of my close association with Admiral Rodman, I concluded from his remarks that he was needling me. I responded that while Admiral Rodman admittedly was not the greatest flag officer ever, he nevertheless had many admirable flag-officer qualities, principal among which was his ability to make firm and, if need be, quick decisions. King grudgingly agreed.

Admiral King spoke most highly of Admiral Henry T. Mayo, on whose staff he had served: "No question about it, Mayo was a fine flag officer, and it is my opinion that his reputation as such was well deserved."

And so the conversation went. We discussed some contemporary officers "on the way up," and the admiral had no hesitancy in appraising them. Then, much to my amazement, the conversation took a personal turn.

"You know, McCrea, I regard you as a good officer, but you could be a lot better. The trouble is that you have one outstanding weakness."

Catching my breath, I responded, "Thank you, Admiral. I have inventoried myself often, and I can come up with many, many weaknesses. Since you say I have one outstanding weakness, I'm wondering if you would tell me what you think it is."

"Your big weakness, McCrea, is that you are not a son of a bitch. A good naval officer has to be a son of a bitch."

Catching my breath again, I said, "Well, Admiral, you may be right. But I feel that I know when to be a son of a bitch. I think I would prefer to be a son of a bitch when the need arises, than to feel that every time I walk down the deck, the universal under-the-breath remark is, 'There goes that son of a bitch.'

"Besides, Admiral," I continued, realizing I had an opportunity to respond in kind to the admiral's needling, "you're a good naval officer and universally regarded as such. And I must say"—looking him dead in the eye—"I have never heard anyone refer to you as a son of a bitch."

Well, Admiral King knew full well that I was lying, but what could he say? He returned my look, arose, and stomped out of my cabin without a word. Our discussion of naval officers was at an end that evening.

As we neared Gibraltar, six British destroyers joined up with us, augmenting our escort screen to a total of nine destroyers. We made landfall off Gibraltar sometime after dark. The night was clear and dark, and many, many shore lights were visible. Searchlights scanned the sky and the horizon.

Around first light, we arrived off Oran. A French pilot boarded *Iowa* and escorted us to the inner harbor. *Iowa* turned around and moored to the quay headed seaward. Fueling began at once. The president, the Joint Chiefs, and their respective staffs left the ship around 8:00 a.m. On arrival ashore, they were driven to the airfield, where they boarded their waiting aircraft and proceeded to Cairo for the first of the president's conferences.

Here I shall backtrack briefly. Prior to *Iowa*'s departure from Hampton Roads, I remarked to Admiral King that his deputy, Admiral Edwards, had informed me I would receive orders regarding *Iowa*'s employment during the two conferences, but I had not received any orders. "You will receive necessary orders in due course," King had said in his iciest tone. From that I inferred that further inquiry was distinctly out of order.

As the voyage progressed, it was only natural to wonder what our employment might be during the conference period. *Iowa*'s executive, Tom Casey, wondered, too. All I could tell him was what Admiral King had told me. Rear Admiral Charles M. Cooke, Admiral King's senior aide, also asked what *Iowa* would be doing. If Cooke didn't know, I was sure Admiral King had not made up his mind, or if he had, he would not issue orders until he felt like it. One thing was certain. Admiral King would eventually tell me what he wanted done. I decided to keep my mouth shut and act as if I didn't give a damn. I determined I would not raise the subject of *Iowa*'s deployment unless King gave an indication of leaving the ship without giving me any instruction. In other words, I wouldn't say anything until he started to step over the side bound for Oran.

As remarked earlier, *Iowa* arrived at Oran in the early hours of the morning watch. As can be imagined, there was much shipboard activity. The disembarking of so many high rankers—civilians, army, navy, and air force—and staff personnel, Secret Service, and others was an important and time-consuming operation. I kept my eye on Admiral King. He had been on the lower bridge during our entry into the harbor and, before leaving the bridge, he remarked as to the smartness of the shiphandling. This was pleasant to hear, of course, but still there were no instructions as to what *Iowa* was to do.

About five minutes before he left the ship, Admiral King handed me a scrap of paper. On it, he had written in pencil in his distinctive fine hand, "When in all respects ready for sea, and no later than 1800 hours tomorrow, *Iowa*, accompanied by its destroyer division escort, to proceed to Bahia, Brazil, and await orders from the commander in chief of the U.S. Fleet."

So *Iowa* had her orders. King's deliberate silence about his plans for *Iowa* was typical. He made it clear he would act in his own good time, and he did so. Admiral Cooke was standing nearby on the quarterdeck. I handed him the unusual operation order for his inspection and information. He smiled, and so did I.

As Admiral King left the ship, he quietly remarked, "*Iowa* has done a good job. Since her shakedown cruise was in Chesapeake Bay, I thought she might profitably enjoy two Atlantic crossings and, of course, two crossings of the Equator. It will be a good opportunity to work the ship up."

Chapter 22

Three Transatlantic Crossings

—⚮—

After discharging our passengers, we commenced the necessary arrangements for *Iowa*'s immediate future. Refueling began as soon as *Iowa* secured to the quay. The tanker conducting this operation stirred much comment among *Iowa*'s crew. She had been the target of a submarine attack and had lost a substantial part of her bow. The gaping hole brought home to all of us the hazards of submarine warfare. Had the torpedo hit thirty feet further aft, no doubt the ship would have been lost.

A number of Royal Navy men-of-war were moored in the harbor. Among them was HMS *Sheffield*, wearing the flag of Admiral Sir John Cunningham, the allied naval commander in the Mediterranean. After the departure of our passengers, I set out for the *Sheffield* to pay my respects to the senior officer present afloat.

Admiral Cunningham received me most cordially and got right down to business. "What are your orders, Captain?" I told him that no later than the following night *Iowa* was to proceed to Bahia, Brazil, and await orders from the commander in chief of the U.S. Fleet.

"I'm afraid I must change your orders somewhat," said Admiral Cunningham. "I want you to depart Oran no later than sunset today, and I shall tell you why. Despite the fact that *Iowa* passed through the Strait of Gibraltar in the dark, the Spanish observation stations near Gibraltar are probably well aware that at least one capital ship accompanied by a heavy escort entered the Mediterranean last night. This information is unquestionably now in the hands of the enemy. *Iowa* is just the sort of target the enemy would like to work over with their buzz bombs. Accordingly, I want you to get back in the Atlantic as soon as practical. I'm sure that Admiral King, were he here, would approve this modification of his orders."

"*Iowa* can leave here tonight," said I, "but only if we can get fueled in time to do so. The single tanker alongside us cannot do the job."

"Another tanker will be sent to you at once," said he, dispatching his flag lieutenant to make the arrangements. "*Sheffield* will join your outbound escort. Hopefully, three American destroyers and the six Royal Navy destroyers can give you safe conduct into the Atlantic."

We spent the afternoon readying *Iowa* for sea. I told the two tankers to pump at their best speed for as long as possible, but they were to clear *Iowa*'s side by five minutes before sunset. Their pumping capacity was not quite equal to the job, but they managed to approximate it.

At sunset, *Iowa* slipped her moorings and proceeded to the open roadstead. There we picked up HMS *Sheffield* and our destroyer escort, and set course for the Strait of Gibraltar. *Iowa* cleared the strait in the latter hours of the midwatch.[78] By daybreak, we were well out of sight of land. About mid-afternoon, our Royal Navy escort fell away, and *Iowa* and its three U.S. destroyers set course for Bahia.

On the passage to Bahia, we took the opportunity to exercise all of *Iowa*'s departments in every way possible. On 27 November,

---

78 Midwatch is between midnight and 4:00 a.m.

Iowa made her first crossing of the Equator—"crossing the line," as we say in the navy. Crossing the line is an event in the life of any navy ship. The ship is given over to Neptune Rex, king of the bounding main, and the ship's "shellbacks"—those of the ship's company who have previously crossed the line—initiate the "polliwogs"—those who have never crossed the line—into the mysteries of the domain of Neptune Rex. The occasion is greeted with much horseplay, and indignities of all sorts are visited upon the lowly polliwogs. Since *Iowa's* crossing the line was entirely unexpected, there was no advance opportunity to acquire the usual accoutrements used on such occasions. I was astonished at the ingenuity of *Iowa's* shellbacks in producing some truly remarkable costumes for the occasion.

All was not relaxation during this fine event. We were in the war zone, and while a certain amount of "let up" could be tolerated, there could be no relaxation in our antisubmarine defenses. But a good time was had, and at the end of the day, all the ship's company were shellbacks.

Shortly after we left the Mediterranean, I sent a dispatch to the commander of the U.S. Fourth Fleet in Bahia, Vice Admiral Jonas H. Ingram, telling him of our estimated time of arrival and our fuel requirements. The reply stated that Admiral Ingram would be in Bahia on *Iowa's* arrival. When we reached port, Admiral Ingram's chief of staff advised me that the admiral had come to Bahia specially because he thought the president would be on board *Iowa*.

As soon as we anchored, I called on Admiral Ingram, an old friend with whom I had served on a couple of occasions. "Why didn't you tell me the president wasn't coming to Bahia?" he remarked with irritation. He had assumed the president would be with me because the two of us had come to Brazil together in January 1943, on the way back from the Casablanca Conference. Soon the humor of the situation struck him, and we had a good laugh. He invited me for lunch the following day, gave me a box of cigars, and we parted in high good spirits.

On my return to the ship, Tom Casey met me at the gangway. He handed me a dispatch, which read in effect: "*Iowa* proceed to Freetown, British West Africa, arriving no later than so-and-so, and there await orders from the Commander in Chief U.S. Fleet."[79] Casey said he and the navigator had already consulted the charts and tide tables. They had determined that *Iowa* could enter Freetown's harbor only at high water. To arrive by the designated time we would have to catch a particular high tide, which meant that *Iowa* would have to leave Bahia no later than 4:00 a.m. the next morning.

I checked the reckoning, and Casey was correct. I wrote a note to Admiral Ingram informing him of *Iowa*'s orders. I thanked him for the lunch invitation and indicated that I assumed I had his permission to leave his jurisdiction. Our visit to Bahia was short indeed.

Upon reaching West Africa, we found the entrance to Freetown harbor most difficult for a ship of *Iowa*'s size, but once inside, there was a fine anchorage and plenty of water. There were a number of Italian men-of-war present. In September 1943, the Italian military had begun to disintegrate under Allied pressure. Many Italian men-of-war had left the Mediterranean and turned up voluntarily in Allied ports. The British had permitted these ships to enter Freetown harbor, but there was doubt as to whether they were still Axis belligerents.

Our two days in Freetown were delightful. We sent as many men ashore on liberty as possible, and they were fascinated with the town and its history. When the slave trade was at its height, tribal chiefs brought great numbers of their tribesmen to Freetown and sold them at slave auctions there.

In due course, *Iowa* received orders to proceed to Dakar, Senegal, to receive our passengers for the return trip to the United

---

79 Freetown is in Sierra Leone, which in 1943 was one of the colonies comprising British West Africa.

States.[80] We reached the harbor entrance buoys shortly after first light on the date of our designated arrival. A French naval officer came on board and acted as pilot during our passage through the channel. At about 8:30 a.m., *Iowa* anchored off the Dakar docks.

The senior United States naval officer stationed at Dakar was Vice Admiral William A. Glassford, another old friend. As soon as we anchored, I received a letter from him about the transfer of the presidential party from the dock to *Iowa*. It read something like this: "The president and his party will arrive at Dakar airfield at about 5:00 p.m. and proceed directly to *Iowa*. The passage from shore to *Iowa* causes me considerable concern. The French insist that since the president is in a French port, they should be given the honor of transporting his party to *Iowa* in a French ship. They have been most sticky about this. I have tried to explain that because of the president's infirmities, he needs special handling, but to no avail. I am sure that acceding to their wishes now will smooth my dealings with them in the future.

"The craft they propose to use for the transfer has an upper bridge about the same height off the water as *Iowa*'s quarterdeck. I do not think it practical to get the president to this upper bridge. Those more agile than he can manage it and cross to *Iowa* via a gangplank. But other arrangements must be made for the president. That I leave to you."

From Admiral Glassford's description, it was evident that the only practical way of transferring the president from the French ship to *Iowa*'s quarterdeck was via a boatswain's chair.[81] Now, there are boatswain's chairs, and there are boatswain's chairs. For the most part, they are used by men working over the side scrubbing paintwork and painting. I had served with President Roosevelt long enough to know that he disliked having attention drawn to

---

80 In 1943, Senegal was one of the colonies of French West Africa.

81 A boatswain's chair consists of a rigid seat attached to a set of ropes that allow the person in the chair to be moved by a rope. More elaborate chairs also have straps to keep the person from falling out.

his lack of mobility. If he had to be brought aboard in a manner different from the rest of his party, I determined to make the event something special. In the hours at our disposal, *Iowa*'s crew whipped up probably the dressiest boatswain's chair ever made. Fancy work and cross pointing of superior quality were evident everywhere.[82] The president deserved the best.

When the French ship arrived alongside *Iowa*, the president was surprised at his boarding arrangements. Like worthy admirals of old, he was hoisted aboard by eight side boys—the number to which his rank entitled him—to the tune of the boatswain's pipe. It was a pleasant ceremony, and the president took it in high good humor.

A narrow gangplank equipped with a steadying line was extended from *Iowa* to the upper bridge of the French ship. The rest of the president's party used the gangplank to board *Iowa*. Harry Hopkins and Pa Watson—landlubbers, of course—did not attempt to walk across using the steadying line. Instead, these two distinguished men crawled on all fours, much to the amusement of the president and everyone else. The president, who regarded him-self as a sailor, taunted them as landlubbers and referred to their "disgraceful" display on boarding.

As soon as all of our passengers were on board, *Iowa* got under way for the United States. I accompanied the president to his cabin, and informed him that I had decided, subject to his approval, that on our westbound passage, we would stay as long as we could in the low latitudes to give him the benefit of as much sun as pos-sible en route. To this he readily agreed.

The French naval authorities sent a naval officer to act as our pilot in leaving port. It would have been helpful if they had sent the same man who had piloted us that morning. In no time, it was clear that this chap's principal and only asset was a fair fluency in English.

---

82 Fancy work and cross pointing are forms of decorative patterned rope work.

It was a dark, dark night. Many of the buoys were not lighted, despite contrary indications on the chart. Our pilot's inexperience was painfully evident. "Ah, no light. I wonder why?" This repeated many, many times did not inspire confidence. Our experience entering port in daylight was most helpful in picking our way out that night. It was a big relief to reach the harbor entrance buoys. We dropped off the pilot, and set course for the first leg of the trip across the Atlantic.

We had been on our merry way about a half hour when I heard the voice of Vice Admiral Wilson Brown on the bridge. "Captain McCrea," said he in a firm, icy tone, "I would like to be informed as to what this ship is up to."

The admiral was right to demand an explanation. Since Admiral King had remained in North Africa, Brown was the senior naval officer on board, and he was also the naval aide to the president. I apologized profusely for my failure to acquaint him with *Iowa*'s plans. I explained my proposal for our Atlantic crossing, showed him the route on the charts, and indicated that I had told the president what I proposed to do and received his approval. I said I hoped the plan met with the admiral's approval as well.

The admiral replied curtly that it did, adding, "I trust that I will be kept informed as to *Iowa*'s employment from here on." I assured him that he would and that I would welcome any thoughts he might have to make the president's passage more comfortable. The admiral was not pleasant, but he was right. I had ignored him, and he had reason to be annoyed.

Iowa's westward passage was uneventful. By the time we entered Chesapeake Bay, we had used enough fuel that we could transit the channel without lightening the ship in any way. We arrived in the lower reaches of the Potomac River in the late afternoon of 16 December 1943.

After we came to anchor, the president consented to make a few remarks to the ship's company. I had the honor of introducing him. He spoke on the quarterdeck as he was about to leave the ship:

Captain McCrea, officers and men of the *Iowa*. I had wanted to say a few words to you on the trip east, but I couldn't do it properly because so many of you were mere miserable polliwogs. Now I understand that I can talk to you as the chief shellback of them all.

I have had a wonderful cruise on the *Iowa*, one I shall never forget. I think that all my staff have behaved themselves pretty well, with one or two lapses. When we came on board from that little French destroyer, I was horrified to note that Major General Watson and Mr. Hopkins came over the rail on all fours. However, landlubbers like that do have lapses.

Outside of that, all the army and navy and civilians have been wonderfully taken care of, and I am impressed with two facts. The first is that you had a happy lot of visitors, fellow shipmates. Secondly, from all that I have seen and all that I have heard, the *Iowa* is a happy ship. And having served with the navy for many years, I know and you know what that means. It is a part and parcel of what we are trying to do, to make every ship happy and efficient.

One of the reasons I went abroad, as you know, was to try, by conversations with other nations, to see that this war that we are now engaged in shall not happen again. We have an idea—all of us, I think—that hereafter we have got to eliminate from the human race nations like Germany and Japan, eliminate them from the possibility of ruining the lives of a whole lot of other nations. And in these talks in North Africa, Egypt, and Persia with the Chinese, the Russians, the Turks, and others, we have made real progress. Obviously, it will be necessary when we win this war to make the possibility of a future upsetting of our civilization an impossible thing. I don't say forever. None of us can look that far ahead. But I do say that, as long as any Americans and others who are alive today are still alive, that objective is worth fighting for. It is a part of democracy, which exists in most of the world.

In upper Tehran, where the prime minister, Marshal Stalin, and I met, in one sense it followed that, as heads of governments, we were representing between two-thirds and three-quarters of the entire population of the world. We all had the same fundamental aims: stopping what has been going on in these past four years. And that is why I believe, from the viewpoint of people, just plain people, this trip has been worthwhile.

We are all engaged in a common struggle. We are making real progress. Take what has happened in the past two years: from Pearl Harbor, from being on the defensive—very definitely so—two years ago; from being in the process of building things up to a greater strength a year ago; to where we are today, when we have the initiative in every part of the world. The other fellows may not be on the run backward, yet. That will be the next stage, and then all of us in the service of the country will have a better chance to go home, even if we have come home to very cold weather like this. I think after what you have seen in Bahia and Freetown and Dakar, that you will agree with me that, in the long run, year in and year out, this American climate is better than any other.

Now I have to leave you for the USS *Potomac*. When I came out on deck a while ago and saw her about a half a mile away, I looked and decided how much she had shrunk since I have been on the *Iowa*.

And so good-bye for a while. I hope that I will have another cruise in this ship. Meanwhile, good luck, and remember that I am with you in spirit, each and every one of you.

Following his remarks, the president left *Iowa* for USS *Potomac*. After *Potomac* had pulled away from *Iowa*, he waved good-bye to us with his hat in his hand. The crew responded with a spontaneous and prolonged cheer. The whole incident was splendid. The president had given an inspiring talk. He was always superb at off-the-cuff remarks.

Early the following morning, *Iowa* got under way for the naval operating base at Hampton Roads to divest ourselves of the president's special equipment. These items were catalogued and stowed against the day when they might be needed for another presidential trip in this or another ship. The square bathtub in the captain's bath was not removed, since its installation was permanent. Thus, I and all subsequent commanding officers of *Iowa* had a "sit-in" tub as well as a shower. Elegance, I assure you.

Chapter 23

War Preparations

———— ⚬⚬⚬ ————

Promptly after *Iowa*'s return from Africa, I called on Admiral Inger-soll to report on our recent employment. He told me that the tor-pedo incident was under investigation. He also informed me that Battleship Division 7, consisting of *Iowa* and her sister ship, *New Jersey*, would depart for the Pacific on 2 January 1944. Our division commander, Rear Admiral Olaf M. Hustvedt, and his staff would be embarked in *Iowa*.[83]

There was plenty to do to prepare *Iowa* for the Pacific. Since leaving Argentia, the ship had steamed many hundreds of miles at relatively high, sustained speeds, generally about twenty-five knots. Much upkeep had to be done, and the navy yard mechanics were most helpful.

Iowa also had a number of personnel changes. Our executive, Tom Casey, was detached. His relief was Commander George A. Leahey, who had been *Iowa*'s first lieutenant and damage control officer. Our senior medical officer, our senior chaplain, and our chief engineer were also detached.

---

83 *Iowa* (BB-61) and *New Jersey* (BB-62) were the first of four *Iowa*-class battleships. The other members of the class are *Missouri* (BB-63) and *Wisconsin* (BB-64).

The loss of the chief engineer caused me concern, because his orders did not identify his relief. When I spoke to the detail officer for engineers about a replacement, he responded nonchalantly that he could appoint *Iowa*'s senior assistant engineer to the job. I responded that the man was a reserve officer with eight months' experience, and that unless I got a qualified engineer at once, I would report to the commander in chief of the Atlantic Fleet that *Iowa* was not ready to go to the Pacific.

The next morning, a qualified engineer officer reported on board. "You certainly got here in a hurry," said I. "That's right," said he. "Yesterday afternoon, I was in dungarees in the engine room of *Tuscaloosa* in the Boston navy yard. I was handed a dispatch ordering my *immediate* detachment and directing me to report to *Iowa*. So here I am. My captain had gone ashore when I got my orders. I didn't even get a chance to say good-bye to him."

I was determined to spend at least Christmas Day with my family in Washington. Since *Iowa* was Pacific-bound, I thought this was a good time to return Vickie, my daughter Meredith's attractive little dog, to his rightful owner. Vickie—short for Victory—had been in *Iowa* since August. About half the size of a Scotch collie, he was a cross between a collie and something else. Vickie had made himself right at home in *Iowa*. He roamed the ship, made friends here and there, and was never without someone to play with. He liked to return tossed tennis balls and always found someone to roll a ball down the deck. In this way, he kept in good condition. When play became too strenuous, he would go to my cabin and lie on his special mat under my desk. There he knew he was safe from annoyance. He was a smart dog.

Admiral Ingersoll was good enough to give me passage to Washington in his airplane. This was Vickie's first flight, and he did not enjoy it. Throughout the trip, he lay at my feet, trembling. I felt sorry for the little mutt, but he would not be consoled. He just trembled and looked at me, conveying his disappointment in me, his friend.

When we put down in Washington, Vickie was first down the ladder. He raced to the front of the plane, and, looking up at the propeller, started to bark, registering his complete disgust with this instrument of torture. He barked and he barked and he barked, looking intently at the aircraft all the while. The ground crew was amused and astonished at the vigorousness of his barking. He continued until he became hoarse, and his bark had diminished to a mere squeak. Only then did he stop. On arrival at 1700 Surrey Lane, Vickie raced from room to room, giving evidence, I thought, of his pleasure at being home again.

I stayed a couple of days in Washington. I took occasion to run into town and call on the president. He was in fine form and told me what a recuperative effect the trip from Dakar had had on him. I thought I had never seen him looking better. I told him *Iowa* was leaving for the Pacific on 2 January. He remarked that when hostilities ended, it would be fine to make another trip in *Iowa*. I had no way of knowing it, of course, but the president and I were not destined to meet again. How fortunate—and also unfortunate—that we do not know we are doing something for the last time.

I left Washington Christmas night aboard the Washington boat headed for Norfolk. My suitcase was packed and lying on its side by the front door. We had decided that Estelle, Meredith, and Anne would come to the Chamberlin Hotel in Hampton Roads for the New Year's festivities and return to Washington after *Iowa* had departed for the Canal Zone.

As I prepared to depart, I was amazed to find my friend Vickie lying on top of my suitcase, head between his paws. I said good-bye to him and opened the front door. Away he went, down the steps to the waiting taxi. I turned to the family and remarked to the effect that Vickie evidently wanted to go with me, wherever that might be. "Any objection if he returns to *Iowa* with me?" There being none, away we went, leash and all. On his return to *Iowa*, Vickie expressed his delight by racing around the ship at a high rate of speed and licking the hands of my marine orderly, who was pleased with Vickie's idea of affection.[84]

The week in Hampton Roads passed quickly. *Iowa* fueled to capacity, revictualed for 125 days (her maximum), and took on all sorts of other provisions. The family came down from Washington, and we had three good days. On 1 January, at a short celebration, we drank to 1944, which we hoped would be the last year of hostilities. The following morning, *Iowa* and *New Jersey,* with their escorting destroyers, weighed anchor for the Canal Zone. Some sixteen months were to pass before I saw my family again.

As we headed for the Pacific war zone, the health of the crew assumed new importance because of its power to affect the ship's performance. I had witnessed the effect of infectious disease in ships during World War I, when I served in *New York*, one of a division of U.S. battleships operating with the British Grand Fleet. In the late fall of 1918, many ships of the Grand Fleet were essentially demobilized by a flu epidemic. I distinctly recall that the battle cruiser HMS *Princess Royal* had to have another ship come alongside to steam for her because her entire firemen's force was incapacitated. Had the Germans attacked at the time, many of the ships could not have given an account of themselves.

Food poisoning was another danger, and *Iowa* did have an incident of that type. When I took command of *Iowa*, I recalled how faint my Catholic daughter became when she attended communion services on Sundays without breakfast. I directed my executive to come up with a solution for this problem in *Iowa*. We worked it out so that when a Catholic received communion on Sundays, the altar boy handed him a ticket that entitled him to coffee and sandwiches at the ship's galley. Why the ticket? We had to ensure that those who had had their breakfast did not show up for a handout.

One Sunday, shortly after noon, *Iowa's* medical officer, Captain Clifford A. Swanson, came to me in great perturbation. "Captain,

84 Vickie became a beloved mascot and crew member of *Iowa*.

what I have always feared is upon us. We have food poisoning in the ship, and a great many men are coming to sickbay." I wished him well and asked to be kept informed.

I pondered the situation. Breakfast for the crew was at 7:00 a.m. Sunday dinner was at noon. "Seems odd," thought I. "If they had been poisoned at breakfast, why had symptoms taken this long to appear? Certainly they could not have been poisoned at lunch." Then my eye hit the Plan of the Day lying on my desk: "10 a.m. – Coffee and sandwiches at galley for Catholics receiving communion."

I told my orderly to dash down and tell Dr. Swanson about the 10 a.m. sandwiches and ask him to determine the religion of the sick men. In a few minutes, Swanson appeared in my cabin. He reported that forty-seven Catholics and one Jew were sick. The galley had served ham sandwiches that morning. He had examined some ham scraps and the bone, and found them to be "alive."

"How did that Jew get in there?" said I. "The sandwich tickets only go to Catholics." The reply: "He was the cook who made the ham sandwiches."

For some time, I had been thinking that it would be good for *Iowa* to broadcast a summary of the day's news over the ship's loudspeaker. We had about 2,800 men in the ship. Daily news summaries were typed and distributed, but it was impractical to turn out enough copies for everyone. When was the best time for a news broadcast? We finally decided on late afternoon when at sea. I appointed as our newscaster a personable young reserve officer who had had some experience in public relations.

The news was compiled from many sources. We decided to limit each broadcast to about ten to twelve minutes a day. A few days after the operation started, we were startled by an item of alleged news. Its dateline was Rome, and the report stated that a large battleship believed to be USS *Iowa* had been severely damaged in the eastern Atlantic by an Italian submarine. I can still hear the roar of laughter and taunts that followed this announcement. Of course, from then on, we knew that the evening news would get a lot of attention.

Also around this time, I adopted a personal practice that I hoped would contribute in a small way to maintaining morale in the ship. A naval vessel is a very small community, and in wartime, particularly, the whole crew must work together smoothly for the ship to function effectively. Rancor and bad feelings cannot be allowed to fester, because ill will can impair personal performance and endanger the men and the vessel. Accordingly, whenever I had occasion to dress someone down, particularly when I did so publicly to make an example of him for others, I made it a point to have a pleasant word with the man later that same day. I did so to take the personal sting out of the reprimand, so the man would not go to bed feeling angry and resentful.

Our task force reached the Panama Canal Zone in routine fashion. The *Iowa*-class battleships had been expressly designed so they could use the canal. The canal's locks are 110 feet wide. The ships have a beam of 108 feet, 2 inches. Thus, in the locks, *Iowa* had twenty-two inches of clearance to split between the port and starboard sides. It was a tight fit.

Admiral Hugh Rodman, with whom I served for a number of years, was the first marine superintendent of the Panama Canal. He once told me that when the United States undertook to build the canal, the original plan called for locks ninety feet in width. This dimension was chosen because the U.S. Army Corps of Engineers insisted that lock gates wider than ninety feet would be too heavy to operate effectively. The Navy Department told the army the width limitation was entirely unacceptable because the navy was then building the *New York*–class of battleships, which had a beam of ninety-six feet.

Major General George Washington Goethals was the chief engineer on the canal construction project. He and his army corps engineers got busy and redesigned the locks. They came up with a lock 110 feet in width, which seemed satisfactory at the time. Of course, as time passed, our big carriers and tankers became too large to use the canal.

Our battleship division had priority to transit the Panama Canal, and on 7 January 1944, we reached the Pacific after a passage of about nineteen hours. We set out to join the Pacific Fleet at Funafuti Atoll in the Ellice Islands.[85] After crossing the Equator and the International Date Line, we reached Funafuti on Saturday, 22 January 1944. Entering the Funafuti lagoon in the forenoon, we saw the fast modern battleships and aircraft carriers of the Fast Carrier Task Force, Task Force 58, assembled and awaiting the arrival of *Iowa* and *New Jersey*.[86] We anchored near the USS *South Dakota*, which was commanded by my close friend, Captain Allan E. "Hoke" Smith.

Hoke promptly sent me a signal of welcome and invited me to luncheon. By way of inducement, he added that a number "of your White House friends will be here." On boarding *South Dakota*, I was pleased to find several press correspondents I had known at the White House. They were homeward bound after visiting the South

---

85 Before WWII, the Ellice Islands were part of a British colony that also included the Gilbert Islands to the north. On December 10, 1941, the Japanese occupied the Gilbert Islands. By August 1943, the United States built bases in the Ellice group and used them to support the November 1943 operation to capture the Tarawa and Makin atolls in the Gilbert Islands. These atolls were subsequently used as forward bases for operations in the Marshall Islands to the north.

86 From January 1944 through the end of the war, the Fast Carrier Task Force was the primary strike force of U.S. naval forces operating in the Central Pacific. The task force consisted of task groups made up of aircraft carriers, fast modern battleships, cruisers, and destroyers. The task force was part of the Central Pacific Force, renamed the Fifth Fleet, under the command of Admiral Raymond A. Spruance. As the war progressed, command of the Fifth Fleet alternated between Admiral Spruance and Admiral William F. "Bull" Halsey Jr. When Spruance was in command, he led the Fifth Fleet and Task Force 58. To confuse the Japanese, when Halsey was in command, the same entities were called the Third Fleet and Task Force 38, respectively.

Pacific and meeting with General MacArthur. One was Raymond Clapper, whom I knew well. A top-flight reporter, he wrote a nationally syndicated column on matters of political and military significance.[87] Day in and day out, his column was a magnificent effort.

Clapper and I hailed each other with enthusiasm. We talked about the war and his appraisal of General MacArthur. "In one respect, my trip was a failure," said he. "This was MacArthur's fault. Just before I left Washington, Grace Tully"—President Roosevelt's secretary—"jokingly asked me to see if General MacArthur would disavow an interest in the Republican nomination for the presidency in 1944. I liked the idea, and I put the question to the general several times. Each time he acted as though he didn't hear me. I know Grace will be disappointed."

The luncheon among friends on board *South Dakota* was a delightful interlude, a short period of calm before the storm that was about to begin.

---

87 Raymond Clapper (1892–1944), a highly respected journalist, wrote a daily column called "Between You and Me," which was syndicated by Scripps-Howard and appeared in 176 newspapers. When the United States entered WWII, he began to report on the war, traveling with the U.S. Navy in the South Pacific.

Chapter 24

Iowa Joins the Fight

———∞∞∞———

Often during 1942 and 1943, I had thought that fate was against me insofar as combat duty was concerned. After I got command of *Iowa*, I worried the war might be over before *Iowa* got to the Pacific. But things didn't work out that way. For the first few months after our arrival in the Pacific, *Iowa*'s activities were well-nigh continuous. It seemed as if the Pacific command had waited until *Iowa* and *New Jersey* got out there before starting the war in earnest. Of course, this wasn't so, but I can assure you that *Iowa* was continually on the jump for the next seven months or thereabouts. To be sure, we had periods of rest and upkeep, but those periods were short indeed.

The day after *Iowa*'s arrival at Funafuti, the campaign to take the Marshall Islands began.[88] Our task force left Funafuti heading north past the recently won Gilbert Islands on an operation to support the army and marines in taking Majuro and Kwaja-

---

88 Japan had controlled the Marshall Islands since WWI, so the Marshalls campaign represented an attack on the soil of the Japanese Empire. The United States planned to take three of the twenty-nine atolls in the Marshall group—Majuro in the southeast, Kwajalein in the center, and Eniwetok in the northwest, closest to the next target, the Mariana Islands.

lein. *Iowa* was assigned to a task group sent west to conduct air strikes on Eniwetok Atoll, to neutralize Japanese forces there during the invasion of Kwajalein.[89] *Iowa* first saw action 31 January to 2 February, maneuvering among the attacking carriers, watching for a Japanese counterattack that never materialized. Afterward, *Iowa* repaired to the harbor of Majuro to the southeast. For the next several months, we used Majuro as a forward base, returning there between operations for rest, upkeep, and provisioning.

During the last day of the Eniwetok operation, *Iowa* received word that Raymond Clapper had been killed. He had been a passenger in a plane from one of our task group carriers. His plane struck another and crashed. All aboard were killed. Sadly, that plane carried to his death one of the brightest ornaments of the American press that I had ever known.

My personal routine during the next eight months of operations was always the same. Whenever *Iowa* got under way, I went to the bridge and stayed there until the ship next came to anchor. I had an emergency cabin adjacent to the charthouse. It had a bed and was well equipped with necessities, but there was little time for rest. My meals were served on a tray. At night, I slept on a cot on deck adjacent to the conning tower door. My sleep there was always troubled, despite the consideration of the people on the bridge. I was there to be kept informed, and I was.

At sea, all hands went to general quarters, or battle stations, in the morning at first light. I had breakfast at about 6:00 a.m. The executive officer came to the bridge at about 7:30 and took over command of the watch. When I had briefed him sufficiently, I retired to my emergency cabin. I exercised, shaved, showered, and tumbled onto my bed, where I got a body massage from a pharma-

---

89 The role of battleships during carrier air strikes was to maneuver with the carriers and protect them from enemy air attack. Occasionally, the battleships also bombarded land targets.

cist's mate who was expert in such things. By the time he finished, I was usually asleep, trying to make up the rest lost during the night. I was called a few hours later at 11:30 a.m., or earlier if required, and the day started all over again.

After an operation, we invariably arrived in port shortly after daybreak. After bringing the ship to anchor, I would repair to my lower cabin, shave, shower, and breakfast. Then I would turn in to sleep for as long as possible, barring an emergency, so as to recharge my batteries for the next operation, usually just a few days off.

On 12 February 1944 *Iowa* departed Majuro for two back-to-back operations. The first was a raid in force on Truk in the Caroline Islands.[90] Our task group of aircraft carriers, battleships, heavy cruisers, and destroyers under the command of Admiral Raymond A. Spruance got under way towards the northwest, poising sixty miles northwest of Truk during the night of 15 February. Shortly before dawn on the morning of 16 February, the carriers began launching air strikes. In the sky above, fighters blinked their red and green wing lights as a rendezvous signal before their westward sweep across our task group to their objective. About fifteen minutes later, Radio Truk went off the air, undoubtedly because the raid had been detected.

Dawn came, and *Iowa*'s bridge received reports of an air battle over Truk. Our carriers began to launch dive-bombers and Hellcats for the second strike. Soon planes returning to their carriers from the initial strike reported that there were many Japanese transports in the Truk lagoon and that warships were attempting to escape to

---

90 The Caroline Islands had been under Japanese control since WWI. Truk was the site of major Japanese naval and air bases and the headquarters of the Combined Fleet of the Japanese Imperial Navy. Some regarded Japanese operations on the atoll as comparable to those of the United States at Pearl Harbor. The U.S. attack was intended to degrade Truk's forces so they could not defend Eniwetok, where another task group from Task Force 58 was supporting a landing operation.

the north. The carriers responded by launching torpedo bombers to attend to the ships.

About 11:30 that morning, *Iowa* and *New Jersey,* because of our speed, together with some cruisers and destroyers, were ordered westward to run down the crippled escapees. This group was under the command of Admiral Spruance, flying his flag in *New Jersey.* As we pulled away from the carrier formation, I received a semaphore message from Hoke Smith in *South Dakota.* "Lucky you," it read. Our task group broke off at twenty-five knots.

It was a murky day with low clouds. I made sure that the ship's company knew what we were doing and ordered that the sky be carefully watched for planes. Observing gunners in a machine gun battery talking and joking, I was about to make an announcement to the ship's company about battle discipline when suddenly, out of the clouds came a whine, and a zero dove upon *Iowa.* There was an ear-splitting explosion fifty feet to starboard, the loudspeaker blared the gunnery officer's cry, "Air attack starboard!" and the machine gun batteries sprang into action. The zero quickly disappeared into the clouds in a hail of tracers. After that, there was no more joking. Every face was lifted to the sky in anticipation of battle.

In an hour or so, *Iowa* raised an enemy light cruiser to port. Evidently it had gotten separated from the others seeking to escape from Truk. We were at battle stations, and I thought that momentarily we would receive orders to open fire. The range, I would suppose, was about eighteen thousand to fifteen thousand yards. An alert lookout spotted a torpedo approaching *Iowa* on the port side. From its wake, I determined it would pass astern of us by one thousand yards or so. It was barely out of the way when we sighted another torpedo on the port side. I estimated this one would pass ahead of *Iowa* by 500 to 750 yards. Meanwhile, our main battery of sixteen-inch guns was trained on the enemy cruiser, and our fire control people had her in hand.

Immediately after we sighted the second torpedo, I gave orders to the main battery to open fire on the cruiser. The response was virtually instantaneous. A salvo of nine sixteen-inch shells was on its merciless way, the first firing of *Iowa*'s big guns at the enemy. A perfect straddle resulted. By the time we got a second salvo off, the cruiser was listing, and her red anti-fouling paint was beginning to show. I ordered "cease fire" at the end of the third salvo, but not in time to prevent the loading of a fourth.

The cruiser was in distress. It rolled over and sank. As I recall it, Admiral Spruance dispatched a couple of destroyers to pick up survivors.

At this point, *Iowa* had nine sixteen-inch guns loaded and ready to fire. In other words, we had a hot gun-load on our hands. I directed the gunnery officer to unload the guns by firing them, which he did. Had we not done this, we would have had to wait hours for the guns and powder to cool to a point where the guns could be safely unloaded.

While in the midst of carrying on as I thought I should, our division commander, Rear Admiral Olaf M. Hustvedt, appeared at the door of the ship's conning tower and would have words with me. As firmly as I have ever been spoken to in the navy, he said, "Why did you, in the presence of two flag officers senior to you, open fire on that cruiser without authority to do so?" The admiral was angry that I had failed to seek permission from himself or his superior, Admiral Spruance in *New Jersey,* before attacking the cruiser.

My reply ran something like this. "Admiral, evidently you didn't see that the cruiser fired two torpedoes at *Iowa* that missed. I had no idea how many more it would fire if not prevented from doing so, and I couldn't be sure that *Iowa*'s luck would hold. The main battery had had the enemy cruiser in hand for some time. In my anxiety to protect *Iowa*, I instinctively gave the order to open fire. Of course, I realize I shouldn't have done as I did in the presence of two senior officers. But, Admiral, the Japanese cruiser is no longer in a position to threaten *Iowa* or any other ship of this task force."

Admiral Hustvedt was absolutely correct. My order to open fire was indefensible. Yet *Iowa*'s salvos had benefitted our task force. Certainly the cruiser was brought under destructive fire far earlier than if I had waited for an order from my senior. I never heard from Admiral Spruance about the incident. Perhaps he thought my breach of discipline was of minor importance. I don't think Admiral Hustvedt forgave my lapse of discipline.

The second of *Iowa*'s February missions was a one-day operation against the Mariana Islands.[91] On 21 February we were under way with Task Force 58 when our commander, Rear Admiral Marc A. Mitscher, announced in a message to the force, "I cannot tell a lie. Dog Day is Washington's birthday. Let's chop down a few Nip cherry trees." Of course, 22 February was also *Iowa*'s first birthday.

During the afternoon of the twenty-first, an enemy plane was sighted. Attempts to shoot it down failed, so unlike our strikes on Eniwetok and Truk, this operation would not have the element of surprise. That evening in the wardroom, the ship's band played popular swing tunes during a celebratory birthday dinner for *Iowa*'s officers. Afterward, the men stripped the ship for battle. Before dawn the following morning, the sky looked like a Fourth of July celebration as the task force fended off heavy torpedo and dive-bomber attacks. After daylight, the carriers launched strikes against Saipan and Tinian and photoreconnaissance flights over Guam.

For some time after reaching the Pacific, I had been toying with the idea of following *Iowa*'s evening news broadcast with a short prayer by one of our chaplains, one Catholic, one Protestant. I had read somewhere that, in British men-of-war in the early days of sail, an evening prayer was said daily at sunset. I thought that a quiet moment of prayer and reflection would be good for morale. However, no matter how well I liked the idea, I knew that the

---

91 The Marianas are a chain of islands to the west of the Marshalls group and considerably closer to Japan. The islands had great strategic importance for both the United States and Japan because they were within U.S. B-29 bomber range of the Japanese homeland.

introduction of such an activity had to be done adroitly, for a good reason, and in good taste.

One afternoon in late February 1944, *Iowa* received news about the U.S. losses during the invasion of Eniwetok.[92] This seemed an appropriate occasion for a prayer. I talked to one of *Iowa's* chaplains. He agreed to keep his prayer shorter than a minute. He would speak of the families at home thousands of miles away, the hope of an early and victorious end to the hostilities, and other comforting thoughts.

The news broadcast that evening reported the Eniwetok losses and announced that following the newscast, the chaplain would lead a short prayer for the repose of the souls of our deceased brothers in arms, and for the comfort of the families of those lost in the service of their country. The newscast concluded with "silence about the decks for evening prayer."

The idea of prayer caught on. The men responded readily to the call for silence. With no further urging, they were on their feet, heads uncovered. I thought how splendidly they had responded. War is serious business. Daily thoughts of home and loved ones are good for morale. I thought then, and still do, that the evening prayer did a lot for the spiritual condition of *Iowa*.

In mid-March, Vice Admiral Willis A. Lee, commander of battleships in the Pacific, decided that *Iowa* should bombard the island of Mili, not far from Majuro.[93] Admiral Lee felt strongly enough about the operation to shift his flag to *Iowa* for the occasion. Our intelligence data indicated that Mili was equipped with 4.7-inch guns. We estimated that we could close to about sixteen thousand yards and be safely out of range. This we did, and opened fire to

---

92 From February 17–23, 1944, U.S. troops overcame stiff resistance to capture Eniwetok. Subsequently, the atoll became a major U.S. forward naval base.

93 Mili is located at the southeast end of the Marshall Islands, next to Majuro, which was then operating as a forward U.S. naval base. Mili was the site of a Japanese airfield and seaplane base.

port. When the Japanese returned our fire, it was quickly evident that their guns were larger than 4.7 inches.

I immediately ordered our exposed gun crews to take cover, namely the crews of the five-inch and the twenty- and forty-millimeter batteries. I so notified the conning tower, where admirals Lee and Hustvedt were stationed, and indicated that *Iowa* was altering course to seaward to open the range.

Suddenly, a shell hit *Iowa* on the face of number two turret, and shell fragments pierced the forward forty-millimeter gun tub on the starboard side. Had that gun crew not sought cover, there would have been casualties. Moments later, *Iowa* sustained a hit on the port side abreast of number three turret. The shell created a large hole in the skin of the ship, but disintegrated against armor and caused negligible damage. In retrospect, I thought this experience of being hit under fire had done *Iowa* good. After the war, I learned that the guns on Mili were seven-inch guns, captured at the fall of Singapore.

From late March through early May, *Iowa* participated in all sorts of operations across the Pacific as a member of Task Force 58. According to *Iowa*'s Private Log Book, there were strikes on the Palau Islands and Woleai in the Carolines, at Hollandia on northern New Guinea, and a second strike on Truk. *Iowa* also bombarded Ponape in the Carolines. Between strikes, *Iowa* engaged in regular drills and fueling operations while under way, and returned to Majuro for rest and maintenance.

On 6 June 1944,[94] *Iowa* left Majuro to participate in the U.S. operation to take Saipan, Tinian, and Guam in the Marianas.[95] After our departure, we were continuously at sea for over two

---

94   June 6, 1944 was "D-Day," the day of the Allied invasion of France.
95   By early 1944, Japan had heavily fortified and garrisoned Saipan, Tinian, and Guam at the southern end of the Marianas chain. Saipan and Tinian had been under Japanese control since shortly after WWI. Guam had long been a U.S. possession until Japan seized it on December 8–10, 1941, days after the Pearl Harbor attack.

months, primarily in and around the islands. Our activities there were many and varied. We maneuvered with the carriers as they conducted air strikes against the islands. On 13 June, *Iowa* bombarded the southern half of Saipan and the northern half of Tinian. I must note that *Iowa* was never detailed to bombard Guam. I had served on Guam in 1936 and 1937, and it would have been a personal tragedy for me to bring Guam under *Iowa*'s punishing gunfire. I had many fine native friends there whose lives would have been in peril.

After U.S. troops invaded Saipan on 15 June, *Iowa*'s task group was operating to the west of Tinian. Early on 19 June, a large group of enemy planes approached. To compress this yarn a bit, I quote from *A Capsule History of Iowa (BB-61)*, issued by the Navy Department:

> *Iowa*, with other battleships, four heavy cruisers, fourteen destroyers, under command of Vice Admiral Lee, formed a battle line around the aircraft carriers as the fleet prepared for the Battle of the Philippine Sea [on 19-20 June]. Thus started the Marianas "Turkey Shoot" [on 19 June], which resulted in the heavy loss of Japanese aircraft.[96]

On the first night of the battle, U.S. forces were moving to the west. Some of our planes were down, and it was hoped that men and planes might be recovered. The night was dark, the state of the sea choppy. Admiral Hustvedt and I were on the bridge. A signalman came racing up to say that he was certain he had heard a whistle from the water level. All aviators carried a loud police

---

96 At the Battle of the Philippine Sea, Japan lost nearly all of her carrier-based aircraft, a substantial number of land-based planes, many pilots, and three aircraft carriers. As a result, her naval air arm, her most effective strike force, was crippled. On the first day of the battle, *Iowa* shot down one torpedo plane and assisted in downing a torpedo plane and a fighter.

whistle as part of their equipment. No one on the navigating bridge had heard a whistle.

We immediately directed one of our screening destroyers to backtrack on *Iowa*'s wake to search for a possible downed aircraft. Shortly thereafter, the destroyer reported that she had recovered a downed aviator, but had been unable to recover the plane. The next afternoon, this destroyer came alongside *Iowa* for topping off with fuel. I had the pleasure of introducing the alert signalman who had heard the whistle to the recovered aviator.[97]

One important battleship function performed by *Iowa* in the Marianas and elsewhere was servicing destroyers. Destroyers steaming at high speed burn a lot of fuel. Almost daily at first light, a destroyer would come alongside, or one on either side, for topping off with fuel and provisions. *Iowa* had refrigeration capacity for 125 days of food for its crew and storage capacity for dry provisions much in excess of that. Many of the destroyers had dogs. Vickie took advantage of such visits to race up and down the deck, barking at the visiting dogs. The men were always amused by Vickie's actions on such occasions.

As I mentioned, starting in early June, *Iowa* was continuously at sea for over two months. I spent sixty-eight consecutive days and nights on *Iowa*'s bridge. Of course, I didn't suffer for lack of creature comforts, but it was the longest period that I spent under way in *Iowa* or any other ship in which I served on the bridge.

I cannot describe the stress produced by sixty-eight days on the bridge in a war zone. The experience was exhausting, yet sleep did not come easily. Body massage helped me get some rest. I managed

---

97 While U.S. troops were fighting on the Marianas, *Iowa* was under way patrolling, fueling from tankers, servicing destroyers, and occasionally supporting the action ashore. In late July, *Iowa* participated in air strikes on Palau and Yap in the Carolines and returned to Guam. U.S. forces subdued Saipan on July 9, Tinian on August 1, and Guam on August 10, 1944. A year later, in August 1945, the B-29s that dropped the atomic bombs on Hiroshima and Nagasaki flew from Tinian.

to stay in pretty good shape by doing exercises. Of course, the bridge area of a ship is extremely small, but before the war, I had become addicted to an exercise regime that could be done in a small space. I might add that, to this day, I still take my morning exercises. I do not enjoy them any more now than when I started them, but there is just enough Presbyterian left in me to punish myself the way I do.

Near the beginning of August, *Iowa* finally came to anchor at Eniwetok. A few days prior to our arrival, *Iowa* received dispatch orders that I was to be relieved of command of *Iowa* by Captain Allan R. McCann, and that I was to assume command of a North Pacific task force, U.S. Pacific Fleet, based in the Aleutian Islands in Alaska.

Although the dispatch was silent on this point, I was certain that my name had been reached on the list of prospective flag officers, and that my new assignment assured me of reaching the rank of rear admiral. I had known for many months that I was on the promotion list. While serving as the president's naval aide, it had been my pleasant duty to submit the list to him for his approval, and in this way I had seen the highly confidential list and my name on it.

My last few days in *Iowa* were busy ones, as I closed out all sorts of ship operations incident to my detachment. Captain McCann relieved me on 16 August 1944. I hated to give up command of this fine ship, but since relief was inevitable, it pleased me to turn the ship over to such capable hands.

As I relinquished command, it hit me that age was creeping up on me. I was at the end of the line insofar as individual ship commands were concerned. Never again would I experience the thrill of handling a ship in close quarters, of making the cranky animal do the necessary under trying and severe conditions. Whatever the rest of my naval career would bring, I would never again have the thrill of giving an order to the helm. Suddenly, at age fifty-three, I was an old man, and I felt a bit sorry for myself.

Upon detachment, I was bound for Pearl Harbor. The change-of-command ceremonies were at 1100 hours. At 1300 hours, a supply ship took off for Pearl with McCrea and luggage on board. I was tired. A light luncheon, a sleeping pill, and I turned in to sleep the sleep of the just until the following morning.

Chapter 25

The War in the North Pacific

—∞∞∞—

About four days after leaving Eniwetok, the store ship, McCrea, and luggage arrived in Pearl Harbor. I reported to the commander in chief of the Pacific Fleet, Admiral Chester W. Nimitz. My call on the admiral was most pleasant. I was to relieve my friend Hoke Smith as commander of the Alaska task force. Nimitz was anxious to get Admiral Smith to his next assignment as commander of a cruiser division, so he had already left Alaska. Nimitz remarked, "If you should come across Smith in either San Francisco or Seattle, tell him he is to take off a couple of days and talk to you about your new job."

I caught up with Hoke in San Francisco. We spent a fine couple of days together, comparing ideas and telling tales. He briefed me on my new commanding officer, Vice Admiral Frank Jack Fletcher, commander of the Alaskan Sea Frontier, and on the task force's operations bombarding the Kuril Islands.[98]

In due course, Hoke left for Pearl, and I took off for Seattle, where I was to get air passage to Adak. At the air command, I got

---

98 The Kuril Islands are just to the northeast of Japan. They had been Japanese since the late 1800s and were the point of embarkation for the Japanese forces that attacked Pearl Harbor.

a hint of things to come. When I was issued a heavily lined over-coat, the issuing officer remarked, "Out where you are going, you'll be glad you have that."

Some background about the North Pacific campaign is in order. As far as the press was concerned, the war in the Pacific was fought in the South and Central Pacific, and that is largely true. Certainly the spectacular and decisive campaigns were fought there. However, the strategic concept of the Pacific war was for a three-pronged attack in the South, Central, and North Pacific.

The North Pacific campaign was fought in and from the Aleutian Islands. The Aleutian Island chain is essentially a partially submerged mountain range of recent volcanic origin. There are about 150 islands, all rugged and steep. Rocks descend precipitously into deep water, so there are few anchorages and areas appropriate for naval bases. The Aleutians are in a class by themselves in one respect. They produce, day in and day out, the worst brand of weather a sailor can encounter.

Early in the war, Japan seized Kiska and Attu at the western end of the chain. The first phase of the U.S. North Pacific campaign was the offensive to retake the islands. When the offensive began in the spring of 1943, we initially intended to make an assault on Kiska, but we did not have enough resources. Instead, we decided to bypass Kiska and attack Attu, some three hundred miles further west. Thus, the practice of island bypassing, used so successfully in the Central and South Pacific, began in the Aleutians. The U.S. took Attu, and shortly afterward, under cover of the dense fog that persists during Aleutian summer, the Japanese quietly withdrew from Kiska without U.S. knowledge. Once again, the Aleutians were in American hands.

The next offensive of the North Pacific campaign consisted of attacks on the Kuril Islands.[99] Their purpose was to harass the Japanese and compel them, out of fear of invasion from the north, to

---

99 The offensive began in July 1943 with air attacks.

keep substantial forces in the Kurils that they might have deployed elsewhere. Thousands of Japanese men, hundreds of airplanes, and many ships were kept pinned down by this tactic.

Our principal base for these operations was Adak. The army and navy had constructed airfields there large enough to accommodate B-29 bombers. Attu, the secondary base, also had large army and navy installations with airfields. For safety reasons, emergency airfields were constructed on many other islands. These were necessary because of the bad weather. Time and time again, planes returning from Kuril strikes, low on gas, would find their fields closed in and have to proceed to other fields.

I arrived in Adak late Sunday afternoon, 27 August 1944. The following morning, I reported to Admiral Fletcher, who received me warmly. "McCrea," said he, "your main target will be the Kurils. By operating against them, we will be keeping pressure on the enemy, and that is what Admiral Nimitz wants. Personally, I don't regard the Kurils as of much importance. Even if we could tip each and every one of the islands over on its side, the war would not end one day sooner, in my judgment.

"While operating under me, your command will be as close to an independent operation as I can imagine. You are in charge. You are to do all the planning. Send me copies of what you propose to do. If I don't like what you're up to, I shall tell you. You can count on limited support from our air forces. It will not be substantial, but it will help.

"Your principal problem here will be one of morale. There are limited facilities in Adak for crew relaxation. If opportunity offers, I shall send your force back to Dutch Harbor from time to time, where it will be more possible to relax."

The admiral continued, "Drop in and see me anytime it may be convenient. What about dinner here tonight?" And that was about it, the sum and substance of my introduction to my North Pacific command and my relationship with my commander. I was impressed at the latitude given me, and said so.

My task force, TF92, consisted of three light cruisers of the *Omaha* class and nine big destroyers of the latest type. The cruiser *Richmond* was my flagship. I inherited Hoke Smith's task force staff, and they were a good lot.

It was immediately evident that the North Pacific would be very different from where I had come from. The climate was vile. High winds and snow or rain were typical, although there were occasionally better spells of two to three days. Conditions were also highly changeable. I never left the ship without consulting the aerographer[100] about the forecast for the next few hours.

At the earliest opportunity, I got my flag staff together and started planning strikes on the Kurils. A number of factors shaped our operations. Our strikes had to be short, because our air forces could not provide air cover throughout our bombardment raids. Although our bombers could give us lookout service until we got to the vicinity of the Kurils, our fighters could not operate far from the Aleutians because of fuel limitations. Very shortly after leaving Attu, the fighters had to return to base, and we would have five to six daylight hours without air cover before getting into bombardment range. My greatest anxiety was that we would be discovered on our approaches. Surprise was our most effective weapon.

Of course, the Japanese planes had the same limitations as ours. The enemy had plenty of in-close air power, but it could not operate as far as the Aleutians. Our intelligence indicated that the Japanese had many airfields and hundreds of planes. An intelligent employment of them could have raised havoc with us. We had anti-aircraft guns, but we could not count on them to drive off a determined air attack.

Since our operations were intended merely to exert pressure on the Kurils, Admiral Fletcher and I agreed that unnecessary risk to ships and personnel was not appropriate. We ruled out daylight

---

100 An aerographer collects meteorological and oceanographic data and predicts the weather.

bombardments as too risky. The weather was always a factor in our operations. I relied heavily on our aerologist to try to ensure that our daylight runs to the target were under cloud cover. Whenever possible, we wanted to bombard during the dark of the moon.

With these factors in mind, I adopted a basic approach to planning, and all our strikes followed the same pattern. Invariably, we took off from Adak and went out to Attu, where we topped off with fuel and got advice on the weather we would encounter. We timed our departure from Attu so that we would reach the "open fire" point just after sunset on bombardment day.

Once off the Kurils, we would bombard for short period—a half to three-quarters of an hour. Upon completion of the bombardment, we would get away quickly, so as to get a night's run from the target before daylight. A night's run would not remove us from Japanese bomber range, but every bit of distance helped. We retired to the east—ships darkened, of course—at a speed of twenty-five knots. We generally reached our air umbrella just after daybreak the following morning.

Of course, things did not always go smoothly. On one sweep, we traveled thirteen hours after the bombardment and found ourselves only 130 miles from our target—this due to heavy seas. It is experiences like these that make a naval officer go prematurely gray.

One of the mysteries of the war to me was why the Japanese never ambushed us. We had to get into minable waters to deliver a bombardment. Once we had established a pattern, it should have been easy to cause us plenty of trouble. If the situation had been reversed, you can be sure that we would have met it decisively.

Each sortie was planned in detail. The plan was then laid out to scale on the game board in a large army warehouse in Adak. Each plan was rehearsed, and the captains and navigators of all ships were required to attend. Throughout these exercises, I stressed that we were rehearsing what I *hoped* to do. I cautioned that enemy countermeasures might be encountered. In that event, the plans would have to be modified as appropriate under the circumstances.

During my eight months with the task force, I hoped to make monthly sweeps to the Kurils. We actually made only four bombardment raids. Our targets were Matsuwa, Kurabu Zaki, and Suribachi Nau, the latter two on Paramashimu Island.

The war in the North Pacific did not receive much publicity. The news correspondents didn't like the area because foul weather and heavy seas made riding in ships extremely unpleasant. One bombardment sweep was generally enough for them. Prior to a sweep, I got the correspondents together and explained what I hoped to accomplish. After the operation, I would reassemble them to answer questions. During one such postmortem, a correspondent from the *Chicago Tribune* told me he would never again go on such an operation, and should he feel the urge to try again, he would sign voluntary commitment papers at the nearest hospital. There was nothing romantic about the North Pacific.

I spent Christmas 1944 in Adak. That Christmas Eve, I had a pleasant surprise that I shall not forget. I was feeling a bit low, wondering where next Christmas would find me, and thinking about my family back in Washington. The mail orderly suddenly appeared at my door with a package from Tiffany & Company, sent registered mail. I opened it, and there was a beautiful gold watch, chain, and knife. Inside the watch was a splendid inscription:

Captain J. L. McCrea
First Commanding Officer
of the
U.S.S. *Iowa*
Best wishes and good luck
From the crew
2-22-43 – 8-16-44

In the same mail, there was a note from Frank Duncan, *Iowa*'s chief police petty officer, telling me that the gift was on its way and that no one had been permitted to contribute more than a quarter. That was pleasant to hear.

Of course, the gift was completely against navy regulations, but I couldn't have returned it, even if I'd wanted to. I just sat there a bit stupefied and overcome at this gesture of goodwill. What a wonderful Christmas present.

From time to time, I heard rumors that the state of the president's health was not good. When I had last seen him in December 1943, he was in fine shape, insofar as I could tell. From time to time, I would receive a note from Grace Tully, which invariably contained a note of cheer from the president. When he returned from the Yalta Conference, I listened by radio to his report to the Congress. He remarked that he was giving his report while seated, because of the strain he experienced standing. While I understood this, nevertheless, it made me a bit apprehensive.

Early in April, I received a letter dated 30 March 1945, from Ross McIntire. Ross remarked lightly about the president's health. "He's a bit thin. I'm trying to get a little meat on him in anticipation of the heavy days ahead, setting up the United Nations in San Francisco during the last week in April." This remark also caused me some apprehension. One of the things I most remembered about Ross was that he was always after the president to cut down on his food. He always thought the president was too heavy.

Ross wound up his letter with a postscript that the position of judge advocate general of the navy would be vacant in September 1945. Would I be interested? I was sure that Ross was not speaking for himself, and that the president had told Ross to sound me out.

Ross's inquiry was problematic for me. My first reaction was negative. I was as qualified as any naval officer for the job of judge advocate general. I had done three tours of duty in the JAG Office, I held the degrees of *Juris Doctor* and LL.M. in law, and I was a member of several bars. However, even though I sensed that the war was beginning to wind down, there remained a lot to do in the Pacific to bring it to a conclusion. I had no idea how long that would take, but so long as there was a war, I wanted to be a part of it. Of course, the war might be over before September.[101] And I would be due for shore duty at that time.

What sort of a reply should I make to Ross? I knew I must respond reasonably promptly, because I was sure the inquiry came from the president. I decided to chew chalk on the matter for a few days. I still had not answered Ross's letter on 12 April 1945.

In the forenoon of 12 April, we set up a game board operation for a raid about ten days hence. Afterward, I returned to the ship, entered my cabin, and snapped on the radio at noon to get the six o'clock news from Los Angeles. (The time in Adak was six hours behind Los Angeles.) The first thing I heard was a fragment of a sentence to the effect that, "Mrs. Roosevelt had sent appropriate word to her sons who were serving in the armed services." I realized that death had come to the president.

In accordance with instructions from the Navy Department, we held memorial services for the president. Our chaplain asked that I say a few words, because I had known the president personally. This I declined to do, feeling in some way that my speaking might be construed as taking advantage of my relationship with the president. The chaplain, the Reverend Michael Duty, Chaplain Corps, gave a wonderful three- or four-minute tribute.

The next day, to my amazement, I received orders detaching me from my command and ordering me to report without delay to the chief of naval operations in Washington for duty in that office. My detachment came as a total surprise. To be sure, I had not expected to remain long in this assignment, if the term of duty of my predecessors was any guide. Rear Admiral Wilder Baker had stayed about six months; Hoke Smith, about four months. When

---

101 The official announcement of the Japanese agreement to surrender was made on August 15, 1945, and the formal surrender ceremony in Tokyo Bay took place on September 2, 1945. Victory was achieved in Europe on May 7, 1945, the date the Allies accepted the unconditional surrender of the German armed forces.

they were detached, they were ordered to command cruiser divisions in the Pacific. I would have been pleased to have a cruiser division command, but I had been at sea in excess of two years, and I knew shore duty was a distinct possibility.

I received my orders with mixed emotions. The job in the Aleutians had been good for me. Although it was removed from the main theater of operations, I had had as near to an independent command as a new flag officer could wish, and the freedom had allowed me to develop professionally. I parted company with Admiral Fletcher with genuine regret. We had had a fine association, and I think we did something more or less worthwhile for the country.

I was concerned about giving up a sea job for a shore job, the importance of which was not evident to me. I was particularly puzzled by the precipitous nature of my detachment, but I had been around the navy long enough to know there is always a reason. Since the officer designated to relieve me was still on duty in Washington, I turned over my command to the senior captain in the task force and departed for the East Coast.

Afterword

———∞∞∞———

McCrea's continuous narrative about his career ends abruptly with his sudden recall to Washington in April 1945. By the time he recorded about this period of his life, he was well into his eighties, and he may simply have run out of steam. However, he didn't think much of the work he was assigned to do when he first returned to Washington, and he may not have been inspired to describe it. He did record a little more, but his recollections were episodic. From his fragmentary recordings and other sources, it is possible to tie up the loose ends of his story.

The president's death was a blow to McCrea, greater than one might have expected from the feelings he expressed about the president when he left the White House. In the days following the president's death, he wrote letters to members of the White House community. On April 13, he sent a short note to Mrs. Roosevelt saying that he was "shocked and grieved beyond expression." Later, in letters to Ross McIntire and Bill Hassett, he was more forthcoming about his feelings about the president and his work for him. To McIntire, he wrote:

> As you know, my orders to the White House came "out of the blue." I had not previously known [the president], and assignment as naval aide had never been one of my ambi-

tions. I therefore entered on my new duties with a completely open mind. It wasn't long until I came to the realization that he was a *great* man. The longer I stayed, the more I realized he was a *good* man as well. He was keen mentally. He saw the heart of a problem with an awareness that was often startling. He was invariably so kind, so considerate, and so thoughtful! Serving him was not alone a duty, but it came to be a labor of love for me. I was constantly asking myself, "How can I be of *more* service to him?" . . . I bore him much affection.

McCrea confessed to McIntire the guilt he had felt at leaving the president to go to sea, guilt that had intensified with the deaths of several members of the president's staff, including Pa Watson.

I felt deeply that I should get to sea . . . So I asked to go. He was understanding, as always, and acceded to my request, although he did ask if I couldn't "get something later." As I look back on it, I did a pretty selfish thing. If I had it to do over again, I would have let the career go and stayed and done the best I could for him.

To Bill Hassett, McCrea wrote:

The news of the loss of our good friend left me shocked and grieved. He was a great man and a good man, too. I have never known any man for whom I bore so much affection . . . We were greatly privileged, Bill, to have known and served him as president. But more than all that, we were particularly privileged to have known and served one so great and so good.

About the same time, McCrea received a letter from Harry Hopkins that must have made him feel gratified. Hopkins wrote:

Since you wrote me your nice note on the 21st of March, the great blow has struck and the whole world mourns the greatest champion of human liberty and freedom that ever lived. He was so fond and devoted to you, and ever since you have been away, he has been asking me how things are going with you. I am sure you could not possibly know how much you helped him during the years you were at the White House.

Given the urgency of his recall orders, McCrea hurried to Washington, arriving at midnight and reporting to the CNO's Office first thing the following morning. Much to his surprise, neither Fleet Admiral King[102] nor his chief of staff broached the topic of his next assignment, and he was told to take a week off to unwind.

McCrea spent some of his unexpected free time visiting friends at the White House. He obtained some insight into his sudden recall from Alaska from Sam Rosenman, former counsel and advisor to President Roosevelt, who was then serving in the same capacity for President Harry S. Truman. Rosenman said that when Truman became president, Admiral King wanted McCrea to serve as his naval aide because Truman knew next to nothing about the navy. However, President Truman chose his own naval aide, Lieutenant Commander James K. Vardaman Jr., U.S. Naval Reserve, the head of a St. Louis shoe manufacturing company. While Rosenman's story made sense, McCrea never received an explanation of his sudden detachment from anyone at the Navy Department.

As it turned out, there was a vacancy in the CNO's Office left by an officer who had suffered a heart attack. McCrea replaced him as director of the central division. Among other duties, he acted as navy liaison with the State Department. He continued in this position through the end of the war.

---

102 Fleet admiral, a five-star rank created during WWII, was the highest rank ever attainable in the Navy. Only four officers ever held the rank: Ernest J. King, Chester A. Nimitz, William D. Leahy, and William F. Halsey Jr.

McCrea went on to hold a number of important senior navy positions. In December 1945, Fleet Admiral Chester A. Nimitz relieved King as CNO, and McCrea was assigned as assistant CNO for administration. In August 1946, on the recommendation of McCrea's immediate boss, Nimitz promoted McCrea to deputy CNO for administration, and he advanced to the rank of vice admiral. As one of five deputy CNOs working directly under the CNO and the vice CNO, he was one of the top seven officers in naval operations.

McCrea found Nimitz to be always a gentleman and "a great guy to work for and with." Nimitz gave him a variety of assignments, some of which McCrea characterized as "odd jobs." One of the latter was using his sense of tact to rewrite letters drafted for the CNO's signature that Nimitz found harsh or insulting.

In January 1948, McCrea was assigned as deputy commander in chief of the Pacific Fleet at the request of the fleet's commander in chief, Admiral DeWitt C. Ramsey. Ramsey was gentle and somewhat retiring. Early as commander in chief, he had had an unpleasant meeting with General of the Army Douglas MacArthur,[103] at which he felt "pushed around." When Pacific Fleet business required a second meeting with the general, Ramsey asked McCrea to go on his behalf. McCrea was happy to take on the assignment. He had met MacArthur before and was not intimidated. After a year with the Pacific Fleet, McCrea returned to Washington, where in June 1949, he became director of staff of the personnel policy board in the office of the secretary of defense.

When it came time for reassignment in 1952, McCrea was one year short of the navy's mandatory retirement age of sixty-two. Rather than leave the navy, he chose to take a cut in rank to rear admiral to become commandant of the First Naval District in Bos-

---

103 General of the army, a five-star general officer rank, is the second highest possible rank in the U.S. Army. During WWII, it was conferred on four officers: Douglas MacArthur, Dwight D. Eisenhower, George Marshall, and Henry H. ("Hap") Arnold.

ton, Massachusetts, where he served primarily in a public relations capacity. On June 1,1953, he retired after thirty-eight years as a commissioned officer, and he was re-promoted to the rank of vice admiral based on his service record.

A month later, McCrea embarked on a second career in client relations with John Hancock Mutual Life Insurance Company, based in Boston. He traveled extensively to visit clients and deliver speeches. He remained with the company until 1966, when he reached John Hancock's mandatory retirement age of seventy-five.

McCrea's wife, Estelle, died on July 6, 1961. A year or so later, he began to pay an increasing amount of attention to Martha Tobey, my widowed mother. She was not keen to remarry, but he was unfazed. He wined and dined her, wrote, phoned, and introduced her to interesting people. He cultivated her family and friends, took an interest in her worries, and repeatedly told her what a wonderful person she was. When she finally agreed to marry him, he had a little plaque made up that read, "On this spot she said 'yes,'" with the date. He liked to display it on the library sofa. He once joked to a friend that it was harder to win the hand of Mrs. Tobey than the Second World War. After their marriage in January 1965, his attentions continued unabated. He celebrated their anniversary monthly to make up for their late start, and he always kept an eye out for her happiness and well-being.

Years later, when I was editing McCrea's reminiscences of World War II, I had a sense of déjà vu. McCrea's efforts to preserve FDR's energies and lighten his load, and his plan to transfer the president to *Iowa* in a fancy boatswain's chair, showed the same thoughtfulness and creativity he had shown my mother. The same was true of his leadership in *Iowa*. In his many initiatives to improve morale—the nightly news broadcast, the evening prayer, the pleasant word before bedtime—I recognized his intuitive grasp of human nature and his personal concern for those in his charge.

McCrea died on January 25, 1990, at the age of ninety-eight. At the reception after his funeral at Arlington National Cemetery, he received an unusual tribute. His leadership had already been well recognized. Admiral King had spoken of "the seeds of discipline" in *Iowa*, high praise from this tight-lipped and critical officer. President Roosevelt described *Iowa* as a "happy ship." Admiral Nimitz awarded McCrea a legion of merit for his skill and courage in fighting *Iowa*, and for his inspiring leadership to the officers and men. McCrea also received a gold star in lieu of a second legion of merit for his leadership in the Aleutians. Yet the recognition he received at the reception was unique.

Among those attending the funeral were five or six middle-aged former bluejackets who had served under McCrea in *Iowa*, more than forty-five years before. None of them knew the family. At the reception, they asked to speak about him, and the gathering quieted down to listen. Unfortunately, little of what they had to say was audible, but they were eloquent nevertheless. As each man stepped forward and began to speak, each choked up or wept openly. The incident was as moving as it was unexpected. It was a fitting tribute to a man whose work in World War II, both as leader and aide, was characterized by personal commitment and caring.

Endnotes

⊱⊰⊱

NOTE: The editor has incorporated into the body of the memoir first person material from McCrea's speeches, interviews and writings. The incorporated material is identified below by page number, quotation, and source.

Abbreviations:
FRUS—Foreign Relations of the United States
NHHC—Naval History and Heritage Command

INTRODUCTION
McCrea, *A Naval Life*, chapters 1, 3–5, 8, 15, 17, 24, 28, 29, 31, 32, 34–37.

P. xii. ". . . popular Capt. John McCrea"
Cassini, Igor, "These Charming People," *Washington Times-Herald*, December, 1942;
Severo, Richard, "Igor Cassini, Hearst Columnist, Dies at 86," *The New York Times*, January 9, 2002.

P. xvi. ". . . the navy's third airplane"
Exhibit on Wright B-1 Flyer, Dahlgren Hall, U.S. Naval Academy, visited April 2011;
Thorn, "Naval aviation pioneers";
Sitz," A History of naval aviation," pp. 5–6.

P. xvii. "Orange war plans"
"War Plan Orange," *GlobalSecurity.com.*, http://www.globalsecurity.org /military/ops/war-plan-orange.htm, last accessed 9.20.15.

P. xviii. "Pan American's trans-Pacific Clipper Service"
"Pan Am Across the Pacific, Passenger service," *Pan Am Clipper Flying Boats*, http://www.clipperflyingboats.com/transpacific-airline-service, last accessed 9.20.15.

P. xx. "temporarily retired from the U.S. Army"
"Douglas MacArthur," *Encyclopedia Britannica Online, s.v. [Britannica]*, last modified 8.6.14, http://www.britannica.com/biography /Douglas-MacArthur, last accessed 10.2.15.

P. xxi. "He also prepared Admiral . . . the president had on his mind." McCrea, *Remembrances N.I.*, p. 139.

CHAPTER 1—THE UNITED STATES GOES TO WAR

1. "Yamamoto Isoroku," *Britannica,* last modified 5.5.14, http://www .britannica.com/biography/Yamamoto-Isoroku, last accessed 10.15.15; Stille, Mark, "Yamamoto and the Planning for Pearl Harbor," *The History Reader,* last modified 11.26.12, http://www.thehistoryreader .com/modern-history/yamamoto-planning-pearl-harbor/, last accessed 9.21.15.

P. 5. "Energetic. . . . Very air-minded," in "Memorandum for Admiral Stark," McCrea, *Remembrances N.I.*, Appendix B, p. 17.

P. 5. "If we had had Horatio . . . simply wasn't ready for it." McCrea, *Remembrances N.I.*, p. 87.

2. United States Department of State, "The Conferences at Washington, 1941–1942, and Casablanca, 1943" [FRUS 1942], p. XIII.

3. McCrea, *A Naval Life*, p. 540.

4. "Ernest King, World War II," *Wikipedia*, https://en.wikipedia.org /wiki/Ernest_King, last accessed 5.3.16; "Fleet Admiral Ernest J. King," *NHHC*, published 12.18.15, http://www.history.navy.mil /browse-by-topic/commemorations-toolkits/cno-and-opnav -centennial/chiefs-of-naval-operations/fleet-admiral-ernest-j-king .html, last accessed 5.3.16.

5. FRUS 1942, p. 233;
Declaration by the United Nations, http://avalon.law.yale.edu/20th _century/decade03.asp, last accessed 10.8.15;
Rearden, Steven L., *Council of War: A History of the Joint Chiefs of Staff 1942–1991* (Washington, D.C.: NDU Press, 2012), pp. 2–7, http:// www.dtic.mil/doctrine/doctrine/history/councilofwar.pdf, last accessed 10.8.15.

CHAPTER 2—REPORTING TO THE PRESIDENT

6. "Aide-de-camp" in "American Heritage Dictionary of the English Language, Fifth Edition," *Houghton Mifflin Harcourt Publishing Company*,

http://www.thefreedictionary.com/aide-de-camp, last accessed 4.28.16;
"White House Military Office," *Wikipedia,* https://en.wikipedia.org
/wiki/White_House_Military_Office, last accessed 5.3.16.

7. "United States presidential election of 1936," *Britannica,* http://
    www.britannica.com/event/United-States-presidential-election
    -of-1936, last accessed 10.2.15.

CHAPTER 3—ZEROING IN

8. "Fleet Admiral Ernest J. King," *NHHC,* published 12.18.15, Op. cit.

CHAPTER 4—THE MAP ROOM

9. McIlvaine, Bill, "Harry Hopkins: President Franklin D. Roosevelt's
    Deputy President," *American History Magazine,* April 2000,
    last modified 6.12.06, http://www.historynet.com/harry-hopkins
    -president-franklin-d-roosevelts-deputy-president.htm, last accessed
    9.10.15.

10. Lerner, Adrienne Wilmoth, "Operation Magic," *Internet FAQ
    Archives, Encyclopedia of Espionage, Intelligence, and Security,* http://
    www.faqs.org/espionage/Nt-Pa/Operation-Magic.html, last accessed
    9.22.15.

CHAPTER 5—PRESS RELATIONS

11. "Drew Pearson, American journalist," *Britannica,* http://www
    .britannica.com/biography/Drew-Pearson, last accessed 10.3.15;
    "Drew Pearson (journalist)," *Wikipedia,* https://en.wikipedia.org
    /wiki/Drew_Pearson_(journalist), last accessed 8.22.15.

12. "Elmer Holmes Davis," *Encyclopedia of World Biography (2004), Ency-
    clopedia.com,* http://www.encyclopedia.com/doc/1G2-3404707996
    /html, last accessed 9.22.15.

13. "Office of War Information," *The Columbia Encyclopedia, 6th Ed.,
    The Columbia, Electronic Encyclopedia, Columbia University Press,*
    2015, https://www.questia.com/read/1E1-OfficeWa/office-of-war
    -information, last accessed 9.22.15;
    "United States Office of War Information," *Wikipedia,* http://
    en.wikipedia.org/wiki/United_States_Office_of_War_Information,
    last accessed 8.22.15.

14. "The Battle of the Coral Sea," *NHHP,* published 3.30.15, http://www
    .history.navy.mil/research/library/online-reading-room/title-list
    -alphabetically/b/battle-of-the-coral-sea.html, last accessed 8.23.15;
    Shmoop Editorial Team, "Coral Sea and Midway (May 7, 1942–Jun
    6, 1942 in World War II: Home Front," Shmoop University, Inc.,

11.11.08, http://www.shmoop.com/wwii-home-front/coral-sea-midway-battle.html, last accessed 9.7.15;

"Battle of the Coral Sea," *Wikipedia,* https://en.wikipedia.org/wiki/Battle_of_the_Coral_Sea, last accessed 9.7.15.

15. "Lexington (CV-2) War Damage Report—June 15, 1942 (Coral Sea)," *WWII Archives Foundation,* http://www.wwiiarchives.net/servlet/action/document/index/1313/0, last accessed 8.22.15;

"Battle of Midway: 4–7 June 1942," *NHHC,* last modified 3.9.15, http://www.history.navy.mil/research/library/online-reading-room/title-list-alphabetically/b/battle-of-midway-4-7-june-1942.html, last accessed 9.7.15.

CHAPTER 6—YARN: A LESSON ON THE WHITE HOUSE STEPS

16. "Alexander Woollcott," *Britannica,* http://www.britannica.com/biography/Alexander-Woollcott, last accessed 10.1.15.

CHAPTER 7—FOREIGN RELATIONS

17. FRUS 1942, "Editorial Note," pp. 448–449;

"Pacific War Council," *Wikipedia,* http://en.wikipedia.org/wiki/Pacific_War_Council, last accessed 8.15.15.

18. "Edward Frederick Lindley Wood, 1st earl of Halifax," *Britannica,* http://www.britannica.com/biography/Edward-Frederick-Lindley-Wood-1st-earl-of-Halifax, last accessed 8.24.15.

19. "World War II and Japanese Occupation," *Philippine Country Guide,* last modified 2006, http://www.philippinecountry.com/philippine_history/japanese_colonization.html, last accessed 10.3.15;

"Commonwealth of the Philippines, World War II," *Wikipedia,* https://en.wikipedia.org/wiki/Commonwealth_of_the_Philippines#World_War_II, last accessed 9.3.15.

20. "Memorandum by the President's Naval Aide (McCrea)," FRUS 1942, pp. 449–453;

"Editorial Note," FRUS 1942, p. 419.

21. "Armistice agreement between the German High Command of the Armed Forces and French Plenipotentiaries, June 22, 1940," *The Avalon Project: Documents in Law, History, and Diplomacy, Yale Law School, Lillian Goldman Law Library,* http://avalon.law.yale.edu/wwii/frgearm.asp, last accessed 9.27.15;

"Foreign Relations of Vichy France," *Wikipedia,* https://en.wikipedia.org/wiki/Vichy_France#Foreign_relations_of_Vichy_France, last accessed 8.24.15;

Brown, Robert L., "Operation Catapult: Naval Destruction at Mers-el-Kébir," *Historynet*, last modified 8.31.06, http://www.historynet.com/operation-catapult-naval-destruction-at-mers-el-kebir.htm, last accessed 8.24.15.

22. "Battle of Madagascar," *War History Online*, last modified 8.18.13, https://www.warhistoryonline.com/war-articles/battle-madagascar.html, last accessed 8.24.15.

CHAPTER 8—INFORMAL DIPLOMACY

23. New World Encyclopedia contributors, "Wilhelmina of the Netherlands," *New World Encyclopedia*, last modified 2.2.08, http://www.newworldencyclopedia.org/p/index.php?title=Categor:Credited&oldid=929385, last accessed 9.24.15;

New World Encyclopedia contributors, "Juliana of the Netherlands," *New World Encyclopedia*, last modified 5.26.14, http://www.newworldencyclopedia.org/p/index.php?title=Juliana_of_the_Netherlands&oldid=981801, last accessed 9.24.15.

24. "Batavia, Dutch East Indies," *Wikipedia*, https://en.wikipedia.org/wiki/Batavia,_Dutch_East_Indies, last accessed 9.24.15.

25. Navy Department Office of Naval Intelligence, "The Battle of Savo Island, 8 August 1942, Combat Narrative," *Ibiblio.org/Hyperwar*, http://www.ibiblio.org/hyperwar/USN/USN-CN-Savo/, last accessed 8.25.15.

CHAPTER 9—WHITE HOUSE VISITORS

26. Rees, Laurence, "Molotov Visits Washington" in "Key Moments, Western Front, 29th May 1942," *WW2History*, http://ww2history.com/key_moments/Western/Molotov_visits_Washington, last accessed 8.26.15.

27. "Editorial Note," FRUS 1942, p. 419.

P. 69. "Out the window . . . relaxation at once." McCrea, *Remembrances N.I.*, p. 144.

CHAPTER 10—YARN: A TOUR OF HYDE PARK

28. "U.S. Merchant Marine in World War II," "The Battle for Control of the Atlantic," and "Convoys," *American Merchant Marine at War*, last modified 1.31.07, http://www.usmm.org/ww2.html, last accessed 9.24.15;

"Operation Drumbeat (January–June 1942)," *Wikipedia*, https://en.wikipedia.org/wiki/Battle_of_the_Atlantic#Operation_Drumbeat_.28January_.E2.80.93_June_1942.29, last accessed 9.24.15;

History.com staff, "Battle of the Aleutians," *A+E Networks*, published 2009, http://www.history.com/topics/world-war-ii/battle-of-the-aleutian -islands, last accessed 9.5.15;

McKillop, Jack, "United States Navy Aircraft Carriers December 7, 1941," *Bluejacket.com*, http://bluejacket.com/ww2_12-07-41_carriers .html, last accessed 9.15.15;

"Battle of Gazala, Fall of Tobruk," *Wikipedia*, https://en.wikipedia .org/wiki/Battle_of_Gazala#Fall_of_Tobruk, last accessed 9.8.15.

CHAPTER 11—SPECIAL JOBS

Pp. 85–86. "On another occasion the White House phone . . . as best I could." McCrea, *Remembrances N.I.*, pp. 204–206.

29. Roosevelt, F.D., "Fireside Chat 21: On Sacrifice (April 28, 1942)," *Miller Center, University of Virginia*, http://millercenter.org/president /speeches/detail/3327, last accessed 9.24.15;

"The Story of Dr. Wassell (1944)," *Wikipedia*, https://en.wikipedia .org/wiki/The_Story_of_Dr._Wassell, last accessed 9.24.15.

30. "U-Boat Happy Time," *American Merchant Marine at War*, last modified 1.31.07, http://www.usmm.org/ww2.html, last accessed 9.24.15.

31. "President Herbert and Lou Henry Hoover's Rapidan Camp," *National Park Service*, www.nps.gov/nr/travel/presidents/hoover _camp_rapidan.html, last accessed 9.24.15.

32. Richard Sassaman, "The Impossible Raid," *America in WWII*, June 2007, http://www.americainwwii.com/articles/the-impossible-raid/, last accessed 5.2.16.

P. 90. "It was interesting to be . . . as the president." McCrea, *Remembrances N.I.*, p. 157.

33. Ardman, Harvey, "World War II: German Saboteurs Invade America in 1942," *HistoryNet*, last modified 6.12.06, http://www.historynet .com/world-war-ii-german-saboteurs-invade-america-in-1942.htm, last accessed 8.30.15.

CHAPTER 12—FDR

P. 100. ". . . there were more important things in store . . . naval officer." McCrea, *Remembrances N.I.*, p. 267.

34. "Messages," *Naval Personnel Command*, http://www.public.navy.mil /bupers-npc/reference/messages/Pages/default2.aspx, last accessed 9.25.15;

Shafroth, J.F., "Bureau of Navigation Circular Letter No. 152-41," *NHHC*, last modified 5.13.14, http://www.history.navy.mil/browse -by-topic/heritage/uniforms-and-personal-equipment/tags/bureau -of-navigation-circular-letter-no-152-41.html, last accessed 9.25.15.

P. 101. "It was startling to be quizzed . . . little about." McCrea, *Remembrances N.I.*, p. 276.

35. "All Purpose Capsule (US DOD pain relief tablet)," *AcronymFinder. com,* http://www.acronymfinder.com/Military-and-Government/APC. html, last accessed 9.25.15.

36. "Office of Civilian Defense," *The Eleanor Roosevelt Papers Project, George Washington University,* http://www.gwu.edu/~erpapers/teachinger /glossary/office-civilian-defense.cfm, last accessed 9.25.11;
"James M. Landis," *Wikipedia,* https://en.wikipedia.org/wiki /James_M._Landis, last accessed 8.3.15.

CHAPTER 13—SEA DUTY AND WAR PRODUCTION
37. "Joseph Grew," *Wikipedia,* https://en.wikipedia.org/wiki/Joseph _Grew, last accessed 8.31.15.

Pp. 112–113. "I recall that . . . no politics.'" McCrea. *Remembrances N.I.*, p. 354.

38. "The President's Party" in Log, FDR Inspection Trip, Part 1.

39. Bellafaire, Judith A., "The Women's Army Corps: A Commemoration of World War II Service," *U.S. Army Center of Military History,* last modified 2.17.05, http://www.history.army.mil/brochures/wac /wac.htm, last accessed 9.25.15.

CHAPTER 14—THE INVASION OF NORTH AFRICA AND PREPARATIONS FOR THE CASSABLANCA CONFERENCE
40. Hickman, Kennedy, "World War II: Operation Torch," *About.com,* http://militaryhistory.about.com/od/worldwarii/p/optorch.htm, last accessed 9.25.15;
"Operation Torch," *Wikipedia,* https://en.wikipedia.org/wiki/Operation _Torch, last accessed 9.25.15;
Eisenhower, Report on Operations in Northwest Africa, pp. 16–17, http://www.ibiblio.org/hyperwar/USA/rep/TORCH/DDE-Torch .html#armistice, last accessed 10.5.15.

41. Reilly, *Reilly of the White House*, pp. 143–151.

42. Hamilton, *Mantle of Command*, pp. 404–405, 415–417;
"Admiral Darlan," *The History Learning Site,* http://www .historylearningsite.co.uk/world-war-two/military-commanders-of -world-war-two/admiral-darlan/, last accessed 9.25.15;
"François Darlan," *Britannica,* http://www.britannica.com/biography /Francois-Darlan, last accessed 9.25.15.

43. "Casablanca Conference," *Britannica,* http://www.britannica.com /event/Casablanca-Conference, last accessed 10.5.15.

CHAPTER 15—THE CASABLANCA CONFERENCE

44. "Itinerary," Log, FDR Casablanca Trip;
    Craven, W.E. & Cate, J.L., eds., "Vol. I, Chapter 9—The Early Development of Air Transport and Ferrying," *The Army Air Forces in World War II*, (Chicago: University of Chicago Press 1948–1958), pp. 319–320, *Ibiblio.org/Hyperwar*, http://www.ibiblio.org/hyperwar/AAF/I/AAF-I-9.html, last accessed 9.26.15.

45. Log, FDR Casablanca Trip, p. 4.

46. Roosevelt, *As He Saw It*, pp. 75–77.

47. "Senegal, The French Period," *Britannica*, http://www.britannica.com/place/Senegal/Government-and-society#toc255602, last accessed 9.26.15.

48. "Elliott Roosevelt (1910–1990)," *The Eleanor Roosevelt Papers Project, George Washington University*, http://www.gwu.edu/~erpapers/teachinger/glossary/roosevelt-elliott-son.cfm, last accessed 9.26.15.

49. "W. Averell Harriman," *Britannica*, http://www.britannica.com/biography/W-Averell-Harriman, last accessed 9.26.15.

50. McCrea, *A Naval Life*, pp. 769–770.

51. Simpkin, John, "Henri Giraud," *Spartacus Educational*, last modified 8.2014, http://spartacus-educational.com/FRgiraud.htm, last accessed 9.26.15.

52. Simpkin, John, "Charles Nogues," *Spartacus Educational*, last modified 8.2014, http://spartacus-educational.com/FRnogues.htm, last accessed 9.26.15.

53. Brands, H.W., *Traitor to His Class: The Privileged Life and Radical Presidency of Franklin Delano Roosevelt* (New York: Anchor Books 2009), p. 704.

54. Hickman, Kennedy, "World War II: Operation Torch, Operation Torch-Planning," *About.com*, http://militaryhistory.about.com/od/worldwarii/p/optorch.htm, last accessed 9.25.15;
    "Robert D. Murphy (1894–1978)," *U.S. Diplomacy: An Online Exploration of Diplomatic History and Foreign Affairs*, http://www.usdiplomacy.org/history/service/history_robertdmurphy.php, last accessed 10.5.15.

55. "Mohammedan" in "Collins English Dictionary, 12th Edition," *Harper Collins Publishers*, http://thefreedictionary.com/mohammedan, last accessed 5.2.16.

56. FRUS 1942, pp. 609, 644 (Giraud), and p. 694 (de Gaulle).

57. FRUS 1942, pp. 839–840;
    Wells, Ann S., "Free French," in *Historical Dictionary of World War II: The War against Germany and Italy* (Baltimore: Scarecrow Press 2013), pp. 134–135.

CHAPTER 16—RETURN TO THE WHITE HOUSE AND DETACHMENT

58. McMillan, Joseph, "Flag Officers of the U.S. Navy," *Sea Flags,* last modified 2001, http://www.seaflags.us/seaflags.html#contents, last accessed 9.30.15;

    Log, FDR Casablanca Trip, picture between pp. 38 and 39.

59. "British West Africa," *Britannica,* http://www.britannica.com/place /British-West-Africa, last accessed 9.26.15.

60. Jalloh, Alustine and Falola, Toyin, *The United States and West Africa: Interactions and Relations* (Rochester: University of Rochester Press 2008), pp. 23–24;

    "Liberia and the United States: A Complex Relationship" in "Global Connections," *PBS.org,* http://www.pbs.org/wgbh/globalconnections /liberia/essays/uspolicy/, last accessed 9.26.15.

61. History.com staff, "FDR becomes the first president to travel by airplane on U.S. official business," *A+E Networks,* last modified 2009, http://www.history.com/this-day-in-history/fdr-becomes-first-president -to-travel-by-airplane-on-u-s-official-business, last accessed 9.3.15;

    History.com staff, "Franklin D. Roosevelt," *A+E Networks,* last modified 2009, http://www.history.com/topics/us-presidents/franklin-d -roosevelt, last accessed 9.26.15;

    Rothman, Lily, "This Was the First Time a Sitting U.S. President Visited Africa," *Time.com,* last modified 7.23.15, http://time.com/3962496 /obama-africa-trip-history-roosevelt/, last accessed 9.26.15.

CHAPTER 17—*IOWA* GOES INTO COMMISSION

62. "Broadside," *Wikipedia,* https://en.wikipedia.org/wiki/Broadside, last accessed 9.25.15.

63. "Chapter 31A-2, The Gunnery Department" and "Chapter 31A-3, Duties of the Gunnery Officer," *Naval Ordnance and Gunnery, Vol. 2 Fire Control* (Washington, D.C.: Bureau of Naval Personnel 1958), http://www.eugeneleeslover.com/USNAVY/CHAPTER-31-A.html, last accessed 9.26.15.

64. *Ibid.*

65 "Master-at-arms," Compilation of Enlisted Ratings and Apprenticeships U.S. Navy 1775-Present, (Washington, D.C.: Bureau of Naval Personnel, 1969); "master-at-arms (2)" in "Dictionary.com," Dictionary.com Unabridged, Random House, Inc., http://www.dictionary. com/browse/master-at-arms, last accessed 6.23.16; "dpcsdan #56" in "Navy Police/Master-at-Arms Badges," U.S. Militaria Forum, http:// www.usmilitariaforum.com/forums/index.php?/topic/199619-navy -policemaster-at-arms-badges/page-3, last accessed 6.23.16.

66. "Gunner (2)" in "Collins English Dictionary—Complete and Una-bridged, 12th Edition 2014, *HarperCollins Publishers*, http.//www .thefreedictionary.com/gunner, last accessed 5.2.16.

P. 159. "The ceremonies were held . . . facing aft." McCrea, *Iowa History*, ch. 1, pp. 1–2.

P. 159. "I expect a clean ship.... must not fail them." McCrea, "*Address at the Commissioning Ceremony*" in *Iowa History*, Appendix 1.

P. 162. "In addition, last minute . . . were routine." *Iowa History*, ch. 2, pp. 1–2.

P. 163. "We passed under the Manhattan . . . Gravesend Bay." *Ibid.*, ch. 2, pp. 3–4.

CHAPTER 18—SHAKEDOWN

67. "Shakedown" and "shakedown cruise," *Seatalk, The Dictionary of English Nautical Language,* (Nova Scotia: Mike MacKenzie 2005), http:// www.seatalk.info/cgi-bin/nautical-marine-sailing-dictionary/db.cgi ?db=db&uid=default&FirstLetter=s&sb=Term&view _records=View+Records&nh=7, last accessed 9.29.15.

68. "Engineering department" in "BMR Training Resources to Help Sea-bees Advance," Ch. 6, p. 6–8, *Seabee Online, Official Online Magazine of the Seabees,* last modified 2.21.14, http://seabeemagazine .navylive.dodlive.mil/2014/02/21/bmr-training-resources-to-help -seabees-advance/, last accessed 9.29.15.

P. 165. "There were day and night . . . first aid training." *Iowa History*, ch. 4, pp. 1, 4.

69. "Conn [nautical]," *Dictionary.com Unabridged,* http://dictionary .reference.com/browse/conn, last accessed 9.5.15.

70. "Side boys" in "Navy Traditions and Customs," *NHHC,* last modified 5.12.14, http://www.history.navy.mil/browse-by-topic/heritage/terminology /nautical-terms-and-phrases-their-meaning-and-origin.html, last accessed 9.14.15.

Pp. 167–170. "Towards the end of the shakedown cruise . . . most power-ful ship in the world." McCrea, "Shakedown Address," *Iowa History*, Appendix 4.

71. U.S. Navy Training Film MN-9321c. "Major Caliber Guns and Tur-rets." 1955. (Iowa Class 16-inch guns and turrets), published 3.17.13, https://www.youtube.com/watch?v=_wT1xkRpCKk, last accessed 10.4.15.

P. 170. ". . . we headed north . . . Maine Coast." *Iowa History*, ch. 5, p. 1.

CHAPTER 20—PLANS FOR A SECRET MISSION

72. "The Atlantic Conference and Charter, 1941" and "The Formation of the United Nations, 1945" in "Milestones: 1937–1945," *Office of the*

Historian, U.S. Department of State, https://history.state.gov
/milestones/1937-1945, last accessed 9.30.15;

Higgins, Jenny, "Argentia," *Newfoundland and Labrador Heritage Web
Site,* last modified 7.07, http://www.heritage.nf.ca/articles/politics
/argentia-base.php, last accessed 9.29.15.

Hamilton, *Mantle of Command,* Chapter 1.

Pp. 175–176. "One bright spot . . . this was the result." McCrea, *Remembrances N.I.,* p. 263.

73. "Cairo Conference 1943," *U.S. Department of State Archive,*
http://2001-2009.state.gov/r/pa/ho/time/wwii/107184.htm, last accessed
9.14.15;

"The Tehran Conference 1943" in "Milestones: 1937–1945," *Office
of the Historian, U.S. Department of State,* https://history.state.gov
/milestones/1937-1945/tehran-conf, last accessed 9.14.15;

United States Department of State, "Introduction, The Conferences
at Cairo and Tehran, 1943" in "The Conferences at Cairo and Tehran" [FRUS 1943], pp. XI–XII.

P. 178. "He was a no-fooling guy . . . wishy-washy type." McCrea, *Remembrances N.I.,* p. 119.

CHAPTER 21—VOYAGE TO ALGERIA

74. Cdr. Charles F. Pick, Jr., U.S. Naval Reserve (Retired), "Torpedo on
the Starboard Beam," *Proceedings Magazine, U.S. Naval Institute,* Vol.
96/8/810, August 1970.

75. *Ibid.*

76. "Primer[2]" in "American Heritage Dictionary of the English Language,
Fifth Edition 2011, *Houghton Mifflin Harcourt Publishing Company,*
http://www.thefreedictionary.com/primer, last accessed 5.2.16.

77. "Crew Recalls How It Nearly Sank Roosevelt," *Boston Sunday Herald*
(Boston, MA), March 16, 1958; "F.D.R. in Peril from Torpedo on
U.S. Ship," *Boston Sunday Globe* (Boston, MA), March 16, 1958;
"U.S. Destroyer's Face Red After Shot at F.D.R.," *Boston Sunday
Globe* (Boston, MA), March 16, 1958;

Freeman, Gregory A., "USS *William D. Porter:* The U.S. Navy
Destroyer's Service in World War II," last modified 6.12.06, http://
www.historynet.com/uss-william-d-porter-the-us-navy-destroyers
-service-in-world-war-ii.htm, last accessed 7.17.15.

CHAPTER 22—THREE TRANSATLANTIC CROSSINGS

78. "Watches" in "Origins of Navy Terminology," *America's Navy,* last
modified 9.15.09, http://www.navy.mil/navydata/traditions/html
/navyterm.html#watches, last accessed 9.15.15.

79. New World Encyclopedia contributors, "Freetown," *New World Encyclopedia,* last modified 4.17.12. http://www.newworldencyclopedia. org/p/index.php?title=Freetown&oldid=960647, last accessed 9.16.15.

80. "Senegal, Government and Society," *Britannica,* last modified 7.30.14, http://www.britannica.com/place/Senegal/Government-and -society#toc255602, last accessed 9.26.15.

81. "Boatswain's chair," *Dictionary.com Unabridged,* http://dictionary .reference.com/browse/boatswain-s-chair, last accessed 10.10.15.

82. "Fancy work'" in "Naval Terminology," *USS Rankin (AKA-103),* last modified 2.8.12, http://www.ussrankin.org/terms/, last accessed 9.30.15.

CHAPTER 23—WAR PREPARATIONS

83. "*Iowa* class battleships," *Wikipedia,* https://en.wikipedia.org/wiki /List_of_battleships_of_the_United_States_Navy#Iowa.C2.A0class, last accessed 9.16.15.

P. 206. "I had witnessed the effect . . . account of themselves." McCrea, *A Naval Life*, pp. 151–152.

84. "Vickie Quits Mighty Iowa for 'Tin Can,'" *U.S.S. Iowa Veterans Association Newsletter* 34, no. 5 (Fall 2007): 12.

Pp. 206-207. "Food poisoning . . . the ham sandwiches." McCrea, Med. Sym. Speech, pp. 4–5.

P. 208. "A naval vessel . . . resentful." McCrea, *Remembrances N.I.*, Appendix C, p. 9.

P. 209. ". . . a passage of about nineteen hours." *Iowa History*, ch. 10, p. 2.

85. "Tuvalu History," *TuvaluIslands.com,* last modified 9.18.12, http:// www.tuvaluislands.com/history2.htm, last accessed 10.1.15;
Unites States Strategic Bombing Survey (Pacific), Chapter IX, pp. 191–193.

P. 209. "Entering the Funafuti . . . *New Jersey.*" *Iowa History,* ch. 10, p. 5.

86. Hickman, Kennedy, "World War II: Admiral Raymond Spruance," *About.com* http://militaryhistory.about.com/od/WorldWarIINavalLeaders /p/World-War-Ii-Admiral-Raymond-Spruance.htm, last accessed 9.15.15;
"Iowa III (BB-61)," *NHHC,* http://www.history.navy.mil/research /histories/ship-histories/danfs/i/iowa-iii.html, last accessed 9.15.15.

87. "Raymond Clapper (1892–1944)," *The Eleanor Roosevelt Papers Project, George Washington University,* http://www.gwu.edu/~erpapers /teachinger/glossary/clapper-raymond.cfm, last accessed 9.15.15.

CHAPTER 24—*IOWA* JOINS THE FIGHT

Pp. 211–212. "The day after *Iowa's* . . . that never materialized." *Iowa History*, ch. 10, p. 6.

88. United States Strategic Bombing Survey (Pacific), Chapter IX, pp.193–195;
Kiste, Robert S., "Marshall Islands History," *Britannica,* last modified 5.15.15, http://www.britannica.com/place/Marshall-Islands#toc53997, last accessed 9.16.15.
P. 212. "During the last day . . . task group carriers." *Iowa History,* ch. 10, p. 7.
P. 213. "On 12 February . . . back-to-back operations." *Ibid.,* ch. 11, p. 3;
89. "Battleships & World War II," GlobalSecurity.org, last modified 22.7.2011, http://www.globalsecurity.org/military/systems/ship/battleship-ww2.htm, last accessed 11.11.2015.
USS *Iowa* War Diary, February 1944.
90. United States Strategic Bombing Survey (Pacific), Chapter IX, pp. 194–195.
"Caroline Islands," *Wikipedia*, https://en.wikipedia.org/wiki/Caroline_Islands, last accessed 9.16.15.
Pp. 213–214. "Our task group . . . About 11:30 that morning . . ." *Iowa History,* ch. 11, pp. 3–5.
P. 214. "It was a murky . . . anticipation of battle." *Ibid.,* ch. 11, pp. 6–7.
P. 216. "The second of *Iowa*'s February . . . flights over Guam." *Ibid.,* ch. 12, pp. 1–4.
91. "Mariana Islands," *Britannica,* http://www.britannica.com/place/Mariana-Islands, last accessed 9.25.15.
92. "The Battle of Eniwetok" in "Pride and Patriotism: Stamford's Role in World War II," *The Stamford Historical Society Online,* http://www.stamfordhistory.org/ww2_eniwetok.htm, last accessed 9.16.15.
93. Spennemann, Dirk H.R. "Mili Island, Mili Atoll, A brief overview of its WWII sites," *Digital Micronesia,* last modified 2000, http://marshall.csu.edu.au/Marshalls/html/WWII/Mili.html, last accessed 9.26.15.
94. "D-Day June 6, 1944," *Army.Mil Features,* http://www.army.mil/d-day, last accessed 5.3.16.
95. "The Battle of Saipan," *The Battle of Saipan, WWII Maritime Heritage Trail,* http://www.pacificmaritimeheritagetrail.com/history-of-the-battle/, last accessed 10.1.15.
96. Trueman, Chris, "The Battle of the Philippine Sea," *The History Learning Site,* http://www.historylearningsite.co.uk/world-war-two/the-pacific-war-1941-to-1945/the-battle-of-the-philippine-sea/, last accessed 10.1.15;
USS *Iowa* War Diary, June 1944, 19 June entry.
97. *Iowa* Private Log, June 11-August 8, 1944;

Budge, Kent G., "Mariana Islands," *Pacific War Online Encyclopedia*, last modified 2011, http://pwencycl.kgbudge.com/M/a/Mariana _Islands.htm, last accessed 10.4.15;

History.com staff, "Bombing of Hiroshima and Nagasaki," *A+E Networks*, last modified 2009, http://www.history.com/topics/world -war-ii/bombing-of-hiroshima-and-nagasaki, last accessed 10.4.15.

CHAPTER 25—THE WAR IN THE NORTH PACIFIC

98. "Kuril Islands, World War II," *Wikipedia*, https://en.wikipedia.org /wiki/Kuril_Islands#World_War_II, last accessed 10.1.15.

P. 224. "As far as the press . . . in American hands." McCrea, Amen Corner Speech, pp. 1, 2.

99. "Kuril Islands, World War II," *Wikipedia, op. cit.*

100. "Aerographer" in "Oxforddictionaries.com," *Oxford University Press,* http://www.oxforddictionaries.com/us/definition/american_english /aerographer, last accessed 10.7.15.

P. 226. "Our strikes had to be short . . . weapon." McCrea, Amen Corner Speech, p. 3.

P. 227. "I relied heavily . . . dark of the moon." *Ibid.*, p. 3.

P. 227. "Upon completion of the bombardment . . . met it decisively." *Ibid.*, p. 3.

P. 228. "The war in the North Pacific . . . about the North Pacific." *Ibid.*, p. 3.

101. Chen, C. Peter, "Japan's Surrender 14 Aug–2 Sep 1945," *World War II Database,* http://ww2db.com/battle_spec.php?battle_id=13, last accessed 9.17.15.

Chen, C. Peter, "Germany's Surrender 7 May 1945," *World War II Database,* http://ww2db.com/battle_spec.php?battle_id=152, last accessed 9.17.15.

AFTERWORD

Pp. 232-234. McCrea to Mrs. Franklin D. Roosevelt, 13 April 1945; McCrea to Vice Adm. Ross T. McIntire, 20 April 1945; McCrea to Mr. William D. Hassett, 20 April 1945; Harry L. Hopkins to McCrea, 21 April 1945. John L. McCrea Papers, Library of Congress.

102. *Fleet Admirals, US Navy* (Washington, D.C: Naval Historical Foundation 1966), http://www.navyhistory.org/fleet-admirals-us-navy/, last accessed 10.1.15.

103. "U.S. Army Five-Star Generals," *U.S. Army Center of Military History,* http://www.history.army.mil/html/faq/5star.html, last accessed 9.18.15.

Stillwell, Paul, "Afterword" to McCrea, *A Naval Life*.
Assorted curricula vitae and fragmentary writings by McCrea, McCrea
    Family Papers.

Bibliography

Borneman, Walter R. *The Admirals: Nimitz, Halsey, Leahy, and King—The Five-Star Admirals Who Won the War at Sea.* New York: Little, Brown and Co., 2012.

De Kay, James Tertius. *Roosevelt's Navy: The Education of a Warrior President 1882–1920.* New York: Pegasus Books, 2012.

Dobbs, Michael. *Saboteurs, The Nazi Raid on America.* New York: Alfred A. Knopf, 2004.

Elsey, George McKee. *An Unplanned Life: A Memoir.* Columbia, MO: University of Missouri Press, 2005.

Goodwin, Doris Kearns. *No Ordinary Time, Franklin & Eleanor Roosevelt: The Home Front in World War II.* New York: Simon & Schuster, 1994.

Hamilton, Nigel. *Mantle of Command: FDR at War, 1941–1942.* Boston: Houghton Mifflin Harcourt, 2014.

Keeney, L. Douglas. *The Eleventh Hour: How Great Britain, The Soviet Union, and the U.S. Brokered the Unlikely Deal That Won the War.* New York: Wiley, 2015.

Lehman, John. *On Seas of Glory: Heroic Men, Great Ships and Epic Battles of the American Navy.* New York: Touchstone, 2001.

McCrea, John L. *Reminiscences of Vice Admiral John L. McCrea, U.S. Navy (Retired), Vol. I.* Edited by Paul Stillwell. Annapolis, MD: U.S. Naval Institute, 1990. [*Reminiscences N.I.*]

Persico, Joseph E. *Roosevelt's Centurions: FDR and the Commanders He Led to Victory in World War II.* New York: Random House, 2013.

Reilly, Michael F. and Slocum, William J. *Reilly of the White House.* New York: Simon & Schuster, 1947.

Roosevelt, Elliot. *As He Saw It.* New York: Duell, Sloan and Pearce, 1946.

Sherwood, Robert E. *Roosevelt and Hopkins, An Intimate Portrait.* New York: Harper & Brothers, 1948.

Ward, Geoffrey C., ed. *Closet Companion, The Unknown Story of the Intimate Friendship between Franklin Roosevelt and Margaret Suckley.* New York: Houghton Mifflin Co., 1995.

INTERNET AND UNPUBLISHED SOURCES

"Captain James K. Vardaman, Jr. (1893–1972) U.S. Navy." *Treespot.net.* http://www.treespot.net/FamilyBios/MilitaryService/WWII /captjamesvardaman.htm. Last accessed 10.1.15.

Chief of Naval Operations. "War warning dispatch of 27 November 1941." *Ibiblio.org/Hyperwar.* http://www.ibiblio.org/hyperwar/PTO /EastWind/CNO-411127.html. Last accessed 9.20.15.

Declaration by the United Nations, January 1, 1942. *The Avalon Project, Yale Law School, Lillian Goldman Law Library,* 2008. http://avalon .law.yale.edu/20th_century/decade03.asp. Last accessed 10.8.15.

Eisenhower, D.D. "Report of the Commander-in-Chief Allied Forces to the Combined Chiefs of Staff on Operations in Northwest Africa." *Ibiblio.org.Hyperwar.* Transcribed and formatted for html. Last modified 3.31.06. http://www.ibiblio.org/hyperwar/USA/rep/TORCH /DDE-Torch.html. Last accessed 10.5.15. [Eisenhower, Report on Operations in Northwest Africa]

History.com Staff. "Battle of the Aleutian Islands." *A+E Networks.* Published 2009. http://www.history.com/topics/world-war-ii/battle-of -the-aleutian-islands. Last accessed 10.7.15.

Howe, George F. "Northwest Africa: Seizing the Initiative in the West." *United States Army in World War II, Mediterranean Theater of Operation.* Washington, D.C.: Office of the Chief of Military History, Department of the Army, 1957. Transcribed and formatted for html. http://www.ibiblio.org/hyperwar/USA/USA-MTO-NWA/index. html. Last accessed 10.5.15.

"Log of the President's Inspection Trip, 17 September—1 October 1942," Parts 1 and 2 (of 2). Grace Tully Papers. Grace Tully Archive. Franklin D. Roosevelt Library [FDR Library]. Part I: http://www .fdrlibrary.marist.edu/resources/images/tully/7_06a.pdf. Part II: http://www.fdrlibrary.marist.edu/_resources/images/tully/7_06b. pdf. Last accessed 1.15.16.

"Log of the President's Trip to Africa and the Middle East, November-December 1943," Parts 1 and 3 (of 3). Grace Tully Papers. Grace Tully Archive. FDR Library. Part I: http://fdrlibrary.marist.edu /_resources/images/tully/7_10a.pdf. Part III: http://www.fdrlibrary .marist.edu/_resources/images/tully/7_10c.pdf. Last accessed 1.15.16.

"Log of the Trip of the President to the Casablanca Conference, 9–31 January 1943." Grace Tully Papers. Grace Tully Archive. FDR Library. http://www.fdrlibrary.marist.edu/_resources/images/tully/7_07.pdf. Last accessed 1.15.16.

McCrea, John L. "Address Before Members of the A-Men Corner at William Penn Hotel, Pittsburgh, Pennsylvania, March 15, 1946." John L. McCrea Papers. Library of Congress.

McCrea, John L. *A Naval Life, The Memoirs of Vice Admiral John L. McCrea, U.S. Navy (Retired)*. Edited by Julia C. Tobey. Unpublished manuscript. [A Naval Life]

McCrea, John L. *History of the USS Iowa (BB 61)* (Unpublished history of *Iowa*'s first year). John L. McCrea Papers. Library of Congress. [*Iowa History*]

McCrea, John L. "Address at the Commissioning Ceremony." *Iowa History*, Appendix 1.

McCrea, John L. "Memorandum for Admiral Stark" (Notebook of trip to Hawaii and the Philippines). *Reminiscences N.I.*, Appendix B.

McCrea, John L. "Remarks at Medical Symposium, Chelsea Naval Hospital, October 27, 1952." McCrea Family Papers. [Med. Sym. Speech]

McCrea, John L. "Setting up Map Room in White House and Other Incidents in Connection with Service There, 19 March 1973." Edited by W.W. Moss. John L. McCrea Papers. FDR Library.

McCrea, John L. "Shakedown Address." *Iowa History*, Appendix 4.

McCrea, John L., Papers. Franklin D. Roosevelt Library, Hyde Park, NY.

McCrea, John L., Papers. Manuscript Division, Library of Congress, Washington, D.C.

McCrea Family Papers. Editor's Possession.

Moskowitz, Daniel B. "Nazi Saboteurs at the Supreme Court." *HistoryNet*. Last modified 9.21.15. http://www.historynet.com/nazi-saboteurs-at-the-supreme-court.htm. Last accessed 9.25.15.

"Private Log Book of USS *Iowa*." John L. McCrea Papers, Library of Congress. [*Iowa* Private Log]

"Richmond IV (CL-9)." *NHHC*. Last modified 6.4.15. http://www.history.navy.mil/research/histories/ship-histories/danfs/r/richmond-iv.html. Last accessed 10.7.15.

Roosevelt, Franklin D. "Joint Press Conference with Prime Minister Churchill at Casablanca," January 24, 1943. Online by Gerhard Peters and John T. Woolley, *The American Presidency Project*. http://www.presidency.ucsb.edu/ws/?pid=16408. Last accessed 9.26.15.

Scott, James M. "The Untold Story of the Vengeful Japanese Attack After the Doolittle Raid." *Smithsonian.com*. Published April 14, 2015. http://www.smithsonianmag.com/history/untold-story-vengeful

-japanese-attack-doolittle-raid-180955001/?no-ist.   Last   accessed
10.3.15.

Sitz, W.H., "A History of Naval Aviation." *Naval History and Heritage
Command.* http://www.history.navy.mil/content/dam/nhhc/research
/histories/naval-aviation/pdf/History%20(1).pdf. Last accessed 9.16.15.

Shuffield, Lynna Kay and Gonyo, Bill. "Thomas Charles Hart, Admiral,
U.S. Navy, U.S. Senator." *Arlington Cemetery.* Last modified 7.30.09.
http://www.arlingtoncemetery.net/tchart.htm. Last accessed 9.24.15.

Thorn, Martha. "Naval aviation pioneers spread wings at Annapolis."
dcmilitary.com: Comprint Military Publications online. Last modified
7.3.2002.   http://ww2.dcmilitary.com/dcmilitary_archives/stories
/070302/17997-1.shtml

United States Department of State. "The Conferences at Washington, 1941–
1942, and Casablanca, 1943" in *Foreign Relations of the United States.*
[FRUS 1942] Washington, D.C.: U.S. Government Printing Office,
1941–43. http://digital.library.wisc.edu/1711.dl/FRUS.FRUS194143.

United States Department of State. "The Conferences at Cairo and Tehran" in *Foreign Relations of the United States diplomatic papers.* [FRUS
1943] Washington, D.C.: U.S. Government Printing Office, 1943.
http://digicoll.library.wisc.edu/cgi-bin/FRUS/FRUS
-idx?type=header&id=FRUS.FRUS1943CairoTehran.

United States Strategic Bombing Survey (Pacific), Naval Analysis Division. "Chapter IX, Central Pacific Operations from 1 June 1943 to 1
March 1944 Including the Gilbert-Marshall Islands Campaign" in
The Campaigns of the Pacific War. Washington, D.C.: U.S. Government Printing Office 1946, transcribed and formatted for html,
http://www.ibiblio.org/hyperwar/AAF/USSBS/PTO-Campaigns
/USSBS-PTO-9.html, last accessed 10.1.15.

USS *Iowa* War Diaries, January—August 1944. McCrea Family Papers.

Acknowledgments

I owe an enormous debt of gratitude to Paul Stillwell, naval historian and former director of oral history at the Naval Institute, for his many contributions to this book, during John McCrea's lifetime and after. *Captain McCrea's War* was taken from McCrea's complete memoir, *A Naval Life*. Without Paul, *A Naval Life* would be nothing more than forty-eight cassette tapes in two shoeboxes. He arranged for transcription of the tapes, and during the editing of *A Naval Life* and *Captain McCrea's War*, he has answered countless questions on naval matters and referred me to experts for specialized issues. He also reviewed the entire edited manuscript of *A Naval Life*, applying his considerable naval knowledge and editorial skills to improving it. His enthusiasm and personal support have been invaluable.

I am especially grateful to Joseph Craig, my editor at Skyhorse Publishing, for his appreciation of the charm and historic importance of *Captain McCrea's War*, and for his insight in developing the material into a significant book. I also want to thank my able map maker, Chris Sampson.

Special thanks are due to Anne Rehill of the U.S. Naval Institute for her gracious permission to quote from John McCrea's USNI oral history, *Reminiscences of Vice Admiral John L. McCrea*, edited by Paul Stillwell.

I want to acknowledge the contributions of a number of others. Sara Bartlett, military researcher and word processor, assembled *A Naval Life,* a document of monumental size, and she indefatigably tracked down correct names and the proper titles of military figures, royalty, and nobility. Robert Clark, Supervisory Archivist at the Franklin D. Roosevelt Library, assisted me with obtaining documents and answered numerous questions. Robert J. Cressman, Historian, History and Archives Division, Naval History and Heritage Command, U.S. Navy, answered questions and generously provided copies of *Iowa's* War Diaries from January 1, 1944, through August 29, 1944. McCrea's personal papers are in the Manuscript Division of the Library of Congress. Daun van Ee, historian in the Manuscript Division, steered me to interesting portions of McCrea's papers. John E. Haynes, historian in the Manuscript Division, supplied copies of documents that saved me an extra trip to Washington.

Richard J. Smethurst, Professor of History at the University of Pittsburgh, and Duncan K. Foley, Professor of Economics at The New School for Social Research, graciously agreed to read the memoir portion of *Captain McCrea's War,* and I am most grateful for their time and helpful commentary. Sarah Jackson also reviewed portions of the memoir and has supplied useful advice and maintained a continuing interest in this project over many years.

Robert A. Kaplan of Rob Kaplan Associates assisted with the editing of *Captain McCrea's War,* provided encouragement and essential help in finding a publisher, and generously volunteered to assist with matters relating to the publishing world. L. Douglas Keeney helped to sustain my motivation over many years by his belief in the value of *A Naval Life,* and he was generous with advice and assistance in the effort to publish *Captain McCrea's War.*

John McCrea's daughter, Anne McCrea Sullivan, and his grandchildren, Jennifer N. Williams, John M. Niles, Rebecca N. Lingard, and Meredith Niles enthusiastically supported the publication of this book and graciously granted me the rights to John

McCrea's dictated memoir. My copyright lawyer, Judith B. Bass, Esq., sorted out rights issues that made the publication of this book possible.

I also wish to thank Kathy Talalay, Susan A. Schwartz, Cynthia M. Koch, Geoffrey C. Ward, Gerald Gneckow, John Shroyer, and Julie Ganz for their advice and help.

In tracking down the rights to the photographs in this book, I received vital assistance from Matthew Hanson, Archivist at the Franklin D. Roosevelt Presidential Library; Holly Reed, Still Picture Reference Team at the National Archives & Record Administration; David Way, Curator of the Battleship USS *Iowa* Museum; and Sean Evans at the Cline Library Special Collections, North Arizona University, which houses the Bill Belknap Collection. Bill Belknap was a navy photographer assigned to the White House in 1942.

Last but not least, I wish to thank members of my family. My husband, Ken Johnson, digitized and organized countless documents and photographs from McCrea's papers, which greatly enhanced my knowledge of, and ability to work with, original materials. He also gave insightful comments and put up with endless editing over many years. My niece, Elizabeth Tobey, helped with word processing and supplied vital information on everything from scanners to lodging near the National Archives. My stepsister, Annie McCrea Sullivan, John McCrea's younger daughter, offered support and boundless enthusiasm for this project. She also mined her basement for McCrea photographs and documents, which she generously gave me.

Index

Adak, 223, 225, 227, 228, 230

Admiralty Map Room, 25, 26–27

Afghan, sent from Eleanor Roosevelt, 175–176

Alaskan Sea Frontier, 223

Aleutian Islands, xv, 82n28, 221, 224, 226, 231, 237

Algeria, x, 55n21, 123, 124n40, 145n54, 184–192

Allied Expeditionary Force, 139

AlNav (All Navy message), 100, 100n34

Amagansett, New York, 92n33

Annapolis Roads, 6, 165

Arcadia Conference (1942–1943), 5–6, 6n2, 10n5

"Are We Ready" paper, xx, xxiv

Argentia, Newfoundland, 175n72, 175–176

Arlington National Cemetery, 72, 178–179, 236

Arnold, Henry H. "Hap," 10n5, 137, 181, 182, 185n74, 235n103

Asiatic Fleet, xxii, 73–74

Astoria. See USS *Astoria*

Atlantic, Battle of the, 82n28

Atlantic Charter, 175n72

Atlantic Conference (1941), 175n72

Attu, 224, 225, 226, 227

Australia, 38n14, 48, 51, 64, 65

Barclay, Edwin J., 151–152

Bathurst, Gambia, West Africa, 128, 129, 133n44, 134–135, 135n46, 149, 150–151, 152

Bayonne, New Jersey, 163

Beardall, John, 2, 8, 13

Berry, Charles Nelson, 41, 117

Bidwell, A. Trood, xx

Bittern. See USS *Bittern*

Bloch, Claude C., 2, 3

Bloedorn, Walter, 16

Boatswain's chair, 197–198

Boettinger, Anna, 113

Brady, Dorothy Jones, 22, 113

British Grand Fleet, xvii, 13, 70, 189, 206

British West Africa, 128, 133n44, 151, 151n59, 196, 196n79

Brooke, Alan F., 7, 137n50

Brooklyn Navy Yard. *See* New York Navy Yard, Brooklyn

Brown University, 118, 119

Brown, Wilson, 121, 122, 153, 181, 182, 199

Bryan, William Jennings, xi

Bureau of Navigation, xix, 7, 111

Bureau of Personnel, U.S. Navy, 120, 122, 156, 157

Byrnes, James F., 71

Cairo Conference, x, 177n73, 178, 191

Camp David. *See* Shangri-La

Camp Shelby, Mississippi, 118–119

Canada, 48, 175n72

Canberra (HMAS). See HMAS *Canberra*

Canberra (USS). *See* USS *Canberra*

Cape of Good Hope, 55

A Capsule History of Iowa (BB-61) (Navy Department), 219

Caroline Islands, 213, 213n90, 218, 220n97

Carpender, Arthur S., 7n3

Casablanca Conference, viii, ix–x, 133–147
    air journey for, 133n44, 133–135
    dates, 128n43
    delivery of note to sultan of Morocco during, 140–142
    departing from, 147–150
    dinner in honor of sultan of Morocco during, 144–146
    dinner party for WAACs at, 140
    FDR Jr. at, 139
    hotel/villas for, 136
    inspection of U.S. Army divisions, 142–143
    meetings during, 136–137
    Pa Watson and, 128, 131–132
    plans for, 125–127
    purpose of, 128n43
    return trip from, 152–153
    Roosevelt and Churchill's first meeting during, 137–139
    secrecy and, 129–130
    sightseeing in Africa, 151–152
    train journey for, 133
    travel arrangements for, 127–129
    USS *Memphis* and, 134, 150–151

Casco Bay, Maine, 170, 171, 172

Casey, Thomas J., 156, 158, 159, 162–163, 171, 176, 177–178, 180, 191, 196, 203

Central Pacific Force, 209n86

Chatfield, Ernle, 70

Chefoo, China, xviii

Chesapeake Bay, 164–165, 170, 179–180, 199

Chiang Kai-shek, 28, 48, 50, 177n73

China, xviii, 28, 48, 50, 89n32, 168, 177

Christmas, xxii, 5, 204, 205, 228–229

Churchill, Randolph, 84–85

Churchill, Winston, xi
    Casablanca Conference and, viii, x, 125, 137–139, 140, 144–146, 147
    Chatfield, Ernle and, 70
    correspondence between FDR and, 28, 48, 56, 123
    de Gaulle, thoughts on, 138
    farewell to FDR at Marrakech by, 149–150
    Hopkins, Harry, and, 29n9
    Iowa's secret mission to North Africa and, 177n73
    the Kremlin, views on, 139
    Madagascar and, 56
    McCrea escorting, xiv, 68–70
    Pacific War Council and, 48, 52, 52n20
    traveling map room of, 25
    visit to White House following Pearl Harbor attack, 5–6, 6n2

Clapper, Raymond, 210, 210n87, 212

Clipper service (Pan American), xix, xxii–xxiii, 128

CNO's Office. *See* Office of the Chief of Naval Operations

Combined Chiefs of Staff, 10n5, 48n17, 137

Cooper, Gary, 86n29

Coral Sea, Battle of the, 37–38, 38n14

Cox, James, 109

Crim, Howell, 22, 25, 73, 106

Cunningham, John, 193–194

Dakar, Senegal, 196–197

Darlan, François, 127, 127n42, 138n51

Dauntless. See USS *Dauntless*

Davis, Elmer, 35n12, 35–37, 38–39, 40

Declaration by the United Nations, 10n5

De Gaulle, Charles, 55, 56, 138–139, 143, 146–147, 147n57

Delano, Laura, 113

DeMille, Cecil B., 86n29

Deyo, Morton L., 173–174

Dispatches
  delivery to Roosevelt, 19, 20
  kept in Map Room, 28–29
  on Madagascar assault, 56–59
  organizing and filing, 26
  war warning, xxv–xxvi

Dixon, Lady, 65–66

Dixon, Sir Owen, 51, 64–65

Doolittle air raid, 89n32, 89–90

Doolittle, James, 89

Douglas Aircraft Corporation, 116, 128

Douglas, Donald W., 116

Duncan, Frank, 157, 228–229

Dunn, James, 48, 58, 59

Dutch East Indies, 62–63, 73–74, 75–76, 86

Duty, Michael, 230

Early, Stephen T., 22
  Drew Pearson incident and, 34–35
  Garner, John Nance and, 117, 118
  Nazi saboteur executions and, 96–97
  press conferences and, 33
  recording of talks and, 71–72
  Roosevelt and McCrea's
    relationship, views on, 98
  Shangri-La and, 87
  war material/training facilities tour,
    travel on, 113
  Willkie's broadcast (1942) and, 124

Edison, Thomas A., xxi

Edwards, Richard S., 178, 191

Eisenhower, Dwight D., 89, 123, 127n42, 139–140, 235n103

Ellice Islands, 209, 209n85

Eniwetok Atoll, 212, 213n90, 216, 217, 217n92, 221

Evatt, Herbert V., 48, 51, 53–54

Fala (dog), 79, 80–81, 103–104, 113

Fast Carrier Task Force, 209, 209n86

Fechteler, William M., 117, 120, 122

Fifth Fleet, 209n86

Fireside chats, viii, 85–86, 86n29

Firestone Tire and Rubber Company, 152

Flag officers, 150n58

Fletcher, Frank Jack, 223, 225, 226, 231

Flu epidemic, 1918, 206

Food poisoning, on USS *Iowa,* 206–207

Ford Motor Company, Willow Run plant, 115

Foreign relations, 47–60
  Dutch royal visit, 61–64
  Madagascar, Marshal Pétain, and, 54–60
  naming of ships, 64–66
  Pacific War Council and, 48–54

Forrestal, James V., 100–101

Forster, Rudolph, 15, 21

Fourteenth Naval District, Pearl Harbor, 2

France, 54–55, 56, 137–138, 218n94.
  See also Vichy French Government

Fredericks, Charles, 22, 72–73, 79, 80–81

Free French Movement, 55, 138, 147n57

Freetown, Sierra Leone, British West Africa, 196

French colonies, 54–55, 55n21, 197n80

French Committee of National Liberation, 147n57

French West Africa, 127n42, 135, 197n80

Funafuti Atoll, 209, 211

Garner, John Nance, ix, 17n7, 117–118

George Washington University, 16, 28

German High Seas Fleet, xi, xxi

German saboteurs, 92–98
Gilbert Islands, 209n85, 211
Giraud, Henri, 138, 138n51,
    146–147, 147n57
Glassford, William C., 85–86, 86n29,
    197
Godwin, Earl, 33
Goethals, George Washington, 208
Grant, Ulysses S., 147
Gravesand Bay, 163
Grew, Joseph C., 112, 112n37
Guam, xix–xx, 38n14, 216, 218,
    218n95, 219, 220n97
Gunnery officer, on USS *Iowa,* 157,
    157n63, 214, 215

Hackmeister, Louise, 22, 39, 40
Hall, John L. "Jimmy," 139
Halsey, William F. "Bull" Jr., 101,
    109n86, 209n86, 234n102
Hampton Roads, Virginia, 176, 180,
    182, 191, 202, 205–206
Harriman, W. Averell, 136, 136n49
Hart, Thomas C.,
    discussing Japan's naval officers
        with, 4–5
    MacArthur and, xxiv
    Queen Wilhelmina visit and, 73–77
    war plans and, xxii, xxiii–xxiv
Harvey, George, 109
Harvey's Weekly, 109
Hassett, William D., 22, 78, 96–97,
    124, 233
Hipsley, Elmer R., 133
HMAS *Canberra* (Australian cruiser), 64
HMS *Sheffield* (British cruiser), 193–194
Holcomb, Thomas, 85
Hollandia, Dutch New Guinea
    (Indonesia), 218
Hooker, Henry, 113
Hopkins, Diana, 31
Hopkins, Harry, vii
    Casablanca Conference and, 129,
        130, 132, 133, 136, 137, 140,
        149, 152

FDR's relationship with, 29n9, 103
Iowa's secret mission to North
    Africa and, 181, 182, 185n74,
    198, 200
letter from, after FDR's death,
    233–234
Map Room and, 29, 30
Pacific War Council and, 49, 51
at Shangri-La christening, 91
Willkie's broadcast (1942) and, 124
Horne, Frederick J., 161
Hornet. See USS *Hornet*
Hotel Anfa, 136
Hudson Valley, viii, 39, 40, 78
Hull, Cordell, ix, 47, 60, 67, 68, 69
Hustvedt, Olaf M., 203, 215–216,
    218, 219–220
Hyde Park, viii, 13, 61, 63, 66, 108
    McCrea's visit to, 78–82

Illiterate troops, 118–119
Informal diplomacy, 61–66
    naming of ship, 64–66
    Queen Wilhelmina's visit to Hyde
        Park, 61–64
Ingersoll, Royal E., 176–177, 180,
    184, 203, 204
Ingram, Jonas H., 195, 196
Investiture ceremony, 72, 73–77
Iowa. See USS *Iowa*

Jacobs, Randall, 7–8, 111, 112, 120
JAG (Judge Advocate General) Office.
    See Office of the Judge Advocate
    General
Jakarta, Indonesia, 62n24
Japan
    Aleutian Islands and, 224, 226
    Ambassador Nomura of, xxv
    Coral Sea, Battle of the, 38n14
    cracking diplomatic code of,
        55–56
    Doolittle raid on, 89n32, 89–90
    Kuril Islands and, 223n98,
        224–225

Marshall Islands and, 211n88
naval officers, 4–5
North Pacific campaign and, xv,
226, 227
Orange war plans against, xxi–xxiv
John Hancock Mutual Life Insurance,
xi, 236
Joint Chiefs of Staff, U.S., 10n5
Juliana, Princess of the Netherlands,
61–63

Kaiser Shipbuilding Company,
Portland, Oregon, 115
Kelly Field, Texas, 114
Khartoum, Sudan, 125
Kimmel, Husband E., xxiv, 5, 162–163
King, Ernest J., ix, xvi, 82n28, 101,
120, 235, 237
Casablanca conference and, 128,
129, 134, 137
as chief of naval operations and
commander in chief of the U.S.
Fleet, 8n4, 19n8
Doolittle air raid and, 89, 90
as fleet admiral, 234n102
Iowa's Casco Bay casualty and, 173
Iowa's inspection by, 165–167
Iowa's post-Oran deployment
orders and, 191–192, 194
Iowa's secret mission to North
Africa and, 177, 178–179, 180,
181, 182, 188–189, 191–192
Lexington's loss and, 38–39, 40
Map Room and, 30
McCrea as naval aide, views on 9,
16–17
McCrea's discussion of naval
officers with, 189–190
McCrea's opinion of, 178, 189
McCrea's reading dispatches in
office of, 19
McCrea's relationship with, ix, 111
as member of joint chiefs of staff, 10n5
Secretary Knox's rebuke to,
104–106

Truman's naval aide and, 234
Kirk, Alan G., 26
Kiska, 224
Knox, Frank, ix, 8
commissioning ceremony for *Iowa*
and, 159, 160, 161
election of 1936, 17, 17n7
McCrea as naval aide, views on
17–18
Pearl Harbor attack and, 2, 3
Kurabu Zaki, 228
Kuril Islands, xv, 223, 223n98,
224–225, 226, 227, 228
Kwajalein Atoll, 211n88, 211–212

Lambrecht, Mary, 84
Landis, James M., 108, 108n36
Landon, Alf, 17, 17n7
League of Nations, 109
Leahey, George A., 172, 203
Leahy, William D., 29, 121–122
as ambassador to Vichy France,
124n40
Casablanca conference and, 133,
134, 152
as chairman of the Joint Chiefs of
Staff, chief of staff to the
commander in chief, 10n5
as fleet admiral, 234n102
Iowa's secret mission to North
Africa and, 181, 182, 185n74
Map Room and, 30
Willkie's broadcast (1942) and, 124
Lee, Willis A., 217, 218, 219
Lexington. See USS *Lexington*
Liberia, 151n60, 151–152
Long Island, New York, 92, 93
Loudon, Alexander, 48, 51, 62, 66,
74, 77
Low, Francis Stuart, 188–189
MacArthur, Douglas, xxiv, 210, 235,
235n103
Madagascar, 54–60
"The Magic Book," 29, 29n10, 30
Mahan, Alfred T., 189

Majuro Atoll, 211–212, 213, 217, 217n93, 218

Manila, xxiv, xxiii, 50n19, 63

Manuscript Room, Library of Congress, xii

Map Room, viii, xiv
Admiralty Map Room and, 25, 26–27
Army and, 27–28
creation of, 24–32
furniture for, 25–26
information kept in, 28–29
Lexington and, 38, 41
location of, 25
McCrea's assistant for, 28–29
McCrea's communications with, 43, 59, 104, 131, 154
Montgomery, Bob and, 26–27, 31–32
personnel, 30–31
recognizing need for, 24–25
Roosevelt visiting, 29, 30
Situation Room and, 32
State Department and, 48
visitors to, 30
visual aids in, 27

Mariana Islands, 211n88, 216, 216n91, 218n95, 218–220, 220n97

Marlette, Michigan, xv

Marquart, Edward J., 112

Marshall, George C., 85, 140, 235n103
Arcadia conference and, 7
Casablanca conference and, 128, 137
on *Iowa*'s secret mission to North Africa, 181, 182, 185n74
Joint Chiefs of Staff and, 10n5
Map Room and, 30

Marshall Islands, 209n85, 211n88, 211–212, 216n91, 217n93

Märtha, Princess of Norway, 68

Mason, Redfield "Rosie," 5

Matsuwa Island, 228

Mayo, Henry T., 190

Mayrant. See USS *Mayrant*

McCann, Allan R., 221

McCarthy, Leighton, 48

McCrea, Annie, xix, 205

McCrea, Estelle, xix, xxii, 2, 176, 205, 236

McCrea, John
as aide to Adm. Rodman, Pacific Fleet, xvii–xviii
as aide to Adm. Stark, CNO, xxiv–xxv, 1–10
Arcadia conference and, 6
childhood of, xv
funeral tribute to, 236–237
Guam duty, xix–xx
legal education and legal work of, xviii, xix, xx
John Hancock Mutual Life Insurance Company and, xi, 236
marriages of, xix, 236
Naval Academy, attendance at, xv–xvi
Naval War College, time at, xviii
navy jobs, post-WW2, of, 235–236
New York and leadership style of, xvii
Pearl Harbor attack and, 1–2, 5
personality and traits of, xvi–xvii
retirement of, 236
sea duty, early assignments of, xvii, xviii–xix

McCrea, John, as naval aide
Casablanca Conference and, ix–x, 125–130, 136–137, 140–142
communication with White House, 20–21, 83–84
desire for sea duty of, xviii, 110–111, 117, 120–121
detached from duties of, 153–155
Churchill, Winston, and, 68–70
Davis, Elmer, and 36–37
Dixon, Sir Owen, and, 64–65
Early, Steve, the "boss," and, 98
Evatt, Herbert, and, 51, 52–54

FDR and two-dollar debt to, 102–103

FDR, opinion of, 81–82, 155, 232–233

FDR, private conversations with, viii–ix, 13–14, 99, 101–102, 108, 109, 205

Hart, Thomas, and, 73–77

Iowa christening and, 111–112

Iowa negotiations for command by, 111, 112, 117, 120–121

Iowa, offer of command to, 117, 120

King, Ernest, advice from, 104–106

King, Ernest, job advice to, 16–17

Knox, Frank, job advice to, 17–18

Map Room and, 24–32

opinion of FDR, 81–82, 232–233

Pacific War Council and, 49–50, 51

Princess Juliana and, 62–63

roles and duties, 14, 19–20, 83

Shangri-La and, 86–89

special assignments of, 84–98

tour of Hyde Park and, 78–82

on war production/training facilities tour, 112–120

Watson, "Pa" and, 11–13, 14–16

Willkie's broadcast (1942) and, 124

McCrea, John, *Iowa* command

choice of personnel and, 156–158

crew compliance with dress regulations and, 162

evening news broadcast and, 207–208

evening prayer and, 216–217

expectations for *Iowa* and crew of, 159–160

FDR, last meeting with, 205

King, Ernest, discussion of naval officers, and, 189–190

mission to North Africa, secrecy plan of, 179–181

pleasant word before bed and, 208

promotion to rear admiral, 221

relief and detachment and, 221

speech at *Iowa* commissioning by, 159

speech during *Iowa* shakedown cruise by, 167–170

McCrea, John, North Pacific task force command

abrupt detachment orders to, 230–231, 234

FDR's death and, 230, 232–234

gift from *Iowa*'s crew to, 228–229

judge advocate general job feeler to, 229–230

on news coverage of bombardment operations, 228

on North Pacific campaign, 224–225

on planning bombardment raids, 226–227

on reports of FDR's health (1945), 229

McCrea, Meredith, xix, 1, 2, 106, 204, 205

McIntire, Ross T., 20, 106–107, 124

Casablanca Conference and, 129, 133, 134, 135, 136, 149, 150, 152

on FDR's health (1945), 229

FDR's medical treatment by, 25, 30, 86, 99, 103

Garner, John Nance and, 118

Iowa's Casco Bay casualty and, 174

Iowa's secret mission to North Africa and, 181

McCrea, judge advocate general job feeler, and, 229

McCrea's condolence letter to, 232–233

Shangri-La and, 86–87, 91

war production and training tour and, 113, 115, 118

McMahon, William T., 157

Medal of Honor award, General Wilbur, 144

Mehdia-Port Lyautey, Battle of, 143

Memphis. See USS *Memphis*

Mers-el-Kébir, Algeria, 55n21, 184
Midway, Battle of, 40–41n15,
    82n28
Mili Island, 217n93, 217–218
Missouri. See USS *Missouri*
Mitscher, Marc A., 216
Molotov, Vyacheslav, 67–68, 68n26
Montgomery, Henry (Robert), 26–27,
    31–32
Morocco, 123, 124n40, 138, 140n52,
    143
Mott, William C., 28, 30, 153
Murphy, Estelle, xix. *See also* McCrea,
    Estelle
Murphy, Robert D., 124n40, 145,
    145n54

Nash, Walter, 48, 51
Naval Academy, xv–xvi, xvii, xx, 8,
    57, 100, 110
*A Naval Life: The Memoirs of Vice
    Admiral John L. McCrea, U.S.
    Navy* (Tobey), xiii
Naval Training Station Great Lakes,
    Illinois, 114
Naval War College, xviii
Nazi saboteurs, 92–98
Nesbitt, Henrietta, 23
Netherlands, the, 48. *See also*
    Wilhelmina, Queen of the
    Netherlands
New Jersey. See USS *New Jersey*
New York. See USS *New York*
New York Herald Tribune, 42
New York Navy Yard, Brooklyn
    (Brooklyn Navy Yard), 111–112,
    158, 162
New Zealand, 48
Nimitz, Chester A., xvi, 101, 223,
    225, 234n102, 235, 237
Noguès, Charles, 140, 140n52, 141, 145
Nomura, Kichisaburo, xxv
North Africa, xxiv, 27, 55, 82n28,
    123, 124–127, 127n42, 130, 131,
    138, 138n51,145n54, 200

North Pacific campaign, 224–225

Oakland Naval Supply Base and
    Army Port of Embarkation,
    California, 114
Office of Naval Intelligence, 26, 125
Office of the Chief of Naval
    Operations (CNO's Office), xxi,
    19, 100n34, 110, 220, 234
Office of the Judge Advocate General
    (JAG Office), xviii, xx, 94,
    100–101, 174, 229
Office of War Information (OWI),
    37n13, 37, 38
Off the Record with FDR (W.D.
    Hassett), 78
Olav, Crown Prince of Norway, 68
Operation Torch, 123, 124n40,
    127n42, 138n51, 140n52, 143
Orange war plans, xxi–xxii, xxiii
Osmena, Sergio, 50, 50n19
OWI. *See* Office of War Information

Pacific Fleet, xvii, xviii, xxv, 13,
    40n15, 162, 209, 221, 223, 235
Pacific War Council, 48n17, 48–52,
    52n20, 64, 67, 155
Palau Islands, 218, 220n97
Palembang, Sumatra, 62–63
Panama Canal Zone, xviii–xix, 208,
    209
Pan American Airways, xix, xxii–xxiii,
    128, 133, 152
Paramashimu Island, 228
Patton, George S., 124n40, 140,
    140n52, 142, 143, 144, 145
Pearl Harbor, xxii, xxiii, xxiv, 213n90,
    222–223
Pearl Harbor attack, vii, xiv, 1–4, 5,
    5n1, 7n3, 8n4, 24, 38n14,
    112n37, 114, 115, 117, 162, 163,
    201, 218
Pearson, Drew, 34n11, 34–35
Pennsylvania. See USS *Pennsylvania*
Pershing, General John J., 139–140

Pétain, Philippe, 55, 56, 57–59, 60, 127n42

Philippines, xix, xxii–xxiii, xxiv, xxv, 50, 50n19, 75

Pick, Charles F. Jr., 185n74, 186n75

Ponape Island, 218

Ponte Vedra Beach, Florida, 92n33

Port Moresby, 38n14

Portal, Sir Charles, 7, 136, 137n50

Potomac. See USS *Potomac*

Pound, Sir Dudley, 7, 136, 137n50

Prendergast, Jacob, 157–158

Press
    coverage of *Iowa* commissioning, 160–161
    false Italian report of damage to *Iowa,* 207–208
    loss of *Lexington* and, 37–40, 40n15
    McCrea on, 41–42
    Pacific War Council members and, 52–54
    press release on Nazi saboteur executions, 96–97
    Willkie broadcast (1942), 123–124

Press conferences, 33–42
    Davis, Elmer and, 35–37
    days and times of, 33
    FDR asking McCrea to attend, 14
    FDR's performance at, 34
    location of, 33
    Pearson, Drew and, 34–35
    reporters/newsmen at, 34
    seating for, 33

Press secretary, 22

Puget Sound navy yard (Bremerton, WA), 115

Quezon, Manuel L., 50, 50n19, 51

Quiggle, Lynne C., 156–157, 163, 172

Quisling, Vidkun, 68

Rabat, Morocco, 125, 140–141

Ramsey, DeWitt C., 235

Randolph Field, Texas, 114

Rayburn, Sam, 72

Reilly, Mike F., 22, 79, 128–129, 135

Republic of Liberia, 151n60, 151–152

Richardson, James O., xxii, xxiii, xxiv

Richmond. See USS *Richmond*

Roberts Field, Monrovia, Liberia, 151, 151n60

Rodman, Hugh, xvii–xviii, 13–14, 189–190, 208

Romagna, John, 71–72

Roosevelt, Eleanor, vii, 44, 45, 61, 108, 113n38, 144, 230
    afghan sent from, 175–176
    at christening of *Iowa,* 112
    McCrea's letter to, after FDR's death, 232
    at Shangri-La christening, 91

Roosevelt, Elliott, 113, 135, 135n46, 135n48, 136, 140, 145

Roosevelt, Franklin D., vii, xi, xii, xiv
    Casablanca conference and, 125–128, 135, 135n46, 136–139, 147
    death of, 230
    elections and, 17n7, 101–102, 143
    flying personal flag in Bathurst, 150–151
    Free French leadership and, 137–139, 143, 146–147
    health in 1945 of, 229
    on illiterate troops, 119
    infirmity of, 99–100
    interest in the navy, 100–101
    intimate associates of, vii
    Iowa's secret mission to North Africa and, 177, 178–179, 181, 182–183, 197–198, 199–202
    jokes and humor of, 13, 80–81, 90, 91, 106–107
    knowledge of world geography, 24
    Knox, Frank and, 17–18, 17n7
    on League of Nations, 109
    Lexington loss publication and, 38–40

Madagascar invasion and, 56, 57–58

Map Room and, 24, 29–30

McCrea, opinion held by, 98, 154–155, 234

McCrea's briefing sessions with, 20, 30, 100–101

McCrea's detachment from White House and, 153–155

McCrea's introduction to, 6, 6n2

McCrea's private conversations with, viii–ix, 13–14, 99, 101–102, 108, 109, 205

McCrea's desire for sea duty and, 110–111, 120–121

McCrea's tour of Hyde Park with, 78–82

Nazi saboteurs and, 93–95, 96

nonpolitical politics and, 112–113

Pacific War Council and, 48–50, 51

press conferences and, 34–35, 36

Queen Wilhelmina's visits and, 61–62, 63, 72, 73, 75, 77

quoting POTUS to the press and, 53–54

relations with White House staff, 106

secretary of state, as his own, and, 47

Shangri-La and, 86–89

sightseeing in Africa, 151–152

sinus problems and treatment of, 103–104

sixty-first birthday of, 152–153

solitaire and, 113

stamp collection and, 113

on the State Department, ix, 47–48

"table talks" at state dinners and luncheons by, 71–72

thoughtfulness and kindness of, 106, 140, 174

tour of war production and training facilities by, 112–120

Willkie, Wendell and, 106–107, 123–124

Roosevelt, Franklin D., Jr., 139, 140

Roosevelt, John, 113

Rosenman, Samuel I., 85, 93–94, 98, 234

Royal Navy, 5–6, 7, 58, 59–60, 70, 136, 184, 193, 194

Royal visitors, 61–64, 67–68, 72

Saipan, 216, 218, 218n95, 219, 220n97

Savo Island, Battle of, 64, 64n25

Second Cairo Conference, 177n73

Secret Service, 62, 113

  Casablanca Conference and, 128–129, 130, 133, 134n45, 161, 148, 150

  on *Iowa's* secret mission to North Africa, 181, 186n75, 191

  White House and, 21–22, 72, 79, 87, 87n30,

Sexton, William, 7

Shangri-La (Camp David), viii

  alterations to, 87–88

  christening of, 91

  Doolittle air raid and, 89–90

  finding location for, 86–87

  furnishings for, 90–91

  Meredith McCrea's birthday gift and, 106

  naming, 88–89

  staff for, 91

  view from, 91

Sheffield. See HMS *Sheffield*

Sherwood, Robert E. "Bob," 85

Simpson, Clarence L., 152

Situation Room, 32, 92

Smith, Alfred E. "Al," 101–102

Smith, Allan E. "Hoke," 209, 214, 215, 223, 226, 256

Solomon Islands, 38n14, 64n25

Somervell, Brehon B., 182

Soong, T.V., 48, 50–51

South Dakota. See USS *South Dakota*

Soviet Union, 29n9, 55, 167, 136n49, 175.

270 • • *Captain McCrea's War*

Special Service Squadron, Panama
   Canal Zone, xviii–xix
Spruance, Raymond A., 209n86, 213,
   214, 215, 216
Stalin, Joseph, 28, 29n9, 48, 128n43,
   146, 177n73
Stark, Harold R. "Betty," xx, xxi, xxii,
   xxiii, xxiv–xxvi, 19n8
   Arcadia conference and, 6, 7
   Map Room and, 30
   on McCrea as naval aide, 8–9, 17,
      111
   McCrea screening visitors to, 4
   Pearl Harbor attack and, 1–3, 4
Starling, Edmund, 21–22, 130
"The Star-Spangled Banner," 63, 178
State Department
   FDR's suspicion of, ix, 47
   Madagascar operation and, 57,
      58–59, 60
   Map Room and, 48
   McCrea acting as navy liaison
      with, 234
Stillwell, Paul, xii–xiii
Stimson, Henry L., 17
The Story of Dr. Wassell (film), 86n29
Suckley, Margaret, 79, 81, 113
Sultan of Morocco, ix–x, 140–142,
   144–146
Summerllin, George, 54, 71
Suribachi Nau, 228

Tanjung Priok, 62
Task Force 38, 209n86
Task Force 58, 209, 209n86, 213n90,
   216, 218
Tehran Conference, x, 177n73, 178
Third Fleet, 209n86
Thompson, Malvina, 91, 111–112
Tinian, 216, 218, 218n95, 219,
   220n97
Tirpitz (German battleship), 175
Tobey, Julia C. "Judy," x, xiii
Tobey, Martha, 236
Tobruk, Libya, 82n28

Tomb of the Unknown Soldier,
   Arlington Cemetery, 178–179
Truk Island, 213, 213n90, 214, 216,
   218
Truman, Harry S., 234
Tully, Grace, 22, 75, 93, 106, 108,
   113, 153, 154, 210, 229
Turkey, 177n73
Turner, Richmond Kelly, xxi–xxii,
   xxv–xxvi, 4
Types of Naval Officers (Mahan), 189

United Nations (organization), 109,
   175n72, 229
U.S. Army at Casablanca
   2nd Armored Division, 142–143
   3rd and 9th Infantry Divisions,
      142–143
   conference organization and, 136
U.S. Naval Hospital, San Diego,
   California, 116–117
USS *Astoria*, 156–157, 161, 172
USS *Bittern*, 62–63
USS *Canberra*, naming of, 64–66
USS *Dauntless*, 181, 182
USS *Hornet*, 40–41n15, 89, 89n32
USS *Iowa*, commissioning and
   training,
   Casco Bay casualty of, 171–174
   commissioning of, 159–161
   dress regulation compliance on,
      162
   Kimmel's visit to, 162–163
   McCrea's responsibilities in, x, xv
   Navy Department schools and,
      158–159
   pre-commissioning work for, 156,
      158–159
   selection of officers and crew for,
      156–158
   shakedown cruise of, 164–170
   Tirpitz watch, Argentia, and,
      175–176
USS *Iowa*, secret mission to North
   Africa

Bahia, Brazil, round trip and,
194–196
bathtub installation for, 177, 181
"crossing the line," 194–195
Dakar, Senegal, and 196–197
destroyer escort for, 184–185
disembarking at Oran and, 191
FDR boarding in boatswain's chair
and, 197–198
FDR's farewell to crew of, 199–201
Freetown, Sierra Leone, and 196
post-Oran orders of, 191–192
post-Oran orders' modification
and, 193–194
return to the United States by,
198–199
secrecy measures for, 178–181,
183, 185
Strait of Gibraltar and, 190–191
William D. Porter torpedo incident
and, 185–188
zigzag steering and, 184, 188–189
USS *Iowa*, Pacific War
evening news broadcast in, 207
evening prayer in, 216–217
first birthday celebration of, 216
food poisoning in, 206–207
Mariana Islands campaign, and
219–220, 220n97
Mariana Islands one-day raid and,
216, 218–220
Marshall Islands campaign and,
211–213, 217–218
McCrea, relief and detachment
from, 221
Mili Island bombardment and,
217–218
Panama Canal and, 208–209
Philippine Sea, Battle of, and, 219,
219n96
servicing destroyers, 220
Truk raid and, 213–216
Vickie and, 204–206, 206n84
war preparations by, 203–204
USS *Lexington*, 37–40, 40n15

USS *Mayrant*, 139
USS *Memphis*, 134, 150–151
USS *Missouri*, 203n83
USS *New Jersey*, 203, 203n83, 206,
209, 211, 214, 215
USS *New York*, xvii, xxi, 70
USS *Pennsylvania*, xx, 15, 181
USS *Potomac*, 86–87, 88, 90, 91, 92,
179, 180, 181, 182, 201–202
USS *Richmond*, 226
USS *South Dakota*, 209–210, 214
USS *Wasp*, 117
USS *William D. Porter*, 185, 186–188
USS *Wisconsin*, 203n83
USS *Yorktown*, 38n14, 40–41n15,
82n28, 117
Uvalde, Texas, 117–118

Vanderbilt mansion, 80
Vardaman, James K., Jr., 234
Vichy French Government, 30, 55,
55n21, 56, 59, 124n40, 127n42,
138n51, 145n54
Vickie (dog), 204–206, 220

WAAC. *See* Women's Army Auxiliary
Corps
WAC. *See* Women's Army Corps
Wallace, Henry, 72
War Plans Division, U.S. Navy
Department, xxi
Wassell, Corydon M., 86n29
Wasp. See USS *Wasp*
Watson, Edwin "Pa," vii, ix, 259
advice to McCrea from, 15
aftershave lotion of, 13
Casablanca conference and, 128,
131–132
chewing tobacco and, 11
FDR's daily appointment list and,
14–15
Iowa's secret mission to North
Africa and, 181, 182, 198,
200
Map Room expansion and, 27–28

McCrea, introduction to White House operations, by, 21, 83

McCrea, reporting to FDR, and, 11, 13, 14–16

as military aide, 11n6, 12

as president's appointment secretary, 12–13

Welles, Sumner, 47, 71

While Rome Burns (Woollcott), 45

White House

communication with, as naval aide, 20–21, 83–84

conversation with Alexander Woollcott on steps of, 43–46

McCrea acquainting himself with inner workings of, 21–23

visitors to, 67–73

Whiteside, William J., 171–172

Wilbur, William H., 140, 141, 142, 144

Wilhelmina, Queen of the Netherlands, 61, 61n23, 62, 63, 72–73, 74, 75, 76, 94

Willkie, Wendell, 107, 123–124

William D. Porter. See USS *William D. Porter*

Willow Run Plant, Ford Motor Company, 115

Wilson, Woodrow, 109

Wisconsin. See USS *Wisconsin*

Woleai Atoll, 218

Women's Army Auxiliary Corps (WAAC), 114, 114n39, 140

Women's Army Corps (WAC), 114n39

Wood, Edward Frederick Lindley (Lord Halifax), 48, 48n18, 50, 68, 69

Woollcott, Alexander, 43n16, 43–46, 108

Wright B-1 Flyer, xx–xxi

Wright brothers, xx

Yamamoto, Isoroku, 5, 5n1

Yap Island, 220n97

Yorktown. See USS *Yorktown*

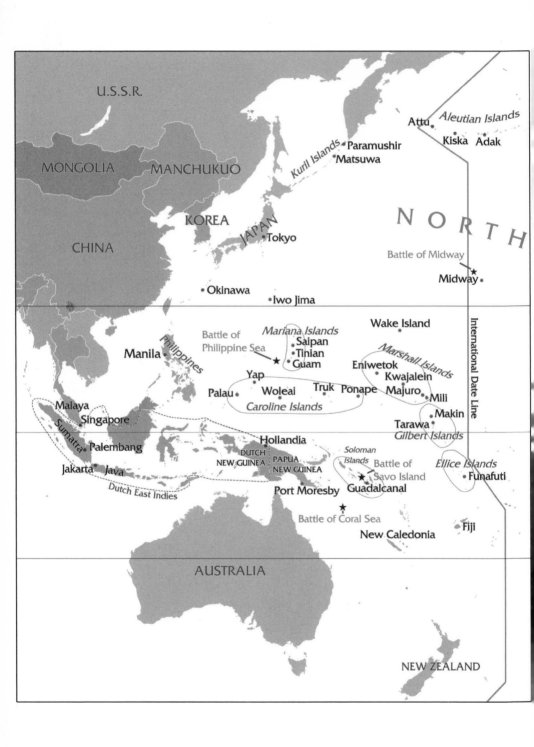